THE NEGRO IN THE UNITED STATES

THE NEGRO
IN THE UNITED STATES

A Selected Bibliography

Compiled by DOROTHY B. PORTER

Librarian of the Negro Collection, Howard University

LIBRARY OF CONGRESS • WASHINGTON • 1970

L.C. Card 78–606085

For sale by the Superintendent of Documents,
U.S. Government Printing Office, Washington D.C. 20402.
Price $3.25

PREFACE

The career of Daniel Alexander Payne Murray, who served as a member of the staff in various capacities "up to an assistant librarian" from 1871 to 1922, is a natural starting point for a discussion of Negro materials in the Library of Congress. While serving in his first position in the Library, as a personal assistant to the Librarian, Ainsworth R. Spofford, Mr. Murray undertook the systematic study of "the origin and historical growth of the colored race throughout the civilized world," which he hoped would result in an encyclopedic history of his race. Almost 30 years later, he was chosen by Herbert Putnam, then just beginning his career as Librarian, to respond to a request from Ferdinand W. Peck, Commissioner General of the United States to the Paris exposition of 1900, that a collection of books and pamphlets by Afro-American authors be made a feature of the American exhibit at the exposition. Within a period of 2 weeks, Mr. Murray prepared a preliminary list of 223 works written by 152 Negro authors. The purpose of this list was to aid in securing a copy of "every book and pamphlet in existence, by a Negro Author, the same to be used in connection with the exhibit of Negro Authorship in the Paris Exposition of 1900, and later placed in the Library of Congress."

It was soon discovered that, owing to Dr. Spofford's foresight, the Library of Congress was "uncommonly rich in such books and pamphlets," but "no little difficulty was encountered then and subsequently in identifying them." By the time the world exposition at Paris opened in May 1900, however, Mr. Murray had located 1,100 titles written by Negro authors, of which about 500 were forwarded to the exposition. Thomas J.

Calloway, special agent for the U.S. Commission at the exposition, wrote that "the most creditable showing in the exhibit is by Negro authors collected by Mr. Daniel Murray of the Library of Congress."

After the close of the Paris exposition, Mr. Murray continued to collect works by Afro-American, Afro-European, and West Indian authors and to amass a varied collection of Afro-Americana. At his death in 1925, the Library of Congress received by provision of his will a unique collection of some "1,448 volumes and pamphlets, 14 broadsides, and 1 map, with the idea that it should form part of the material especially selected by him for exhibit purposes." The books that had been sent to the Paris exposition were kept together upon their return to the Library. This small collection, along with Mr. Murray's bequest and a few volumes presented to the Library by Mrs. Anna Murray after her husband's death, became the "Colored Author Collection." Many of the titles have since been cataloged and added to the general collections.

The *Preliminary List of Books and Pamphlets by Negro Authors, for Paris Exposition and Library of Congress* (1900), compiled by· Daniel Murray, appears to have been the first effort on the part of the Library to draw attention to works by and about Negroes.

In 1906 Appleton Prentiss Clark Griffin, chief of the Division of Bibliography, directed the compilation of a *Select List of References on the Negro Question,* published by the Library. It contained entries for 232 books and 286 periodical articles published during the period 1879-1906. The Library also published in the same year a *List of Discussions of the Fourteenth and Fifteenth Amendments,* which comprised 103 entries. Both bibliographies included titles relating primarily to Negro suffrage and the Negro in the South and were compiled to "meet requests by letter upon topics of current interest."

In 1940, for the 75th anniversary of the proclamation of the 13th amendment to the Constitution of the United States, which abolished slavery, the Library prepared and issued a bibliography of its special materials on the Negro. In connection with this anniversary, the Library also mounted an exhibition of books, manuscripts, and works of art and arranged a series of concerts. The festival of music and the exhibits that opened on December 18, 1940, vividly presented the contribution of the American Negro to American culture.

Without question both scholars and the general public are aware that the Library of Congress has extensive holdings on the Negro, not only printed books and periodicals but also manuscripts, music, prints, photographs, motion pictures, and sound recordings. This awareness is reflected in the steady flow of requests for bibliographies and other guides to Negro studies that the Library receives. The factors that stimulate such requests are rooted in the national—indeed, the worldwide—interest in the

American Negro which recent social and cultural events in this country have intensified. For many years the Library has responded to this interest by issuing from time to time typed lists relating to various aspects of Negro life.

The mounting interest in Negro history and culture, manifested particularly by the introduction of courses in these subjects in high school, college, and university curricula, has given rise to a demand for lists of books that can be used to support such studies. The present bibliography is designed to meet the current needs of students, teachers, librarians, researchers, and the general public for introductory guidance to the study of the Negro in the United States.

This bibliography is selective rather than exhaustive. Among the topics covered are the urban Negro, relations between the races, discriminatory practices in all areas, and efforts to obtain political and economic freedom, as well as the education and cultural history of the Negro, his religious life, the social conditions under which he lives, and his historical past. Included are works depicting the lives of outstanding Negroes—abolitionists, fugitive slaves, educators, civil rights leaders, scientists, journalists, religious leaders, artists, athletes, and literary figures.

The selection of many of the titles, especially in the fields of literature and history, was based on the frequency of requests for particular works in large library collections on the Negro and on their inclusion in the numerous bibliographies and reading lists now being compiled for use in junior colleges, colleges, and universities. In addition, bibliographic lists and essays appended to such works as *From Slavery to Freedom,* by John Hope Franklin; *North of Slavery,* by Leon F. Litwack; *The Burden of Race; a Documentary History of Negro-White Relations in America,* by Gilbert Osofsky; *The Negro in the Civil War,* by Benjamin Quarles; *The Black Power Revolt,* edited by Floyd B. Barbour; and *The Negro in the United States,* by E. Franklin Frazier, were consulted. Use was also made of previously published bibliographies such as Monroe Work's *Bibliography of the Negro in Africa and America* and Erwin A. Salk's *A Layman's Guide to Negro History.*

While some books written especially for children and young people are included, and some of the other publications cited are well adapted to their use, no systematic effort was made to represent material of this type. Lists such as Miles M. Jackson's *Bibliography of Negro History & Culture for Young Readers* may be used as guides in this field.

Identification of writers by race has not been attempted except in the section on fiction, which lists only novels and short stories written by representative Negro authors. While the writings of white novelists are not cited, the importance of the treatment of Negro characters and the educational, moral, and artistic value of works by such authors as Howard Fast,

William Faulkner, Harper Lee, Du Bose Heyward, Julia Peterkin, Lillian Smith, Harriet Beecher Stowe, T. S. Stribling, and Mark Twain are undisputed. Apart from fiction, the publications of both white and Negro writers are included throughout the bibliography.

The compiler gratefully acknowledges the invaluable editorial assistance of Mary Jane Gibson, assistant head of the Bibliography and Reference Correspondence Section, General Reference and Bibliography Division, Library of Congress. Miss Gibson also prepared the index. The compiler wishes to express her appreciation as well to Ruth S. Freitag, head of the Bibliography and Reference Correspondence Section, for helpful suggestions and for assistance in indexing and proofreading, and to Robert H. Land, chief of the General Reference and Bibliography Division, for emphasizing the need for the bibliography and offering encouragement while the work was in progress.

Dorothy B. Porter

April 1969

CONTENTS

NOTE TO THE USER

Scope. The emphasis of this bibliography is on recent monographs in the collections of the Library of Congress, although a number of important older works, a few periodicals, and several titles from the holdings of other American libraries are included.

Arrangement. Entries are arranged alphabetically by author under broad subject headings that reveal the Negro's part in numerous aspects of American life, culture, and history. An index of names and subjects is provided.

Annotations. Entries have been given brief annotations where clarification seemed necessary. Because of the increasing importance for the building of library collections of scholarly reprints of long unavailable classics in Negro literature and history, indication of reprint editions has been made where possible.

Call numbers and location symbols. Location of items is indicated either by a Library of Congress call number or location symbol, or, for material in another library, by the National Union Catalog symbol for that library. A key to the symbols used is given on the next page.

KEY TO SYMBOLS

DHU   Howard University, Washington, D.C.

DLC   Library of Congress (uncataloged)

DLC-LL Library of Congress, Law Library (unclassified)

FU   University of Florida, Gainesville

ICN   Newberry Library, Chicago, Ill.

ICU   University of Chicago

MH   Harvard University, Cambridge, Mass.

NNC   Columbia University, New York, N.Y.

NcD   Duke University, Durham, N.C.

NcU   University of North Carolina, Chapel Hill

PSt   Pennsylvania State University, University Park

TxU   University of Texas, Austin

Vi   Virginia State Library, Richmond

THE NEGRO IN THE UNITED STATES

Bibliographies, Guides, Indexes

1

Abrahamson, Julia. Race relations; a selected list of readings on racial and cultural minorities in the United States, with special emphasis on Negroes, by Julia Waxman. Chicago, Julius Rosenwald Fund, 1945. 47 p.

Z1361.N39A3

2

Baker, Augusta. Books about Negro life for children. Rev. New York, New York Public Library, 1963. 33 p.   Z1361.N39B2 1963

> A new edition is in preparation.

3

Bennett, Elaine C. Calendar of Negro-related documents in the records of the Committee for Congested Production Areas in the National Archives. Prepared for the Committee on Negro Studies of the American Council of Learned Societies. Washington, American Council of Learned Societies, 1949. 100 leaves.   E185.6.B47

3a

Bibliographic survey: the Negro in print. v. 1+ May 1965+ Washington, Negro Bibliographic and Research Center. bimonthly.   Z1361.N39N39

> At head of title, May 1965-Mar. 1968: Bibliographic Survey.
> Title varies: May 1965-Mar. 1968, *The Negro in Print*.
> An annotated list of fiction and nonfiction, paperbacks, and books

for young readers, with occasional periodical articles and references on poetry and art.

4

Brooks, Alexander D. Civil rights and liberties in the United States, an annotated bibliography. With a selected list of fiction and audio-visual materials collected by Albert A. Alexander and Virginia H. Ellison. New York, Civil Liberties Educational Foundation, c1962. 151 p.

Z7164.L6B7

5

Brown, Warren H. Check list of Negro newspapers in the United States (1827-1946). Jefferson City, Mo., School of journalism, Lincoln University, 1946. 37 p. (Lincoln University journalism series, no. 2)

Z6951.B88

6

Chapman, Abraham. The Negro in American literature, and a bibliography of literature by and about Negro Americans. Stevens Point, Wisconsin State University [c1966] 135 p. (Wisconsin Council of Teachers of English. Special publication, no. 15)   DHU; TxU

7

Dickinson, Donald C. A bio-bibliography of Langston Hughes, 1902-1967. With a preface by Arna Bontemps. [Hamden, Conn.] Archon Books, 1967. 267 p. port.   PS3515.U274Z62

An expansion of the author's dissertation, University of Michigan. Bibliography: p. 257-262.

8

Dodds, Barbara. Negro literature for high school students. [Champaign, Ill.] National Council of Teachers of English [1968] 157 p.

Z1361.N39D62

9

DuBois, William E. B., *ed*. A select bibliography of the Negro American. A compilation made under the direction of Atlanta University, together with the Proceedings of the Tenth Conference for the Study of the Negro Problems, held at Atlanta University, on May 30, 1905. 3d ed. Atlanta, Atlanta University Press, 1905. 71 p. (Atlanta University publications, no. 10)   E185.5.A88 v. 10

Z1361.N39D85

10

Dumond, Dwight L. A bibliography of antislavery in America. Ann Arbor, University of Michigan Press [1961] 119 p.   Z1249.S6D8

11

Ellis, Ethel M. V., *comp.* The American Negro: a selected checklist of books. Washington, Negro Collection, Howard University Library, 1968. 46 leaves.   Z1361.N39E4

12

Guzman, Jessie P. George Washington Carver, a classified bibliography. [Tuskegee Institute, Ala.] Dept. of Records and Research, Tuskegee Institute, 1953 [i.e. 1954] 26 p. (Records and research pamphlet no. 3)
Z8150.7.G8

13

Hall, Woodrow W. A bibliography of the Tuskegee gerrymander protest; pamphlets, magazine and newspaper articles chronologically arranged. Tuskegee Institute, Ala., Dept. of Records and Research, Tuskegee Institute, 1960. 54 leaves. (Records and research pamphlet no. 8) DLC

14

Hampton Institute, *Hampton, Va. Collis P. Huntington Library.* A classified catalogue of the Negro collection in the Collis P. Huntington Library, Hampton Institute. Compiled by workers of the Writers' Program of the Works Projects Administration in the State of Virginia. Sponsored by Hampton Institute. [n.p.] 1940. 255, [35] p.   Z1361.N39H3

15

Haywood, Charles. A bibliography of North American folklore and folksong. 2d rev. ed. v. 1. The American people north of Mexico, including Canada. New York, Dover Publications [1961] xxx, 748 p. maps (on lining papers)   Z5984.U5H32 v. 1
    Section on the Negro: p. 430-560.

16

Heartman, Charles F. Phillis Wheatley (Phillis Peters); a critical attempt and a bibliography of her writings. New York, For the author, 1915. 44 p. facsims. (part fold.), port. (Heartman's historical series, no. 7)
PS866.W5Z6
    "The following essay was written by me originally in German . . . now translated by another person."
    "A short list of books with contents relating to Phillis Wheatley": [1] p. at end.

17

Historical Records Survey. *District of Columbia.* Calendar of the writings of Frederick Douglass in the Frederick Douglass memorial home,

Anacostia, D. C. Prepared by District of Columbia Historical Records Survey, Division of Professional and Service Projects, Work Projects Administration. Sponsored by the Board of Commissioners of the District of Columbia. Washington, District of Columbia Historical Records Survey, 1940. 93 leaves.   Z6616.D7H57

18

Howard University, *Washington, D. C. Library. Moorland Foundation.* The Arthur B. Spingarn collection of Negro authors. Washington [1948] [12] p. facsim.   Z733.W31M6

18a

Hussey, Edith L., Mary Henderson, *and* Barbara Marx. The Negro American; a reading list. [New York, Dept. of Racial and Cultural Relations, National Council of Churches of Christ in the USA, 1957] 40 p. (Interracial publication, no. 96)   Z1361.N39I5 no. 96

18b

Index to periodical articles by and about Negroes. Mar. 1950+ Boston, G. K. Hall. quarterly.   A13.O4

Vols. for 1961+ called v. 2+

Title varies: Mar. 1950-summer 1954, *Index to Selected Negro Periodicals.*—Fall 1954-fall 1965, *Index to Selected Periodicals.*

Vols. for 1960+ compiled by Hallie Q. Brown Memorial Library, Central State College, Wilberforce, Ohio, and the Schomburg Collection, New York Public Library.

Vols. for Mar. 1950-fall 1959 issued by the Library, Central State College (called Mar.-Dec. 1950 College of Education and Industrial Arts).

Decennial cumulation, 1950-59; annual cumulation, 1960+

19

Jackson, Miles M. A bibliography of Negro history & culture for young readers. Assisted by Mary W. Cleaves and Alma L. Gray. [Pittsburgh] University of Pittsburgh Press, published for Atlanta University [c1969] xxxi, 134 p.   Z1361.N39J3

20

Johnson, Clifton H., *and* Carroll G. Barber. The Negro American, a selected and annotated bibliography for high schools and junior colleges. Nashville, Tenn., Amistad Research Center [c1968] 113 p.   DHU

21

Kaplan, Louis. A bibliography of American autobiographies, compiled by Louis Kaplan in association with James Tyler Cook, Clinton E. Colby, Jr. [and] Daniel C. Haskell. Madison, University of Wisconsin Press, 1961. 372 p.   Z1224.K3

See the index for autobiographies relating to the Negro.

22

Koblitz, Minnie W. The Negro in schoolroom literature; resource materials for the teacher of kindergarten through the sixth grade. [New York, Center for Urban Education, 1967?] 67 p.   Z1037.K6

"Research . . . was performed pursuant to a contract with the United States Department of Health, Education, and Welfare, Office of Education."

23

Lancaster, Emmer M. A guide to Negro marketing information. [Washington] U.S. Dept. of Commerce, Business and Defense Services Administration; [for sale by the Supt. of Docs., U.S. Govt. Print. Off.] 1966. 50 p. illus.   HC110.C6L3

Bibliography: p. 7-20.

24

Lewinson, Paul. A guide to documents in the National Archives: for Negro studies, compiled for the Committee on Negro Studies of the American Council of Learned Societies. Washington, 1947. 28 p. (American Council of Learned Societies Devoted to Humanistic Studies. Committee on Negro Studies. Publications, no. 1)   NNC

25

McNamee, Lawrence F. Dissertations in English and American literature; theses accepted by American, British, and German universities, 1865-1964. New York, Bowker, 1968. 1124 p.   Z5053.M32

Chapter 32 is on Negro literature.

26

Merriam, Alan P. A bibliography of jazz. With the assistance of Robert J. Brenford. Philadelphia, American Folklore Society, 1954. 145 p. (Publications of the American Folklore Society. Bibliographical series, v. 4, 1954)   ML128.J3M4

27

Miller, Elizabeth W. The Negro in America; a bibliography compiled for the American Academy of Arts and Sciences. With a foreword by Thomas F. Pettigrew. Cambridge, Harvard University Press, 1966. xvii, 190 p.   Z1361.N39M5

28

Murray, Daniel A. P. Preliminary list of books and pamphlets by Negro authors, for Paris Exposition and Library of Congress. [Washington, U.S. Commission to the Paris Exposition, 1900] 8 p.   Z1361.N39M9

29

National Association for the Advancement of Colored People. *Education Dept.* Integrated school books; a descriptive bibliography of 399 preschool and elementary school texts and story books. New York, NAACP Special Contribution Fund, 1967. 55 p.   Z5814.D5N3

30

National Council of the Churches of Christ in the United States of America. *Division of Christian Education.* Negro heritage resource guide; a bibliography of the Negro in contemporary America. [New York, Council Press, c1967] 21 p.   Z1361.N39N16

31

National Urban League. *Dept. of Research and Community Projects.* Selected bibliography on the Negro. New York, Dept. of Research, National Urban League, 1937. 13 leaves.   Z1361.N39N18

––– ––– Supplement, no. 1. Compiled by the Dept. of Research, National Urban League. [New York, 1938] 13 leaves.

Z1361.N39N18 Suppl.

32

New Jersey Library Association. *Bibliography Committee.* New Jersey and the Negro; a bibliography, 1715-1966. [Trenton] 1967. 196 p.

Z1361.N39N45

33

New York. Public Library. The Negro; a list of significant books. Compiled by Dorothy R. Homer. 8th rev. ed. New York, 1960. 25 p.   DHU

34

New York. Public Library. *Schomburg Collection of Negro Literature and History.* Dictionary catalog. Boston, G.K. Hall, 1962. 9 v. (8473 p.)

Z881.N592S35

A first supplement (2 v.) was published in 1968.

35
Oberlin College. *Library.* A classified catalogue of the collection of anti-
slavery propaganda in the Oberlin College Library, compiled by
Geraldine Hopkins Hubbard, edited by Julian S. Fowler. [Oberlin]
1932. 84 p. (*Its* Bulletin, v. 2, no. 3)   Z1249.S6O2

"Formed the bibliographical portion of a thesis submitted in June,
1932, in partial fulfillment of the requirements for the degree of master
of arts at Oberlin College."–Preface.
"The main list contains all printed items . . . which can be classed as
American anti-slavery propaganda published before January 1, 1863 . . .
An appendix describes the smaller collections of pro-slavery literature
and of the British anti-slavery propaganda."

36
Porter, Dorothy B. Early American Negro writings: a bibliographical
study. *In* Bibliographical Society of America. Papers, v. 39, 3d quarter
1945: 192-268.   Z1008.B51P, v. 39

37
Porter, Dorothy B. North American Negro poets, a bibliographical checklist of their writings, 1760-1944. Hattiesburg, Miss., Book Farm, 1945.
90 p. ([Heartman's historical series, no. 70])   Z1361.N39P6

A new edition is in preparation.

37a
Porter, Dorothy B., *and* Ethel M. V. Ellis, *comps.* The journal of Negro
education. Index to vols. 1-31, 1932-1962. Washington, Howard University Press, 1963. 82 p.   DHU

38
[Pride, Armistead S.] Negro newspapers on microfilm; a selected list.
Washington, Library of Congress, Photoduplication Service, 1953. 8 p.
                                                                Z6944.N39P7
39
Princeton University. *Program in American Civilization.* The Negro in
America; bibliographies, conference 1966. [Lincoln University, Pa.,
American : Studies Institute, c1966] 90 p.   DLC

40
Reid, Ira De A. Negro youth, their social and economic backgrounds; a
selected bibliography of unpublished studies, 1900-1938. Washington,
American Youth Commission of the American Council on Education
[c1939] 71 leaves.   Z1361.N39R35

Largely unpublished theses of a selected list of colleges and universities in the United States.

41

Reisner, Robert G. The literature of jazz, a selective bibliography. With an introduction by Marshall W. Stearns. [2d ed. rev. and enl.] New York, New York Public Library, 1959. 63 p.   ML128.J3R4 1959

42

Rollins, Charlemae H., *ed.* We build together; a reader's guide to Negro life and literature for elementary and high school use. Contributors: Augusta Baker [and others] 3d ed. [Champaign, Ill., National Council of Teachers of English, 1967] xxviii, 71 p.   Z1361.N39R77 1967

43

Ross, Frank A., *and* Louise V. Kennedy. A bibliography of Negro migration. New York, Columbia University Press, 1935. 251 p.

Z1361.N39R8

Annotated.

"The fifth volume produced under the project, Negro Migration, conducted in the Department of Sociology at Columbia University, under subsidy by the Social Science Research Council, and the Columbia University Council for Research in the Social Sciences."–Preface.

"Bibliographies": p. [191]-194.

44

Salk, Erwin A. A layman's guide to Negro history. Chicago, Quadrangle Books, 1966. xviii, 170 p. port.   Z1361.N39S23

45

Scally, Mary Anthony, *Sister.* Negro Catholic writers, 1900-1943, bio-bibliography. Detroit, W. Romig [1945] 152 p.   Z1361.N39S35

"Sources": p. 11-12.

46

Schomburg, Arthur A., *comp.* A bibliographical checklist of American Negro poetry. New York, L. F. Heartman, 1916. 57 p. (Bibliographica americana; a series of monographs, v. 2)   Z1231.P7S3

"Bibliography of the poetical works of Phillis Wheatley (copyrighted by Charles F. Heartman) [reprinted from Heartman's 'Phillis Wheatley (Phillis Peters)'] ": p. 47-57.

47

Sieg, Vera. The Negro problem: a bibliography. Madison, Wis., 1908. 22 p. (Wisconsin Free Library Commission. American social questions, no. 1)
Z7164.S66A5, no. 1
Z1361.N39S5

Prepared in fulfillment of requirements for graduation, Wisconsin Library School.

48

Spangler, Earl. Bibliography of Negro history: selected and annotated entries, general and Minnesota. Minneapolis, Ross and Haines, 1963. 101 p. Z1361.N39S65

49

Texas. Southern University, *Houston. Library.* Heartman Negro collection; catalogue. v. 1. Houston [1955?] 1 v. (unpaged) Z881.H84

50

Thompson, Edgar T., *and* Alma M. Thompson. Race and region, a descriptive bibliography compiled with special reference to the relations between whites and Negroes in the United States. Chapel Hill, University of North Carolina Press, 1949. 194 p. Z1361.N39T5

Material in the libraries of Duke University, the University of North Carolina, and North Carolina College.

51

Treworgy, Mildred L., *and* Paul B. Foreman. Negroes in the United States; a bibliography of materials for schools, approvable for purchase in Pennsylvania under NDEA provisions. With a supplement of recent materials on other American minority peoples. University Park, Pa. [Available from the Office of the Director of Libraries, Pennsylvania State University] 1967. 93 p. (Pennsylvania. State University. Libraries. School series, no. 1) PSt

52

Tuskegee Institute. *Dept. of Records and Research.* A bibliography of the student movement protesting segregation and discrimination, 1960. Tuskegee Institute, Ala., 1961. 10 leaves. (*Its* Records and research pamphlet no. 9) Z7164.R12T8

53

Tuskegee Institute. *Dept. of Records and Research.* A selected list of references relating to the elementary, secondary, and higher education of Negroes, 1949 to June 1955. [Tuskegee Institute, Ala.] 1955. 18 leaves. (*Its* Records and research pamphlet no. 5)   Z1361.N39T8

54

Tuskegee Institute. *Dept. of Records and Research.* A selected list of references relating to the Negro teacher, 1949 to June 1955. [Tuskegee Institute, Ala.] 1955. 3 leaves. (*Its* Records and research pamphlet no. 7)   Z1361.N39T83

55

U.S. *Dept. of Housing and Urban Development. Library.* Bibliography of Robert C. Weaver. [Washington, 1966] 9 leaves.   Z7164.H8U446

56

U.S. *Library of Congress.* 75 years of freedom; commemoration of the 75th anniversary of the proclamation of the 13th amendment to the Constitution of the United States. The Library of Congress. [Washington, U.S. Govt. Print. Off., 1943] 108 p. col. plates.   E185.6.U597

"The contribution of the American Negro to American culture was the theme of a series of exhibits and concerts in the Library of Congress commencing on December 18th, the 75th anniversary of the proclamation of the Thirteenth amendment, which ended slavery in the United States."–p. v.

57

U.S. *Library of Congress. Division of Bibliography.* List of discussions of the fourteenth and fifteenth amendments with special reference to Negro suffrage. Compiled under the direction of Appleton Prentiss Clark Griffin. Washington, Govt. Print. Off., 1906. 18 p.   Z881.U5
Z1361.N39U5

58

U.S. *Library of Congress. Division of Bibliography.* Select list of references on the Negro question. Compiled under the direction of Appleton Prentiss Clark Griffin. 2d issue, with additions. Washington, Govt. Print. Off., 1906. 61 p.   Z881.U5
Z1361.N39U6 1906

59

Weinberg, Meyer. School integration; a comprehensive classified bibliography of 3,100 references. Chicago, Integrated Education Associates, 1967. 137 p.   Z5814.D5W4

60

Welsch, Erwin K. The Negro in the United States; a research guide. Bloomington, Indiana University Press, 1965. 142 p.   Z1361.N39W4 1965

Bibliography: p. 108-138.

61

Whiteman, Maxwell. A century of fiction by American Negroes, 1853-1952; a descriptive bibliography. Philadelphia, 1955. 64 p.

Z1361.N39W5

62

Williams, Daniel T., *and* Carolyn L. Redden. The Black Muslims in the United States: a selected bibliography. [Tuskegee, Ala.] Hollis Burke Frissell Library, Tuskegee Institute, 1964. 19 leaves.   Z7835.B5W5

63

Work, Monroe N. A bibliography of the Negro in Africa and America. New York, Argosy-Antiquarian, 1965. xxi, 698 p.   Z5118.N4W6 1965

Reprint of the 1928 ed.

"A bibliography of bibliographies on the Negro in the United States": pt. 2, p. [630]-636.

Encyclopedias, Biographical Dictionaries, Annuals

64

Bicknell, Marguerite E., *and* Margaret C. McCulloch. Guide to information about the Negro and Negro-white adjustment. [Memphis, Brunner Print. Co.] 1943. 39 p.   E185.61.B5

65

Davis, John P., *ed.* The American Negro reference book. Englewood Cliffs, N.J., Prentice-Hall [1966] xxii, 969 p. illus.   E185.D25

Includes bibliographical references.

66

Directory of U.S. Negro newspapers, magazines & periodicals. 1966. [New York] U.S. Negro World. 30 leaves.   Z6944.N39D5

Editor: F. B. Sawyer.

67

Ebony. The Negro handbook, compiled by the editors of Ebony. Chicago,
Johnson Pub. Co., 1966. 535 p.   E185.E2

   Includes bibliographies.

68

Encyclopedia of the Negro, preparatory volume with reference lists and
reports, by W. E. B. DuBois and Guy B. Johnson; prepared with the
cooperation of E. Irene Diggs, Agnes C. L. Donohugh, Guion Johnson
[and others]. Introduction by Anson Phelps Stokes. Rev. and enl. ed.
New York, Phelps-Stokes Fund, 1946. 215 p. group port.

                                                        HT1581.E5 1946

   "Bibliography of bibliographies": p. [191]-198.

69

Fleming, George J., *and* Christian E. Burckel. Who's who in colored America. An illustrated biographical dictionary of notable living persons of
African descent in the United States. 7th ed. New York, C. E. Burckel,
1950. 648 p. illus.   DHU

   ——— ——— Supplement. New York, C. E. Burckel, 1950. 34 p.   DHU

70

[Gibson, John W.] Progress of a race; or, The remarkable advancement of
the American Negro, from the bondage of slavery, ignorance, and poverty to the freedom of citizenship, intelligence, affluence, honor and
trust. Rev. and enl. by J. L. Nichols and William H. Crogman, with
special articles by well known authorities, Mrs. Booker T. Washington,
Charles M. Melden, M. W. Dogan, Albon L. Holsey, and an introduction
by Robert R. Moton. Naperville, Ill., J. L. Nichols [1929] 480 p. illus.,
ports.   E185.G453

   Cover title: *The New Progress of a Race.*
   1901 ed. by J. W. Gibson and W. H. Crogman, published under title:
The Colored American.

71

Haley, James T., *comp.* Afro-American encyclopaedia; or, The thoughts,
doings, and sayings of the race, embracing addresses, lectures, biographical sketches, sermons, poems, names of universities, colleges, semi-
naries, newspapers, books . . . as discussed by more than 100 of their
wisest and best men and women. Nashville, Haley & Florida, 1895.
639 p. illus.   DHU

72
Julius Rosenwald Fund. Directory of agencies in race relations, national,
State and local. Chicago, 1945. 124 p.   E184.A1J8
"The burden of the responsibility for compilation and editing . . .
has been upon Elizabeth Linn Allen."–Introduction.

73
The National cyclopedia of the colored race. Montgomery, Ala., National
Pub. Co., 1919. [622] p. illus., ports.   E185.N27
    Editor: Clement Richardson.

74
The Negro handbook. 1942-49. New York, Malliet. tables.   E185.5.N382
    Editor: 1942-49, Florence Murray.
    "Books and periodicals, a list of books by and about Negroes":
    1942, p. 194-200.
    Ceased publication with 1949.

75
Negro year book. New York, W. H. Wise, 1912-52. illus., diagrs., maps.
                                                           E185.5.N41
    No editions were published for 1920/21, 1923/24, 1927/28-
1929/30.
    Editor: 1912-38, M. N. Work.
    Vols. for 1912-47 issued by Tuskegee Institute.
    Ceased publication with 1952.

76
Plans for Progress. Directory of Negro colleges and universities, March,
    1967. Washington [1967] 103 p.   LC2801.P55 1967

77
Ploski, Harry A., *and* Roscoe C. Brown, *comps.* The Negro almanac. New
    York, Bellwether Pub. Co. [1967] 1012 p. illus., maps, ports.
                                                           E185.P55
        Bibliography: p. 946-965.

78
Who's who in colored America; a biographical dictionary of notable living
    persons of Negro descent in America. 1927–1938-40. New York, T.
    Yenser. ports.   E185.96.W54
        Ceased publication with 1938-40.

79

Who's who of the colored race; a general biographical dictionary of men
and women of African descent. Chicago, 1915. 296 p. illus.

E185.96.W6

Edited by Frank Lincoln Mather.

Memento ed., "Half-Century Anniversary of Negro Freedom in
U.S."

80

Williams, Ethel L. Biographical directory of Negro ministers. New York,
Scarecrow Press, 1965. 421 p.   BR563.N4W5

Bibliography: p. 407-412.

81

Wright, Richard R., *ed.* The encyclopaedia of the African Methodist Episcopal Church, containing principally the biographies of the men and
women, both ministers and laymen, whose labors during a hundred and
sixty years, helped make the AME Church what it is; . . . and other
matters concerning African Methodism and the Christian church in general. Compiled by R. R. Wright, Jr., assisted by associate editors, W. A.
Fountain [and others] Introduction by William A. Fountain, foreword
by Reverdy Cassius Ransom. 2d ed. Philadelphia, 1947 [i.e. 1948]
688 p. illus., maps, ports.   BX8443.W8 1948

First ed., 1916, has title: *Centennial Encyclopedia of the African
Methodist Episcopal Church.*

82

Albany Institute of History and Art, *Albany*. The Negro artist comes of age; a national survey of contemporary American artists. Albany Institute of History and Art, January 3rd through February 11th, 1945. [Albany, 1945] [77] p. illus., ports.   MH

    Foreword signed: John Davis Hatch, Jr.

    "Up till now" (p. iii-vii) signed: Alain Locke.

    Contains biographies.

83

Bowdoin College. *Museum of Fine Arts.* The portrayal of the Negro in American painting; [exhibition] the Bowdoin College Museum of Art. [Catalogue. Brunswick? Me.] 1964. 1 v. (unpaged) illus., ports.

N8232.B6

84

Dover, Cedric. American Negro art. [Greenwich, Conn.] New York Graphic Society [1960] 186 p. illus., col. plates, ports.

N6538.N5D6 1960

    "Bibliography by Maureen Dover": p. 57-60.

85

Harmon Foundation. Negro artists, an illustrated review of their achievements. New York [1935] 59 p. illus., ports.   N6538.N5H34

Includes exhibition of paintings by Malvin Gray Johnson and sculptures by Richmond Barthé and Sargent Johnson, presented by the Harmon Foundation in cooperation with the Delphic Studios, April 22-May 4, 1935, inclusive.

86

Locke, Alain L. Negro art: past and present. Washington, Associates in Negro Folk Education, 1936. 122 p. (Bronze booklet no. 3)

E185.5.B85 no. 3
E185.82.L74

"Reading references" at end of each chapter.

87

Locke, Alain L. The Negro in art; a pictorial record of the Negro artist and of the Negro theme in art; edited and annotated by Alain Locke. Washington, Associates in Negro Folk Education, 1940. 224 p. illus., plates.

N6538.N5L6

"Selected bibliography": p. 224.

88

Murray, Freeman H. M. Emancipation and the freed in American sculpture; a study in interpretation. Introduction by John Wesley Cromwell. Washington, The author, 1916. xxviii, 239 p. plates. (Black folk in art series)   E185.89.I2M9

"This monograph is chiefly the expansion of papers which were read as lectures . . . at the Summer School and Chautauqua of the National Religious Training School at Durham, N.C., in 1913. Some of the matter has also appeared in the *A.M.E. Church Review*."–Preface.

89

The Negro in American art. An exhibition co-sponsored by the California Arts Commission, UCLA Art Galleries, September 11 to October 16, 1966; University of California, Davis, November 1 to December 15, 1966; Fine Arts Gallery of San Diego, January 6 to February 12, 1967; Oakland Art Museum, February 24 to March 19, 1967. [Los Angeles?] UCLA Art Galleries, Dickson Art Center [1967?] 63 p.   DLC

90

New York (City) City University of New York. The evolution of Afro-American artists, 1800-1950. New York, 1967. 70 p. illus.

N6538.N5N4

Catalog of an exhibition organized by the City University of New York in cooperation with the Harlem Cultural Council and the New York Urban League, and held at Great Hall, the City College.

91

Porter, James A. Modern Negro art. With eighty-five halftone plates. New York, Dryden Press, 1943. 272 p. illus.   N6538.N5P6

Bibliography: p. 183-192.

Reprint issued by Arno Press, 1969.

92

Porter, James A. Ten Afro-American artists of the nineteenth century. Washington, Gallery of Art, Howard University [1967] 33 p. illus.

N6538.N5P62

Catalog, prepared by J. A. Porter, of an exhibition commemorating the centennial of Howard University held Feb. 3-Mar. 30, 1967, Gallery of Art, Howard University.

Bibliography: p. 32-33.

93

Rodman, Selden. Horace Pippin, a Negro painter in America. New York, Quadrangle Press, 1947. 88 p. illus., plates (part mounted col.), ports.

ND237.P65R6

94

Roelof-Lanner, T. V., ed. Prints by American Negro artists. Los Angeles, Cultural Exchange Center [1965] [11] p., [51] illus. (part col.)

NE508.R6

95

Schoener, Allon, *comp.* Harlem on my mind; cultural capital of Black America, 1900-1968. Preface by Thomas P. F. Hoving. Introduction by Candice Van Ellison. New York, Random House [1969, c1968] 255 p. illus., ports.   F128.68.H3S3

Supplements an exhibition held at the Metropolitan Museum of Art in 1969 and organized by the museum in association with the New York State Council on the Arts.

96

United States Committee for the First World Festival of Negro Arts. Dix artistes nègres des États-Unis; premier Festival mondial des arts nègres, Dakar, Sénégal, 1966. Ten Negro artists from the United States; first World Festival of Negro Arts, Dakar, Senegal, 1966. An exhibition produced and sponsored by the United States Committee for the First World Festival of Negro Arts, Inc., and the National Collection of Fine Arts, Smithsonian Institution. [Text translation prepared by Denise and Michel Berthier. New York, Distributed by October House, 1966] 1 v. (unpaged) illus., ports.   N6538.N5U513

"The exhibition will be circulated in the United States by the American Federation of Arts."
English and French.

97
White, Charles. Images of dignity: the drawings of Charles White. Foreword by Harry Belafonte. Introduction by James Porter. Commentary by Benjamin Horowitz. [Los Angeles] W. Ritchie Press [1967] 121 p. illus., port.   NC1075.W55H6

BIOGRAPHY AND AUTOBIOGRAPHY

Collective

98

Adams, Russell L. Great Negroes, past and present. Illustrations by Eugene Winslow. David P. Ross, Jr., editor. Chicago, Afro-Am Pub. Co. [c1963] 182 p. illus. (part col.), maps (part col.), ports. (part col.)

E185.96.A4

Bibliography: p. 178-179.

99

Bardolph, Richard. The Negro vanguard. New York, Rinehart [1959] 388 p. E185.96.B28

Bibliography: p. 343-369.

99a

Barton, Rebecca C. Witnesses for freedom; Negro Americans in autobiography. Foreword by Alain Locke. New York, Harper [1948] 294 p.

E185.96.B3

Bibliography: p. 286-287.

100

Bennett, Lerone. Pioneers in protest. Chicago, Johnson Pub. Co., 1968. 267 p. ports. E185.96.B4

101

Bontemps, Arna W. Famous Negro athletes. New York, Dodd, Mead [1964] 155 p. ports. (Famous biographies for young people)

GV697.A1B575

102

Bontemps, Arna W., *and* Jack Conroy. Anyplace but here. New York, Hill
and Wang [1966] 372 p.   E185.6.B75 1966

"A revised and expanded version of *They Seek a City*."–Dust jacket.
Bibliography: p. 349-360.

103

Bontemps, Arna W. We have tomorrow. Illustrated with photographs by
Marian Palfi. Boston, Houghton Mifflin Co., 1945. 131 p. ports.

E185.96.B6

Biographical sketches of 12 young Negro men and women.

104

Brawley, Benjamin G. Negro builders and heroes. Chapel Hill, University
of North Carolina Press, 1937. 315 p. ports.   E185.96.B797

"Bibliographical notes": p. 293-304.

105

Brown, Hallie Q., *comp.* Homespun heroines and other women of distinction. Foreword by Mrs. Josephine Turpin Washington. [Xenia, Ohio,
Aldine Pub. Co., c1926] 248 p. ports.   E185.96.B84

106

Brown, William W. The black man, his antecedents, his genius, and his
achievements. New York, T. Hamilton, 1863. 288 p.   E185.96.B86

"Memoir of the author": p. 11-29.

107

Bruce, John E., *comp.* Short biographical sketches of eminent Negro men
and women in Europe and the United States, with brief extracts from
their writings and public utterances. Yonkers, N.Y. [Gazette Press]
1910. 103 p.   E185.96.B88

108

Bryant, Lawrence C. Negro lawmakers in the South Carolina Legislature,
1869-1902. Orangeburg, School of Graduate Studies, South Carolina
State College [1968] 142 p.   E185.93.S7B75

Bibliographical footnotes.

109
Bryant, Lawrence C. Negro senators and representatives in the South Carolina Legislature, 1868-1902. Orangeburg, S. C. [1968] 199 p.
                                                    E185.93.S7B76
Bibliographical footnotes.

110
Bullock, Ralph W. In spite of handicaps; brief biographical sketches with discussion outlines of outstanding Negroes now living who are achieving distinction in various lines of endeavor. With a foreword by Channing H. Tobias. Freeport, N.Y., Books for Libraries Press [1968] 140 p. ports. (Essay index reprint series)   E185.96.B93 1968
    Reprint of the 1927 ed.
    Bibliography: p. 131-140.

111
Cherry, Gwendolyn, Ruby Thomas, and Pauline Willis. Portraits in color; the lives of colorful Negro women. New York, Pageant Press [1962] 224 p. illus.   E185.96.C45
    Bibliography: p. 207-224.

112
Child, Lydia M. F. The freedmen's book. New York, Arno Press, 1968. 277 p. (The American Negro, his history and literature)
                                                    E185.86.C46 1968
    Reprint of the 1865 ed.

113
Christmas, Walter, ed. Negroes in public affairs and government. Contributors: Clifford A. Bradshaw [and others] Photographic editor: Roland Mitchell. Preface: Alfred E. Cain. v. 1. Yonkers [N.Y.] Educational Heritage [1966] 352 p. illus., ports. (Negro heritage library)
                                                    E185.96.C47
    Bibliography: p. 342-345.

114
Daniel, Sadie I. Women builders. Washington, Associated Publishers [c1931] xviii, 187 p. plates, ports.   E185.96.D23

    Contents.—Lucy Craft Laney.—Maggie Lena Walker.—Janie Porter Barrett.—Mary McLeod Bethune.—Nannie Helen Burroughs.—Charlotte Hawkins Brown.—Jane Edna Hunter.

115
Dannett, Sylvia G. L. Profiles of Negro womanhood. Illustations: Horace Varela. Roll of honor portraits: Tom Feelings. Yonkers, N.Y., Educational Heritage [1964-66] 2 v. illus., facsims., ports. (Negro heritage library)   E185.96.D25

Includes bibliographies.
Contents.–v. 1. 1619-1900.–v. 2. 20th century.

116
David, Jay, *comp.* Growing up black. New York, Morrow, 1968. 256 p.
E185.96.D283

Includes well-known personalities such as Ethel Waters, Richard Wright, Dick Gregory, and Booker T. Washington.

117
Dobler, Lavinia G., *and* Edgar A. Toppin. Pioneers and patriots: the lives of six Negroes of the Revolutionary era. Illustrated by Colleen Browning. Garden City, N.Y., Doubleday, 1965. 118 p. illus., facsims., ports. (Zenith books)   E185.96.D6

118
Embree, Edwin R. 13 against the odds. New York, Viking Press, 1944. 261 p. ports.   E185.96.E4

Contents.–Mary McLeod Bethune, Amazon of God.–Richard Wright, native son.–Charles S. Johnson, a scholar and a gentleman. –Walter White, little David.–George Washington Carver, sweet potato wizard.–Langston Hughes, Shakespeare in Harlem.–Marian Anderson, deep river of song.–W. E. B. DuBois, elder statesman.–Mordecai W. Johnson, Lord high chancellor.–William Grant Still, music maker.–A. Philip Randolph, Saint Philip of the Pullman porters.–Joe Louis, champion of the world.– Paul Robeson, voice of freedom.

119
Foley, Albert S. God's men of color; the colored Catholic priests of the United States, 1854-1954. With a foreword by Richard J. Cushing, Archbishop of Boston. New York, Farrar, Straus [1955] 322 p.
BX4670.F6

Reprint issued by Arno Press, 1969.

120
Haynes, Elizabeth R. Unsung heroes. New York, DuBois and Dill, 1921. 270 p. illus., ports.   E185.96.H4

Contents.—Frederick Douglass.—Paul Laurence Dunbar.—Booker T. Washington.—Harriet Tubman.—Alexander S. Pushkin.—Blanche Kelso Bruce.—Samuel Coleridge-Taylor.—Benjamin Banneker.—Phillis Wheatley.—Toussaint L'Ouverture.—Josiah Henson.—Sojourner Truth. —Crispus Attucks.—Alexandre Dumas.—Paul Cuffé.—Alexander Crummell.—John Mercer Langston.

121
Hill, Roy L. Who's who in the American Negro press. Dallas, Royal Pub. Co. [1960] 80 p.   PN4888.N4H5
Bibliography: p. 70.

122
Hughes, Langston. Famous Negro heroes of America. Illustrated by Gerald McCann. New York, Dodd, Mead, 1958. 202 p. illus. (Famous biographies for young people)   E185.96.H82

123
Hughes, Langston. Famous Negro music makers: illustrated with photographs. New York, Dodd, Mead, 1955. 179 p. illus. (Famous biographies for young people)   ML3556.H9

124
Huie, William B. Three lives for Mississippi. With an introduction by Martin Luther King, Jr. [New York] New American Library [1968] 160 p. illus., maps, plans, ports. (A Signet book)   F347.N4H8 1968
Concerns civil rights workers Andrew Goodman, James E. Chaney, and Michael H. Schwerner.

125
Lomax, Louis E. To kill a black man. Los Angeles, Holloway House Pub. Co.; [distributed by: All America Distributors Corp., 1968] 256 p.
E185.97.L5L6
Malcolm X and Martin Luther King are the subjects of this study.

126
Majors, Monroe A. Noted Negro women, their triumphs and activities. Chicago, Donohue & Henneberry [c1893] xvi, 365 p. illus., ports.
E185.96.M23

127
Metcalf, George R. Black profiles. New York, McGraw-Hill [1968] 341 p.
E185.96.M48

Bibliographical references included in "A note on sources" (p. 337-340).

Contents.—Martin Luther King, Jr.—William E. B. DuBois.—Roy Wilkins.—Thurgood Marshall.—Jackie Robinson.—Harriet Tubman. —Medgar Wiley Evers.—James H. Meredith.—Rosa Parks.—Edward W. Brooke.—Whitney Moore Young, Jr.

128

Moseley, J. H. Sixty years in Congress and twenty-eight out. New York, Vantage Press [1960] 99 p. illus.   JK1021.M75

129

[Mott, Abigail F., *and* M. S. Wood], *comps.* Narratives of colored Americans. Printed by order of the trustees of the residuary estate of Lindley Murray. New York, W. Wood, 1877. 276 p.   E185.96.M92

130

Murray, Pauli. Proud shoes; the story of an American family. New York, Harper [1956] 276 p.   E185.97.M95

131

The National register; pertinent facts about colored Americans. Louisville, Ky., Register Publications, 1952. 632 p.   E185.96.N37

Editor: T. J. Johnson.

132

Newbold, Nathan C., *ed.* Five North Carolina Negro educators; prepared under the direction of N. C. Newbold. Chapel Hill, University of North Carolina Press, 1939. 142 p. ports.   LC2802.N8N4

Biographical sketches composed by committees organized in nine North Carolina colleges, each committee consisting of one faculty adviser and one or more students.

"Published under the auspices of the Division of Cooperation in Education and Race Relations; cooperating organizations: State Department of Public Instruction, University of North Carolina [and] Duke University."

Contents.—Simon Green Atkins.—James Benson Dudley.—Annie Wealthy Holland.—Peter Weddick Moore.—Ezekiel Ezra Smith.

133

Nichols, Charles H. Many thousand gone; the ex-slaves' account of their bondage and freedom. Leiden, Brill, 1963. xvi, 229 p. (Studies in American literature and history, 1)   E444.N5

Bibliography: p. [213]-224.

134
Ovington, Mary W. Portraits in color. New York, Viking Press, 1927.
241 p.   E185.96.O96
   Contents.—James Weldon Johnson.—Marcus Garvey.—Max Yergan.
—Mordecai W. Johnson.—Lucy Laney.—Robert Russa Moton.—W. E.
Burghardt DuBois.—Scipio Africanus Jones.—Walter White.—Robert S.
Abbott.—Maggie Lena Walker.—Eugene Kinckle Jones.—Louis Tomp-
kins Wright.—Ernest Everett Just.—George Washington Carver.—Janie
Porter Barrett.—Langston Hughes.—Paul Robeson.—Meta Vaux Warrick
Fuller.—Roland Hayes.

135
Redding, Jay Saunders. The lonesome road; the story of the Negro's part
in America. New York, Doubleday, 1958. 355 p. (Mainstream of America series)   E185.61.R298
   Bibliography: p. 335-340.
   The lives of 12 Negro men and women and their struggle for equal
rights.

136
Richardson, Ben A. Great American Negroes; rev. by William A. Fahey,
illustrated by Robert Hallock. New York, Crowell [1956] 339 p. illus.
                                                          E185.96.R5 1956

137
Robinson, Wilhelmena S. Historical Negro biographies. New York, Pub-
lishers Co. [1967] 291 p. ports. (International library of Negro life and
history)   DT18.R57
   Published under the auspices of the Association for the Study of
Negro Life and History.
   Bibliography: p. 271-281.

138
Rogers, Joel A. World's great men of color. New York, J. A. Rogers
[1946-47] 2 v. illus., ports.   DT18.R59
   On cover: 3000 B.C. to 1946 A.D.
   Paged continuously.
   Includes bibliographies.

139
Rollins, Charlemae H. Famous American Negro poets. New York, Dodd,
Mead [1965] 95 p. ports. (Famous biographies for young people)
                                                          PS153.N5R6

140
Rollins, Charlemae H. Famous Negro entertainers of stage, screen, and TV.
New York, Dodd, Mead [1967] 122 p. ports. (Famous biographies for
young people)   PN2286.R6

  Contents.—Ira Aldridge.—Marian Anderson.—Louis "Satchmo"
Armstrong.—Josephine Baker.—Harry Belafonte.—Nat "King" Cole.
—Sammy Davis, Jr.—"Duke" Ellington.—Lena Horne.—Eartha Kitt.
—Sidney Poitier.—Leontyne Price.—Paul Robeson.—Bill "Bojangles"
Robinson.—"Bert" Williams.—Thomas "Fats" Waller.

141
Rollins, Charlemae H. They showed the way; forty American Negro
leaders. New York, Crowell [1964] 165 p.   E185.96.R6

142
Scruggs, Lawson A. Women of distinction: remarkable in works and invin-
cible in character. Introduction by Mrs. Josephine Turpin Washington.
Special contributions by T. Thomas Fortune, William Still. Raleigh, L.
A. Scruggs, 1893. xxiii, 382 p. illus., ports.   E185.96.S4

143
Simmons, William J. Men of mark; eminent, progressive and rising. New
York, Arno Press, 1968. 1141 p. ports. (The American Negro, his his-
tory and literature)   E185.96.S45 1968

  Reprint of the 1887 ed.

144
Spellman, A. B. Four lives in the bebop business. New York, Pantheon
Books [1966] xiv, 241 p.   ML394.S74

145
Sterne, Emma G. I have a dream. Illustrated by Tracy Sugarman. New
York, Knopf [1965] x, 229, iv p. illus.   E185.96.S79

  Bibliography: p. [i]-iv (3d group).
  Contents.—Lift every voice and sing: Marian Anderson.—For life,
liberty, and the pursuit of jobs: Asa Philip Randolph.—Freedom on the
seas: Hugh Mulzac.—Hammer of justice: Thurgood Marshall.—Tired feet
and rested hearts: Rosa Lee Parks.—At the point of the bayonet: Daisy
Bates.—When freedom is a cup of coffee: James Farmer.—The man with
the bulletproof soul: Fred Shuttlesworth.—We shall overcome: John
Lewis.—One day out of a long tomorrow.

146
Styles, Fitzhugh L. The Negro lawyers' contribution to seventy-one years of our progress. 71st anniversary celebration of Negro progress, Philadelphia, 1863-1934. [Philadelphia, Summer Press, c1934] [13] p. ports.   E185.96.S83

147
Troup, Cornelius V. Distinguished Negro Georgians. Dallas, Royal Pub. Co. [1962] 203 p.   E185.93.G4T7
   Bibliography: p. 195-199.

148
Washington, John E. They knew Lincoln. With an introduction by Carl Sandburg. New York, E. P. Dutton, 1942. 244, [21] p. facsims., plates, ports.   E457.15.W32
   "Personal narrative of a Negro boy and man who sought all that could be possibly known about Abraham Lincoln from Negroes having impressions or facts he considered worth record."–Introduction.

149
Wright, Richard R. The bishops of the African Methodist Episcopal Church. [Nashville] Printed by the A.M.E. Sunday School Union, 1963. 389 p.   BX8442.W7

150
Young, Andrew S. N. Great Negro baseball stars, and how they made the major leagues. New York, A. S. Barnes [1953] 248 p. illus.
                                                                                    GV865.Y6A3

Individual

151
Allen, Walter C., *and* Brian A. L. Rust. King Joe Oliver. London, Sidgwick and Jackson [1958] 224 p. illus.   ML419.O4A6 1958
   Biography of a great jazz musician.

152
Anderson, Marian. My Lord, what a morning; an autobiography. New York, Viking Press, 1956. 312 p. illus.   ML420.A6A3

153

Armstrong, Henry. Gloves, glory, and God; an autobiography. [Westwood, N.J.] F. H. Revell Co. [1956] 256 p. illus.   GV1132.A7A3

154

Ashe, Arthur. Advantage Ashe, by Arthur Ashe, Jr., as told to Clifford George Gewecke, Jr. New York, Coward-McCann [1967] 192 p. illus.
                                                                GV994.A7A3

The achievements to date of an outstanding tennis player.

155

Aunt Sally; or, The cross the way to freedom. A narrative of the slave-life and purchase of the mother of Rev. Isaac Williams, of Detroit, Michigan. Cincinnati, American Reform Tract and Book Society, 1862. 216 p. illus., ports.   E444.W79

Slave life in North Carolina and Alabama.

156

Bailey, Pearl. The raw Pearl. New York, Harcourt, Brace & World [1968] 206 p. ports.   ML420.B123A3

157

[Ball, Charles] Fifty years in chains; or, The life of an American slave. New York, H. Dayton, 1859. 430 p.   E444.B184

Prepared by ――― Fisher from the verbal narrative of Ball, a slave.
Earlier editions published under title: *Slavery in the United States.*

158

Bartlett, Irving H. Wendell Phillips, Brahmin radical. Boston, Beacon Press [1961] 438 p.   E449.P5594

Bibliographical references included in "Notes" (p. 402-432).
An abolitionist leader.

159

Beckwourth, James P. The life and adventures of James P. Beckwourth [edited by] T. D. Bonner. New York, Arno Press, 1969. 537 p. illus. (The American Negro, his history and literature)   F592.B388 1969

Reprint of the 1856 ed.

160

Bennett, Lerone. What manner of man; a biography of Martin Luther King, Jr. With an introduction by Benjamin E. Mays. [3d rev. ed.] Chicago, Johnson Pub. Co., 1958. 251 p. illus., ports.

E185.97.K5B4 1968

161

Bernard, Jacqueline. Journey toward freedom; the story of Sojourner Truth. New York, Norton [1967] xiv, 265 p. illus., ports.

E185.97.T82

Bibliography: p. [255]-259.

Upon gaining her freedom in 1828, Sojourner Truth became a lecturer advocating immediate emancipation for her people and the right to vote for women.

162

Bibb, Henry. Narrative of the life and adventures of Henry Bibb, an American slave, written by himself. With an introduction by Lucius C. Matlack. New York, The author, 1949. 204 p. illus.   E444.B58

163

Bleiweiss, Robert M., Jacqueline L. Harris, *and* Joseph R. Marfuggi. Marching to freedom; the life of Martin Luther King, Jr. Middletown, Conn., American Education Publications [1968] 152 p. illus., ports.

E185.97.K5B55

164

Bradford, Sarah E. H. Harriet Tubman, the Moses of her people. Introduction by Butler A. Jones. New York, Corinth Books [1961] 149 p. illus. (The American experience series)   E444.T894

First ed. published in 1869 under title: *Scenes in the Life of Harriet Tubman.*

"Reprint of the expanded second edition of 1886."

165

Branch, Hettye W. The story of "80 John," a biography of one of the most respected Negro ranchmen in the Old West. New York, Greenwich Book Publishers [1960] 59 p.   F392.M6B7

A brief story of Daniel Webster Wallace, a Negro rancher.

166

Brawley, Benjamin G. Paul Laurence Dunbar, poet of his people. Chapel Hill, University of North Carolina Press, 1936. 159 p. port.   PS1557.B7

"Appendix. The Praise of Dunbar": p. 127-140.

Bibliography: p. 141-151.

167

Broderick, Francis L. W. E. B. DuBois, Negro leader in a time of crisis. Stanford, Calif., Stanford University Press, 1959. 259 p. illus.

E185.97.D73B7

Bibliography: p. [233]-236.

168

Brown, Claude. Manchild in the promised land. New York, Macmillan [1965] 415 p.   E185.97.B86A3

Autobiographical study of life in Harlem.

169

Brown, John. Slave life in Georgia: a narrative of the life, sufferings, and escape of John Brown, a fugitive slave, now in England. Edited by L. A. Chamerovzow. London [W. M. Watts] 1855. 250 p. port.   E444.B87

170

Buckle, Richard, *ed.* Katherine Dunham, her dancers, singers, musicians. Illustrations by Roger Wood and other photographers. London, Ballet Publications [1949] xvi, 79 p. (chiefly illus.)   GV1631.B8

English and French.

171

Buckler, Helen. Doctor Dan, pioneer in American surgery. Boston, Little, Brown [1954] 381 p. illus.   R154.W5225B8

Daniel Hale Williams was the first surgeon to operate on the heart.
2d ed. published in 1968 under title: *Daniel Hale Williams, Negro Surgeon.*

172

Byrd, James W. J. Mason Brewer, Negro folklorist. Austin, Tex., Steck-Vaughn Co. [1967] 44 p. (Southwest writers series, no. 12)
                                                                        GR55.B7B9
Bibliography: p. 43-44.

173

Cade, John B. Holsey, the incomparable. New York, Pageant Press [1964] 221 p.   BX8473.H58C3

Bibliography: p. 208-211.
Lucius Henry Holsey was a bishop in the Colored Methodist Episcopal Church in America.

174

Campanella, Roy. It's good to be alive. Boston, Little, Brown [1959] 306 p. illus.   GV865.C3A3

Life of one of the greatest baseball catchers.

175

Chesnutt, Helen M. Charles Waddell Chesnutt, pioneer of the color line. Chapel Hill, University of North Carolina Press [1952] 324 p. port.

PS1292.C6Z68

See Fiction section for his novels.

176

Christian, Malcolm H. My country and I; the interracial experiences of an American Negro. With essays on interracial understanding. New York, Exposition Press [1963] 96 p.   E185.97.C5A3

177

Clark, Septima P., *and* LeGette Blythe. Echo in my soul. Foreword by Harry Golden. New York, Dutton, 1962. 243 p. illus.   E185.97.C59A3

An autobiography of Septima Clark.

177a

Conrad, Earl. Harriet Tubman. Washington, Associated Publishers [1943] xiv, 248 p.   E444.T896

"Documentation": p. 227-238.

178

Cotton, Ella E. A spark for my people; the sociological autobiography of a Negro teacher. New York, Exposition Press [1954] 288 p.

LA2317.C64A3

179

Cronon, Edmund D. Black Moses; the story of Marcus Garvey and the Universal Negro Improvement Association. Madison, University of Wisconsin Press, 1955. 278 p. illus.   E185.97.G3C7

180

Cunningham, Virginia. Paul Laurence Dunbar and his song; illustrated with photographs. New York, Dodd, Mead, 1947. 283 p. illus.   PS1557.C8

Bibliography: p. 267-283.

181

Daly, John J. A song in his heart. Introduction by Harry F. Byrd; illustrated by Marian L. Larer. Philadelphia, Winston [1951] 102 p. illus.

ML410.B627D3

Songs: p. 71-102.

Biography of James A. Bland, composer of "Carry Me Back to Old Virginny."

182

Dancy, John C. Sand against the wind; the memoirs of John C. Dancy. With a foreword by Frank Angelo. Detroit, Wayne State University Press, 1966. 249 p. illus., ports. E185.97.D22A3

The author was a political leader in Detroit.

183

Davis, Edwin A., *and* William R. Hogan. The barber of Natchez, wherein a slave is freed and rises to a very high standing; wherein the former slave writes a two-thousand-page journal about his town and himself; wherein the free Negro diarist is appraised in terms of his friends, his code, and his community's reaction to his wanton murder. Baton Rouge, Louisiana State University Press [1954] 272 p. illus., facsim., port.
E185.97.J697D3

A memoir of William Johnson.

184

Davis, Sammy, Jane Boyar, *and* Burt Boyar. Yes I can; [the story of Sammy Davis, Jr. New York, Farrar, Straus & Giroux, 1965] 612 p. ports. PN2287.D322A3

185

Douglass, Frederick. Life and times of Frederick Douglass: his early life as a slave, his escape from bondage, and his complete history, written by himself. With a new introduction by Rayford W. Logan. New York, Collier Books [1962] 640 p. (Collier books, BS74) E449.D744 1962

Reprinted from the rev. ed. of *My Bondage and My Freedom*, published in 1892.

Includes bibliography.

186

Douglass, Frederick. Narrative of the life of Frederick Douglass, an American slave, written by himself. Edited by Benjamin Quarles. Cambridge, Mass., Belknap Press, 1960. xxvi, 163 p. map, port. (The John Harvard library) E449.D74905

187

Douty, Esther M. Forten, the sailmaker; pioneer champion of Negro rights. Chicago, Rand McNally [1968] 208 p. illus., ports. E185.97.F717D6

Bibliography: p. 200-201.

James Forten, an inventor and sailmaker, fought for civil rights of the Negro in the eighteenth century. He was a prominent Philadelphia Negro leader.

188
DuBois, William E. B. The autobiography of W. E. B. DuBois; a soliloquy on viewing my life from the last decade of its first century. [New York] International Publishers [1968] 448 p. ports.   E185.97.D73A3

A selected bibliography of the published writings of W. E. B. DuBois: p. 431-437.

189
DuBois, William E. B. John Brown. Centennial ed. New York, International Publishers [1962] 414 p. illus.   E451.D81 1962

First published in 1909.

Bibliography: p. [405]-408.

190
Dunham, Katherine. A touch of innocence. New York, Harcourt, Brace [1959] 312 p.   GV1785.D82A3

A well-known dancer and choreographer relates her experiences.

191
Elliott, Lawrence. George Washington Carver: the man who overcame. Englewood Cliffs, N.J., Prentice-Hall [1966] 256 p. port.   S417.C3E4

Bibliography: p. 255-256.

192
Emanuel, James A. Langston Hughes. New York, Twayne Publishers [1967] 192 p. (Twayne's United States authors series, TUSAS 123)
PS3515.U274Z64

Bibliography: p. 184-188.

193
English, James W. Handyman of the Lord: the life and ministry of the Rev. William Holmes Borders. New York, Meredith Press [1967] 177 p.
BX6455.B63E5

194
Farr, Finis. Black champion; the life and times of Jack Johnson. New York, Scribner [1964] 245 p. ports.   GV1132.J73F3

The first Negro heavyweight champion of the world.

195
Feldman, Eugene P. R. Black power in old Alabama; the life and stirring times of James T. Rapier, Afro-American Congressman from Alabama,

1839-1883. Illustrations by Margaret T. Burroughs [and] Jennie Washington. [Chicago] Museum of African American History [1968] 69 p. illus., map, port.   E185.97.R3F4

Bibliographical references included in "Footnotes" (p. [70]-[72]). Bibliography (annotated): p. [73]-[74].

196

Fisher, Miles M. The Master's slave, Elijah John Fisher; a biography, by his son, Miles Mark Fisher. With an introduction by the Rev. Lacey Kirk Williams, and an appreciation by the Hon. Martin B. Madden. Philadelphia, Judson Press [1922] 194 p. plates, ports.   BX6455.F5F5

197

Flipper, Henry O. The colored cadet at West Point. New York, Arno Press, 1969. 322 p. illus. (The American Negro, his history and literature)
                                                                U410.P1F6 1969
    Reprint of the 1878 ed.

198

Flipper, Henry O. Negro frontiersman: the Western memoirs of Henry O. Flipper, first Negro graduate of West Point. Edited with an introduction by Theodore D. Harris. El Paso, Texas Western College Press, 1963. 54 p. ports.   E185.97.F5 1963

"Sequel to . . . *The Colored Cadet at West Point* . . . published in 1878."

199

Foley, Albert S. Bishop Healy: beloved outcaste; the story of a great priest whose life has become a legend. New York, Farrar, Straus and Young [1954] 243 p. illus.   BX4705.H37F6

The life of James Augustine Healy, a bishop in the Catholic Church.

200

Foner, Philip S. Frederick Douglass, a biography. New York, Citadel Press [1964] 444 p. port.   E449.D755

"Reference notes": p. [377]-434.

201

Forman, James. Sammy Younge, Jr.: the first black college student to die in the black liberation movement. New York, Grove Press [1968] 282 p. illus., map, ports.   E185.97.Y64F6

202

Garvey, Amy J. Garvey and Garveyism. [Kingston, Jamaica, c1963] 287 p. ports.   E185.97.G3G3

    Biography of Marcus Garvey.

203

Garvey, Marcus. Philosophy and opinions. New York, Arno Press, 1968. 102 p. (The American Negro, his history and literature)

E185.97.G3A25 1968

    Reprint of 1923 ed. with a new introduction.

204

Gibson, Althea. I always wanted to be somebody. Edited by Ed Fitzgerald. New York, Harper [1958] 176 p. illus.   GV994.G5A3

    The story of the rise to fame of a Negro woman tennis star.

205

Gilbert, Olive. Narrative of Sojourner Truth. New York, Arno Press, 1968. 320 p. illus., facsims., ports. (The American Negro; his history and literature)   E185.97.T882

    First published in 1850.
    Reprint of the 1878 ed.
    "Book of life [by Frances W. Titus] ": p. [127]-320.
    Life of one of the few Negro women abolitionists.

206

Graham, Shirley. Paul Robeson, citizen of the world. Foreword by Carl Van Doren. New York, J. Messner [1946] 264 p. ports.   E185.97.R64

    Bibliography: p. 259.
    The story of an all-American football star who became an internationally famous singer and actor.

207

Graham, Shirley. Your most humble servant. New York, Messner [1949] 235 p.   QB36.B22G7

    "Notes on sources": p. 227-235.
    The story of Benjamin Banneker, mathematician and astronomer, who helped L'Enfant plan the city of Washington.

208

Gregory, Dick. Nigger; an autobiography, by Dick Gregory with Robert Lipsyte. New York, Dutton, 1964. 224 p. illus., ports. PN2287.G68A3

209
Hammon, Briton. A narrative of the uncommon sufferings, and surprizing deliverance of Briton Hammon, a Negro man . . . servant to General Winslow, of Marshfield, in New-England; who returned to Boston, after having been absent almost thirteen years. Containing an account of the many hardships he underwent from the time he left his master's house, in the year 1747, to the time of his return to Boston.—How he was cast away in the capes of Florida; . . . the horrid cruelty . . . of the Indians in murdering the whole ship's crew; . . . the manner of his being carried by them into captivity. Also, an account of his being confined four years and seven months in a close dungeon. Boston, Printed and sold by Green & Russell, 1760. 14 p.   F314.H22

Probably the earliest imprint by an American Negro.

210
Handy, William C. Father of the blues; an autobiography of W. C. Handy, edited by Arna Bontemps, with a foreword by Abbe Niles. New York, Macmillan, 1941. xiv, 317 p. plate, port.   ML410.H18B6

Includes music.
"Compositions, arrangements and books by W. C. Handy": p. 305-308.

211
Hardwick, Richard. Charles Richard Drew, pioneer in blood research. New York, Scribner [1967] 144 p.   QP26.D7H3

212
Hare, Maud C. Norris Wright Cuney: a tribune of the Black people. Introduction by Robert C. Cotner. Austin, Tex., Steck-Vaughn [c1968] xv, 230 p. illus., ports. (Steck-Vaughn's Life and adventure series)
                                                        E185.97.C97H3 1913a

A facsimile reproduction of the 1913 edition with new introduction. The story of a prominent Texas politician in the 1870's.

213
Harrison, Deloris. We shall live in peace: the teachings of Martin Luther King, Jr. Edited, and with commentary, by Deloris Harrison. Illustrated by Ernest Crichlow. New York, Hawthorn Books [1968] 64 p. illus.
                                                        E185.97.K5H3

214
Hawkins, Hugh, *ed.* Booker T. Washington and his critics; the problem of Negro leadership. Boston, Heath [1962] 113 p. (Problems in American civilization)   E185.97.W235

Includes bibliography.

215

Hawkins, William G. Lunsford Lane; or, Another helper from North Carolina. Boston, Crosby & Nichols, 1863. 305 p. port.   E444.L26

Lane, an antislavery lecturer, spent 32 years in slavery. He served as "waiter and messenger" to two Governors of the State of North Carolina.

216

Hayden, William. Narrative of William Hayden, containing a faithful account of his travels for a number of years, whilst a slave, in the South. Cincinnati [Published for the author] 1846. 156 p. plates, port.
E444.H41

217

Henson, Josiah. Father Henson's story of his own life. Introduction by Walter Fisher. New York, Corinth Books [1962] 212 p. illus. (The American experience series, AE18)   E444.H523 1962

First published in 1858 under title: *Truth Stranger than Fiction: Father Henson's Story of His Own Life.*

218

Henson, Matthew A. A Negro explorer at the North Pole. With a foreword by Robert E. Peary and an introduction by Booker T. Washington; with illustrations from photographs. New York, F. A. Stokes Co. [1912] xx, 200 p. illus., plates, ports.   G670.1909.H5

Reprint issued by Arno Press, 1969.

219

Hickey, Neil, *and* Ed Edwin. Adam Clayton Powell and the politics of race. New York, Fleet Pub. Corp. [1965] 308 p. illus., ports.
E748.P86H5

Bibliography: p. 299-300.

220

Holdredge, Helen O. Mammy Pleasant's partner. New York, Putnam [c1954] 300 p. illus.   F869.S3B4 1954

The story of Thomas Frederick Bell in San Francisco.

221

Holt, Rackham. George Washington Carver, an American biography. Rev. ed. Garden City, N.Y., Doubleday [1963] 360 p. illus.
S417.C3H6 1963

222

Holt, Rackham. Mary McLeod Bethune; a biography. Garden City, N.Y., Doubleday, 1964. 306 p. illus., ports.   E185.97.B34H6

An outstanding educator and political figure.

223

Horne, Lena, *and* Richard Schickel. Lena. Garden City, N.Y., Doubleday, 1965. 300 p. illus., ports.   ML420.H65A35

224

Hoyt, Edwin P. Paul Robeson, the American Othello. Cleveland, World Pub. Co. [1967] 228 p.   ML420.R73H7

Bibliographical footnotes.

225

Hughes, Langston. The big sea, an autobiography. New York, Hill and Wang [1963, c1940] 335 p. (American century series)

PS3515.U274Z5   1963

"AC65."

226

Hughes, Langston. I wonder as I wander; an autobiographical journey. New York, Rinehart [1956] 405 p.   PS3515.U274Z58

227

Hughes, William H., *and* Frederick D. Patterson. *eds.* Robert Russa Moton of Hampton and Tuskegee. Chapel Hill, University of North Carolina Press [1956] 238 p. illus.   E185.97.M92H8

"Volume of tributes to the life of Dr. Robert Russa Moton."

228

Huie, William B. Ruby McCollum; woman in the Suwannee jail. Rev. ed. [New York] New American Library [1964] 190 p. illus., port. (A Signet book)   DLC-LL

229

Hunton, George K. All of which I saw, part of which I was; the autobiography of George K. Hunton as told to Gary MacEóin. Introduction by Roy Wilkins. Garden City, N.Y., Doubleday, 1967. 283 p.

E185.61.H96

A crusader for racial justice.

230
Jackson, Mahalia. Movin' on up. With Evan McLeod Wylie. New York, Hawthorn Books [1966] 212 p. illus., ports.   ML420.J17A3
Discography: p. [215], [218]-[219].
Probably the best known gospel singer.

230a
Jefferson, Isaac. Memoirs of a Monticello slave, as dictated to Charles Campbell in the 1840's by Isaac, one of Thomas Jefferson's slaves. Edited by Rayford W. Logan. Charlottesville, Published by the University of Virginia Press for the Tracy W. McGregor Library, 1951. 45 p. port.   E444.J4
"Appeared simultaneously in the autumn 1951 *William and Mary Quarterly.*"
"Bibliographical note": p. 37-38.

231
Johnson, James W. Along this way; the autobiography of James Weldon Johnson. New York, Viking Press, 1933. 418 p. plates, ports.
                                                               E185.97.J69
Life of a diplomat, poet, and anthologist.

232
Keckley, Elizabeth H. Behind the scenes; or, Thirty years a slave, and four years in the White House. New York, G. W. Carleton, 1868. xvi, 371 p. port.   E457.15.K26
An unusual portrait of Mary Todd Lincoln by her dressmaker and "confidante" who served her while in the White House.
Reprint issued by Arno Press, 1968.

233
Kitt, Eartha. Thursday's child. New York, Duell, Sloan and Pearce [1956] 250 p. illus.   ML420.K5A3
Autobiographical.

234
Kytle, Elizabeth L. Willie Mae. New York, Knopf, 1958. 243 p.
                                                            E185.97.W62K9
Story of a Negro servant by one of her white employers.

235
Lee, Reba, *pseud.* I passed for white, by Reba Lee as told to Mary Hastings Bradley. New York, Longmans, Green, 1955. 274 p.   E185.97.Z9L4

236
Lewis, Claude. Adam Clayton Powell. Greenwich, Conn., Fawcett Publications [1963] 127 p. (Gold medal books)   E748.P86L4
"K1361."

237
Lichello, Robert. Pioneer in blood plasma: Dr. Charles Richard Drew. New York, J. Messner [1968] 190 p.   R154.D75L5
Bibliography: p. 185.

237a
Little, Malcolm. The autobiography of Malcolm X. With the assistance of Alex Haley. Introduction by M. S. Handler. Epilogue by Alex Haley. New York, Grove Press [1965] xvi, 455 p. illus., ports.   E185.61.L58

238
Lokos, Lionel. House divided; the life and legacy of Martin Luther King. New Rochelle, N.Y., Arlington House [1968] 567 p.   E185.97.K5L6

Bibliographical references included in "Notes" (p. [505]-555).

239
Louis, Joe. The Joe Louis story. [Written with the editorial aid of Chester L. Washington and Haskell Cohen] New York, Grosset & Dunlap [1953] 197 p. illus.   GV1132.L6A3 1953

First ed. published in 1947 under title: *My Life Story.*

240
Love, Nat. The life and adventures of Nat Love. New York, Arno Press, 1968. 162 p. illus., ports. (The American Negro, his history and literature)   F594.L89 1968

Reprint of the 1907 ed., with new introduction by W. L. Katz.
A pioneer in the westward movement.

241
McFeely, William S. Yankee stepfather: General O. O. Howard and the freedmen. New Haven, Yale University Press, 1968. 351 p. port. (Yale publications in American studies, 15)   E467.1.H8M3

Bibliography: p. [329]-346.
Oliver Otis Howard was one of the founders of Howard University.

242

Magdol, Edward. Owen Lovejoy, abolitionist in Congress. New Brunswick, N.J., Rutgers University Press [1967] 493 p. facsims., map, port.
E415.9.L89M3

Bibliography: p. [457]-468.

243

Magoun, F. Alexander. Amos Fortune's choice; the story of a Negro slave's struggle for self-fulfillment. Photographs by the author. Freeport, Me., Bond Wheelwright Co. [1964] 237 p. illus., facsims., maps.
E185.97.F73M3

Bibliographical footnotes.

244

Malvin, John. North into freedom; the autobiography of John Malvin, free Negro, 1795-1880. Edited and with an introduction by Allan Peskin. Cleveland, Press of Western Reserve University, 1966. 87 p.
E185.97.M26A3   1966

"A book from Cleveland State University."

Bibliographical references included in "Notes to the introduction" (p. 22-24).

245

Mann, Arthur W. The Jackie Robinson story. New York, Grosset & Dunlap [1951] 224 p. ports. (The Big league baseball library)
GV865.R6M3   1951

246

Marrant, John. A narrative of the life of John Marrant, of New York, in North America: giving an account of his conversion when only fourteen years of age: his leaving his mother's house from religious motives . . . and being at last taken by an Indian hunter among the Cherokees. Leeds, Printed by Davies, 1810. 24 p.   E99.C5M35

Preface signed: W. Aldridge. London, July 19, 1786.

247

Marshall, Herbert, *and* Mildred Stock. Ira Aldridge, the Negro tragedian. London, Rockliff [1958] 355 p. illus.   PN2598.A52M3

Includes bibliographies.

248

Martin Luther King, Jr.; man and teacher. [Baltimore, Printed by Vinmar Lithographing Co., 1968] 1 v. (unpaged) illus., ports.   E185.97.K5M34

249

Mays, Willie. Born to play ball, by Willie Mays, as told to Charles Einstein. New York, Putnam [1955] 168 p. illus.   GV865.M38A3

250

Mays, Willie. Willie Mays: My life in and out of baseball, as told to Charles Einstein. New York, Dutton, 1966. 320 p. illus., ports.

GV865.M38A32

251

Melbourn, Julius. Life and opinions of Julius Melbourn; with sketches of the lives and characters of Thomas Jefferson, John Quincy Adams, John Randolph, and several other eminent American statesmen. Edited by a late member of Congress. Syracuse, Hall & Dickson, 1847. 239 p. port.   E338.M51

252

Meltzer, Milton. Langston Hughes; a biography. New York, Crowell [1968] 281 p.   PS3515.U274Z68

Bibliography: p. 269-274.

253

Miller, Floyd. Ahdoolo: The biography of Matthew A. Henson. New York, Dutton, 1963. 221 p. illus.   G635.H4M5 1963

254

Miller, Margery. Joe Louis: American. New York, Current Books, A. A. Wyn [1945] 181 p. plates, ports.   GV1132.L6M5

255

Moore, Archie. The Archie Moore story. New York, McGraw-Hill [1960] 240 p. illus.   GV1132.M75A3

256

Morrow, Everett F. Black man in the White House; a diary of the Eisenhower years by the administrative officer for special projects, the White House, 1955-1961. New York, Coward-McCann [1963] 308 p.

E835.M58

257

Moton, Robert R. Finding a way out; an autobiography. Garden City, N.Y., Doubleday, Page, 1920. 295 p.   E185.97.M9

While president of Tuskegee Institute, Moton raised the standard of its secondary academic work to that of an accredited college.

258
Mulzac, Hugh. A star to steer by; by Hugh Mulzac, as told to Louis Burnham and Norval Welch. New York, International Publishers [1963] 251 p. illus. E185.63.M8

Life of a member of the merchant marine.

259
Newman, Shirlee P. Marian Anderson: lady from Philadelphia. Philadelphia, Westminster Press [c1965] 175 p. ports. ML420.A6N5

Bibliography: p. 163-165.

260
Olsen, Otto H. Carpetbagger's crusade; the life of Albion Winegar Tourgée. Baltimore, Johns Hopkins Press, 1965. xiv, 395 p. illus., facsims., ports. PS3088.O5

"Bibliography of Tourgée's writings": p. 355-362. "General bibliography": p. 363-382.

261
Ottley, Roi. The lonely warrior: the life and times of Robert S. Abbott. Chicago, H. Regnery Co., 1955. 381 p. illus. PN4874.A23O7

Bibliography: p. 369-370.
Abbott was editor for many years of the *Chicago Defender,* a major Negro newspaper.

262
Parker, Robert A. The incredible messiah; the deification of Father Divine. Boston, Little, Brown, 1937. 323 p. port. BX7350.P3

Bibliography: p. 321-323.
Self-named Father Divine, George Baker was the leader for many years of a religious sect.

263
Parks, Gordon. A choice of weapons. New York, Harper & Row [1966] 274 p. PS3566.A73C5

The story of a successful photographer-historian for *Life* magazine.

264
Parks, Lillian R. My thirty years backstairs at the White House [by] Lillian Rogers Parks in collaboration with Frances Spatz Leighton. New York, Fleet Pub. Corp. [1961] 346 p. E176.1.P37

265
Patterson, Floyd. Victory over myself. With Milton Gross. [New York] B. Geis Associates; distributed by Random House [1962] 244 p. illus.
GV1132.P3A3

266
Pauli, Hertha E. Her name was Sojourner Truth. New York, Appleton-Century-Crofts [1962] 250 p.   E185.97.T89

Bibliography: p. 242.244.
An abolitionist and lecturer until her death in 1883.

267
Pennington, James W. C. The fugitive blacksmith; or, Events in the history of James W. C. Pennington . . . formerly a slave in the state of Maryland, United States. 3d ed. London, C. Gilpin, 1850. xix, 84 p.
E444.P41

268
Preston, Edward. Martin Luther King: fighter for freedom. Garden City, N.Y., Doubleday [1968] 142 p. illus., ports. (Doubleday signal books)
E185.97.K5P7

269
Quarles, Benjamin, *comp.* Frederick Douglass. Englewood Cliffs, N.J., Prentice-Hall [1968] 184 p. (Great lives abserved)   E449.Q18

A Spectrum book.
"Bibliographical note": p. 179-181. Bibliographical footnotes.

270
Reddick, Lawrence D. Crusader without violence; a biography of Martin Luther King, Jr. New York, Harper [1959] 243 p. illus. E185.97.K5R4

271
Reisner, Robert G. Bird: the legend of Charlie Parker, New York, Citadel Press [1962] 256 p. ports.   ML419.P4R4

Discography: p. 241-256.

272
Robeson, Eslanda G. Paul Robeson, Negro. New York, Harper, 1930.
178 p. ports.   E185.97.R65

273
Robeson, Paul. Here I stand. New York, Othello Associates [1958] 128 p.
E185.97.R62

274
Robinson, James H. Road without turning, the story of Reverend James H. Robinson; an autobiography. New York, Farrar, Straus [1950] 312 p.   BX9225.R715A3

The founder of "Crossroads Africa" and religious leader of today.

275
Robinson, John R. Jackie Robinson, my own story, as told to Wendell Smith; foreword by Branch Rickey. New York, Greenberg [1948] 170 p. illus., ports.   GV865.R6A3

276
Robinson, John R., *and* Alfred Duckett. Breakthrough to the big league; the story of Jackie Robinson. New York, Harper & Row [1965] 178 p. ports. (A Breakthrough book)   GV865.R6A27

277
Roper, Moses. A narrative of the adventures and escape of Moses Roper, from American slavery; with a preface, by the Rev. T. Price. 4th ed. London, Harvey and Darton, 1840. 120 p. illus., port.   E444.R785

278
Rowan, Carl T. Wait till next year; the life story of Jackie Robinson, by Carl T. Rowan with Jackie Robinson. New York, Random House [1960] 339 p. illus.   GV865.R6R64

279
Rowland, Mabel, *ed.* Bert Williams, son of laughter; a symposium of tribute to the man and to his work, by his friends and associates, with a preface by David Belasco. New York, English Crafters [c1923] xvii, 218 p. illus., facsims., plates, ports.   PN2287.W46R6

Egbert Austin Williams was a comedian loved by theatergoers of the last generation.

280
Rudwick, Elliott M. W. E. B. DuBois; a study in minority group leadership. Philadelphia, University of Pennsylvania Press [1960] 382 p.
                                                                    E185.97.D73R8
Bibliography: p. 350-368.

281
Rudwick, Elliott M. W. E. B. DuBois, propagandist of the Negro protest. With a new preface by Louis Harlan and an epilogue by the author.

New York, Atheneum, 1968. 390 p. (Studies in American Negro life,
NL6)   E185.97.D73R8 1968
Atheneum paperbacks.
Bibliographical references included in "Notes": p. 319-376.

282
Schuyler, George S. Black and conservative; the autobiography of George
S. Schuyler. New Rochelle, N.Y., Arlington House [1966] 362 p.
                                                        PN4874.S35A3
Long-time columnist for the *Pittsburgh Courier,* a Negro newspaper.

283
Schuyler, Philippa D. Adventures in black and white. Foreword by Deems
Taylor. New York, R. Speller [1960] 302 p. illus.   ML417.S42A3
An account of the author's travels in sixty countries. This child
prodigy, musician, and composer, died in Vietnam while on a visit to
entertain the troops.

284
Singleton, George A. The autobiography of George A. Singleton. Boston,
Forum Pub. Co. [1964] 272 p. illus., ports.   BX8449.S5A3
The story of a minister in the African Methodist Episcopal Church.

285
Smith, Amanda B. An autobiography; the story of the Lord's dealings with
Mrs. Amanda Smith, the colored evangelist; containing an account of
her life work of faith, and her travels in America, England, Ireland,
Scotland, India and Africa, as an independent missionary. With an
introduction by Bishop Thoburn. Chicago, Meyer, 1893. xvi, 506 p.
plates, ports.   BV3785.S56A3 1893

286
Somerville, John A. Man of colour; an autobiography. With a foreword by
P. M. Sherlock. Kingston, Jamaica, Pioneer Press [1951] 134 p. illus.
                                                    E185.97.S65 1951

287
Spencer, Samuel R. Booker T. Washington and the Negro's place in Ameri-
can life. Boston, Little, Brown [1955] 212 p. (The Library of
American biography)   E185.97.W272

288
Sterling, Dorothy. Captain of the Planter; the story of Robert Smalls. Illustrated by Ernest Crichlow. Garden City, N.Y., Doubleday, 1958. 264 p. illus.   E185.97.S6S8

Bibliography: p. 247-264.
The *Planter* was a Confederate gunboat seized and turned over to the Union by Smalls, a slave crewman.

289
Steward, Austin. Twenty-two years a slave, and forty years a freeman; embracing a correspondence of several years, while president of Wilberforce Colony, London, Canada West. 3d ed. Rochester, N.Y., Allings & Cory, 1861. 360 p. plates, port.   E444.S845

290
Still, James. Early recollections and life of Dr. James Still. [Philadelphia] Printed for the author by J. B. Lippincott, 1877. 274 p. port.
E185.97.S85
James Still was the brother of William Still, the author of *The Underground Railroad.*

291
Tarry, Ellen. The third door; the autobiography of an American Negro woman. New York, D. McKay Co. [1955] 304 p.   E185.97.T37A3

292
Tarry, Ellen. Young Jim; the early years of James Weldon Johnson. New York, Dodd, Mead [1967] 230 p. facsims., ports.   PS3519.O2625Z89

293
Tatum, E. Ray. Conquest or failure? Biography of J. Frank Norris. Dallas, Baptist Historical Foundation [1966] 295 p. illus., ports.
BX6495.N59T3
Bibliographical footnotes.

294
Terrell, Mary C. A colored woman in a white world. Washington, Ransdell [c1940] 436 p. port.   E185.97.T47

295
Thomas, Jesse O. My story in black and white; the autobiography of Jesse O. Thomas. Foreword by Whitney M. Young, Jr. New York, Exposition Press [1967] 300 p. (An Exposition-banner book)   E185.97.T49A3

296

Thomas, Piri. Down these mean streets. New York, Knopf, 1967. 333 p.

F128.9.P8T5

Autobiographical account of life among the Puerto Ricans and Negroes in New York City.

297

Thomas, Will. The seeking. New York, A. A. Wyn [1953] 290 p.

E185.97.T52A3

Autobiographical; the author is a journalist and writer from Vermont.

297a

Thompson, Era B. American daughter. Chicago, University of Chicago Press [1946] 300 p.   E185.97.T53

Autobiographical.

298

Thompson, John. The life of John Thompson, a fugitive slave; containing his history of 25 years in bondage, and his providential escape. Worcester, J. Thompson, 1856. 143 p.   E444.T47

299

Thornbrough, Emma L., *comp.* Booker T. Washington. Englewood Cliffs, N.J., Prentice-Hall [c1969] 184 p. (Great lives observed)

E185.97.W277

A Spectrum book.
"Bibliographical note": p. 178-182.

300

Ward, Samuel R. Autobiography of a fugitive Negro: his anti-slavery labours in the United States, Canada, & England. New York, Arno Press, 1968. 412 p. port. (The American Negro: his history and literature)   E449.W27 1968

Reprint of the 1855 ed.

301

Washington, Booker T. Up from slavery; an autobiography. New York, Doubleday, Page, 1901. 330 p. port.   E185.97.W3

Originally published in the *Outlook*.

An illustrated edition with an introduction by Langston Hughes was published by Dodd, Mead, New York, in 1965.

302
Webb, Constance. Richard Wright; a biography. New York, Putnam [1968] 443 p. illus.   PS3545.R815Z9
Bibliography: p. 423-429.

303
Wesley, Charles H. Richard Allen, apostle of freedom. Washington, Associated Publishers [c1935] 300 p. port.   BX8449.A6W4
Bibliography: p. 277-285.
The first bishop of the African Methodist Episcopal Church.

304
White, Walter F. A man called White, the autobiography of Walter White. New York, Viking Press, 1948. 382 p.   E185.97.W6A3
Writer and former director of the NAACP.

305
Wright, Richard. Black boy; a record of childhood and youth. Illustrated by Ashley Bryan. Introductory note by Dorothy Canfield Fisher. Cleveland, World Pub. Co. [1950] 298 p. illus. (The Living library [L22])
PS3545.R815Z5 1950

306
Wright, Richard R. 87 years behind the black curtain; an autobiography. Philadelphia, Rare Book Co., 1965. 351 p.   BX8449.W7A3
Richard Robert Wright was a leader in the African Methodist Episcopal Church.

307
Yates, Elizabeth. Howard Thurman, portrait of a practical dreamer. New York, John Day Co. [1964] 249 p. port.   BX6455.T5Y3
"Chronological bibliography of works by Howard Thurman": p. 241-242.
A Negro philosopher, author, and religious leader.

308
Young, Andrew S. N. Sonny Liston, the champ nobody wanted. Chicago, Johnson Pub. Co. [1963] 224 p. illus.   GV1132.L5Y6

CIVIL RIGHTS

309
Ames, William C. The Negro struggle for equality in the twentieth century [Teachers ed.] Boston, Heath [1965] 182, 16 p. illus., maps. (New dimensions in American history)   E185.61.A49

Bibliography: p. 177-179.

310
Barbour, Floyd B., *comp*. The Black Power revolt; a collection of essays. Editor: Floyd B. Barbour. Boston, P. Sargent [1968] 287 p. (Extending horizons books)   E185.615.B2

Includes bibliographies.

311
Belfrage, Sally. Freedom summer. New York, Viking Press [1965] 246 p.
                                    E185.93.M6B4
A personal account of a civil rights worker who spent the summer of 1964 in Mississippi.

312
Blaustein, Albert P., *and* Robert L. Zangrando, *comps*. Civil rights and the American Negro; a documentary history. New York, Trident Press [1968] xv, 671 p.   E185.61.B66

313

Brink, William J., *and* Louis Harris. Black and white; a study of U.S. racial attitudes today. New York, Simon and Schuster [1967] 285 p.

E185.615.B7

314

Bureau of National Affairs, *Washington, D.C.* The Civil Rights Act of 1964: text, analysis, legislative history; what it means to employers, businessmen, unions, employees, minority groups. Washington [1964] 424 p. forms. (A BNA operations manual)   DLC-LL

315

Burns, William H. The voices of Negro protest in America. With a foreword by John Hope Franklin. New York, Oxford University Press [1963] 85 p.   E185.61.B96 1963b

"Issued under the auspices of the Institute of Race Relations, London."

Bibliography: p. [87]-[89].

316

Cable, George W. The Negro question; a selection of writings on civil rights in the South. Edited by Arlin Turner. Garden City, N.Y., Doubleday, 1958. 286 p. (Doubleday anchor books)   E185.61.C19 1958a

317

Cable, George W. A southerner looks at Negro discrimination; selected writings of George W. Cable, edited, with a biographical sketch, by Isabel Cable Manes. With an introduction by Professor Alva W. Taylor. [New York, 1946] 48 p.   E185.61.C197

"References": p. 48.

318

Carmichael, Stokely, *and* Charles V. Hamilton. Black Power: the politics of liberation in America. New York, Random House [1967] xii, 198 p.

E185.615.C32

Bibliography: p. 187-189.

319

Carter, Wilmoth A. The new Negro of the South; a portrait of movements and leadership. New York, Exposition Press [1967] 58 p. (An Exposition-university book)   E185.61.C285

Bibliography: p. [57]-58.

320

Chambers, Bradford, *comp.* Chronicles of Negro protest; a background book for young people, documenting the history of black power, compiled and edited with a commentary by Bradford Chambers. New York, Parents' Magazine Press [1968] 319 p. illus., facsims., ports. (Background books)   E185.61.C5

321

Clark, Mary T. Discrimination today; guidelines for civic action. Foreword by John J. Wright. New York, Hobbs, Dorman [1966] 372 p.

E185.61.C63

Includes bibliographies.

322

Clarke, Jacquelyne J. These rights they seek; a comparison of goals and techniques of local civil rights organizations. Washington, Public Affairs Press [1962] 85 p.   E185.93.A3C55

Bibliographical references included in "References" (p. 78-85).

323

Commager, Henry S., *comp.* The struggle for racial equality: a documentary record, selected and edited by Henry Steele Commager. New York, Harper & Row [1967] 260 p. (Harper torchbooks. The Academy library, TB1300)   E185.61.C72

"Originally published as part 4, chapter 14, of *Living Ideas in America* . . . revised and greatly expanded."

324

Congressional Quarterly Service, *Washington, D.C.* Revolution in civil rights. 4th ed. Washington, 1968. 119 p. (CQ background)

KF4757.Z9C6 1968

325

Cooke, Paul P. Civil rights in the United States. [Washington] Meridian House Foundation [1966] 32 p. illus., ports.   E185.61.C775

325a

Cox, Archibald, Mark D. Howe, *and* James R. Wiggins. Civil rights, the Constitution, and the courts, Cambridge, Harvard University Press, 1967. 76 p.   KF4757.A5C6

"Papers . . . originally presented in 1965-1966 as a series of evening lectures at the Massachusetts Historical Society."
Bibliographical footnotes.

326

Dorman, Michael. We shall overcome. [New York, Delacorte Press]; distributed by the Dial Press [1964] 340 p. E185.61.D69

327

Dumond, Dwight L. America's shame and redemption. Marquette, Northern Michigan University Press [1965] xvi, 171 p. port. E185.D9

328

Facts on File, *New York.* Civil rights, 1960-63; the Negro campaign to win equal rights and opportunities in the United States, compiled by the editors of Facts on file and News year. New York [1964] 152 p. illus., ports. (Interim history) E185.61.F16

A Facts on File publication.

329

Farmer, James. Freedom, when? With an introduction by Jacob Cohen. New York, Random House [1966, c1965] xxiv, 197 p. E185.61.F19

330

Fleishman, Stanley, *and* Sam Rosenwein. The new Civil Rights Act, what it means to you! [Los Angeles, Blackstone Book Co., 1964] 191 p.

DLC-LL

331

Franklin, John H., *and* Isidore Starr, *comps.* The Negro in twentieth century America; a reader on the struggle for civil rights. New York, Vantage Books [1967] xxii, 542 p. illus. E185.61.F79

Bibliography: p. [539]-542.

332

Friedman, Leon, *comp.* The civil rights reader; basic documents of the civil rights movement. Foreword by Martin Duberman. New York, Walker [1967] xxi, 348 p. E185.61.F857

Bibliography: p. [347]-348.

333

Golden, Harry L. Mr. Kennedy and the Negroes. Cleveland, World Pub. Co. [1964] 319 p. group port. E185.61.G58

Bibliography: p. 309-314.

334

Grant, Joanne, *comp.* Black protest; history, documents, and analyses, 1619 to the present, edited with introduction and commentary by

Joanne Grant. [New York, Fawcett World Library, 1968] 505 p. (The Political perspectives series)   E185.G75

A Fawcett premier book.

Bibliography: p. [506]-[507].

335

Gregory, Dick. The shadow that scares me. Edited by James R. McGraw. Garden City, N.Y., Doubleday, 1968. 213 p.   E185.615.G7

336

Handlin, Oscar. Fire-bell in the night; the crisis in civil rights. Boston, Little, Brown [1964] 110 p.   E185.61.H23

337

Hansberry, Lorraine. The movement; documentary of a struggle for equality. New York, Simon and Schuster, 1964. 127 p. (chiefly illus., ports)
E185.61.H24

338

Harris, Janet. The long freedom road; the civil rights story. Foreword by Whitney M. Young, Jr. New York, McGraw-Hill [1967] 150 p.
E185.61.H27

Bibliography: p. 147.

339

Hedgeman, Anna A. The trumpet sounds; a memoir of Negro leadership. New York, Holt, Rinehart and Winston [1964] 202 p.   E185.97.H44

340

Holt, Len. The summer that didn't end. New York, Morrow, 1965. 351 p.
E185.61.H75

The struggle for civil rights in Mississippi.

341

Imari, *Brother.* War in America; the Malcolm X doctrine. Detroit, Malcolm X Society [1968] 64 p. port.   E185.615.I45

342

Isaacs, Harold R. The new world of Negro Americans. A study from the Center for International Studies, Massachusetts Institute of Technology. New York, John Day Co. [1963] 366 p.   E185.61.I75

Includes bibliography.

343
Jackson, Joseph H. Unholy shadows and freedom's holy light. Nashville, Townsend Press [1967] 270 p. group ports. E185.61.J15

Bibliography: p. 264-266.

344
Jacobs, Paul. Prelude to riot; a view of urban America from the bottom. New York, Random House [1968, c1967] 298 p. E185.615.J3 1968
"Sponsored by the Center for the Study of Democratic Institutions."

345
Kahn, Tom. Unfinished revolution. [With forewords by Norman Thomas and James Lawson] New York [Socialist Party-Social Democratic Federation] 1960. 64 p. illus. E185.61.K335

Bibliography: p. 60-63.

346
Kalven, Harry. The Negro and the First amendment. Chicago, University of Chicago Press [1966, c1965] 244 p. (Phoenix books, P240)
DLC-LL
"Lectures . . . originally given for the Ohio State Law Forum on April 7, 8, and 9, 1964."
Bibliographical references included in "Notes" (p. [215]-244).

347
Kennedy, Robert F. Rights for Americans; the speeches of Robert F. Kennedy. Edited and with commentary by Thomas A. Hopkins. Indianapolis, Bobbs-Merrill [1964] 262 p. E185.61.K367

348
Killian, Lewis M. The impossible revolution? Black power and the American dream. New York, Random House [1968] xx, 198 p. (Studies in sociology, SS40) E185.615.K48

Bibliography: p. [189]-191.

349
Killian, Lewis M., *and* Charles Grigg. Racial crisis in America; leadership in conflict. Englewood Cliffs, N.J., Prentice-Hall [1964] 144 p. (A Spectrum book) E185.61.K49

Includes bibliographies.

350

King, Martin Luther. A Martin Luther King treasury. Photographs by Roland Mitchell. Yonkers, N.Y., Educational Heritage [1964] 352 p. illus., ports. (Negro heritage library)   E185.61.K535

Bibliographical references included in "Notes" (p. 338-348).
Contents.—Stride toward freedom; the Montgomery story.—Strength to love.—The days of Martin Luther King, Jr.: a photographic diary. —An appeal to the President of the United States.

351

King, Martin Luther. Where do we go from here: Chaos or community? New York, Harper & Row [1967] 209 p.   E185.615.K5

Bibliographical references included in "Notes" (p. 203-204).
London ed. (Hodder & Stoughton) has title: *Chaos or Community?*

352

King, Martin Luther. Why we can't wait. New York, Harper & Row [1964] 178 p. illus., ports.   E185.61.K54

353

Konvitz, Milton R. A century of civil rights. With a study of State law against discrimination, by Theodore Leskes. New York, Columbia University Press, 1961. 293 p.   DLC-LL

"Table of statutes": p. [278]-280.
Bibliographical footnotes.

354

Kunstler, William M. Deep in my heart. Forewords by James Forman and Martin Luther King, Jr. New York, Morrow, 1966. xxvi, 384 p.

DLC-LL

Autobiographical.

355

Leinwand, Gerard, *comp.* The Negro in the city. New York, Washington Square Press [1968] 191 p. illus. (Problems of American society)

E185.61.L513

Bibliographical references included in "Notes" (p. 179-182).

356

Levy, Charles J. Voluntary servitude; whites in the Negro movement. New York, Appleton-Century-Crofts [1968] 125 p.   E185.92.L46

Bibliographical footnotes.

357

Lewis, Anthony. Portrait of a decade; the second American revolution [by] Anthony Lewis and the New York times. New York, Random House [1964] 322 p. illus.   E185.61.L52 1964

London ed. (Faber) has title: *The Second American Revolution: a First-hand Account of the Struggle for Civil Rights.*

358

Lincoln, Charles Eric, *comp.* Is anybody listening to black America? New York, Seabury Press [1968] 280 p. (A Seabury paperback SP-54)
                                                                                E185.615.L48
Includes bibliographical references.

359

Lomax, Louis E. The Negro revolt. New York, Harper [1962] 271 p.
                                                                                E185.61.L668
Includes bibliography.

360

Mendelsohn, Jack. The martyrs: sixteen who gave their lives for racial justice. New York, Harper & Row [1966] 227 p. ports.   E185.61.M54

361

Moral crisis; the case for civil rights, as stated by John F. Kennedy [and others] Minnesota, Gilbert Pub. Co. [1964] 185 p. illus., ports.
                                                                                E185.61.M79
On spine: *The Case for Civil Rights.*

362

Muse, Benjamin. The American Negro revolution; from nonviolence to black power, 1963-1967. Bloomington, Indiana University Press [1968] 345 p.   E185.615.M83

363

Nelson, Bernard H. The Fourteenth amendment and the Negro since 1920. New York, Russell & Russell [1967, c1946] 185 p.
                                                                                E185.61.N44 1967
Bibliography: p. 172-181.

363a

Nye, Russel B. Fettered freedom; civil liberties and the slavery controversy, 1830-1860. [Rev. ed. East Lansing] Michigan State University Press [1964, c1963] 353 p.   JC599.U5N9 1964
Bibliography: p. 319-[343].

364

Pain, William. To do justice, by the photographers and editors of Black star. [New York] Pyramid Publications, c1965. 104 p. illus., ports. (A Pyramid publication)   E185.615.P3

On cover: *To Do Justice; the Heroic Struggle for Human Rights.*

365

Pettigrew, Thomas F. Epitaph for Jim Crow. New York, Anti-Defamation League of B'nai B'rith [1964] 59 p. illus.   E185.61.P48

"G415."

366

Proctor, Samuel D. The young Negro in America, 1960-1980. New York, Association Press [1966] 160 p.   E185.61.P76

Bibliographical references included in "Notes by chapters" (p. 159-160).

367

Saunders, Doris E., *ed.* The Kennedy years and the Negro, a photographic record. Introduction by Andrew T. Hatcher. Designed by Herbert Temple. Chicago, Johnson Pub. Co., 1964. 143 p. illus., ports.   E185.6.S3

368

Segal, Ben D., William Korey, *and* Charles N. Mason, *eds.* Civil rights in the Nation's Capital: a report on a decade of progress. [New York] National Association of Intergroup Relations Officials, 1959. 90 p. illus.   E185.93.D6S4

"Appeared originally as volume 1, no. 5, of the *Journal of Intergroup Relations.*"

369

Smith, Lillian E. Our faces, our words. New York, W. W. Norton [1964] 128 p. illus.   E185.61.S647

370

Sobel, Lester A., *ed.* Civil rights, 1960-66. New York, Facts on File [1967] 504 p. (Interim history)   E185.61.S66

A Facts on File publication.

371

Southern, David W. The malignant heritage; Yankee progressives and the Negro question, 1901-1914. Chicago, Loyola University Press, 1968. 116 p. (William P. Lyons master's essay award, 1967)   E185.61.S685

Bibliography: p. 101-111.

372
Stahl, David, Frederick B. Sussmann, *and* Neil J. Bloomfield, *eds.* The community and racial crises. New York, Practising Law Institute [1966] xvii, 364 p. E185.615.S7

Outgrowth of a forum devoted to the community and racial crisis, held in New York City in December 1964.

373
Sterling, Dorothy. Tear down the walls! A history of the American civil rights movement. Garden City, N.Y., Doubleday [1968] 259 p. illus., facsims., ports. E185.6.S76

Bibliography: p. [251]-252.

374
Sugarman, Tracy. Stranger at the gates; a summer in Mississippi. Illustrated by the author. Foreword by Fannie Lou Hamer. New York, Hill and Wang [1966] xiv, 240 p. E185.93.M6S88

375
Thomas, Howard E., *and* Sister Mary Peter. Organizing for human rights; a handbook for teachers and students. Dayton, Ohio, G. A. Pflaum [c1966] 64 p. illus. E185.615.T5

"Resource section": p. 39-58.

376
U.S. *Commission on Civil Rights.* Freedom to the free: century of emancipation, 1863-1963; a report to the President. [Washington, For sale by the Supt. of Docs., U.S. Govt. Print. Off., 1963] 246 p. E185.61.U582

Bibliography: p. 209-240.

377
U.S. *Commission on Civil Rights.* Hearing held in Cleveland, Ohio, April 1-7, 1966. Washington, For sale by the Supt. of Docs., U.S. Govt. Print. Off., 1966. 888 p. illus., maps. F499.C6A43

378
U.S. *President, 1961-1963 (Kennedy)* Civil rights. Message relative to civil rights, and a draft of a bill to enforce the constitutional right to vote, to confer jurisdiction upon the District Courts of the United States to provide injunctive relief against discrimination in public accommodations, to authorize the Attorney General to institute suits to protect

constitutional rights in education, to establish a community relations service, to extend for four years the Commission on Civil Rights, to prevent discrimination in Federally assisted programs, to establish a Commission on Equal Employment Opportunity, and for other purposes. [Washington, U.S. Govt. Print. Off., 1963] 24 p. (88th Congress, 1st session. House of Representatives. Document no. 124)

E185.61.U5865

379
Warren, Robert Penn. Who speaks for the Negro? New York, Vintage Books [1966] 454 p.   E185.61.W22 1966

380
Williams, Robert F. Negroes with guns. Edited by Marc Schleifer. New York, Marzani & Munsell [c1962] 128 p. illus.   F264.M75W5

Concerns the Monroe, North Carolina, confrontation.

381
Wright, Nathan. Black power and urban unrest; creative possibilities. New York, Hawthorn Books [1967] 200 p.   E185.615.W7

Bibliographical references included in "Notes" (p. 195).

382
Young, Whitney M. To be equal. New York, McGraw-Hill [1964] 254 p.
E185.61.Y73

383
Bivins, S. Thomas. The southern cookbook; a manual of cooking and list of menus, including recipes used by noted colored cooks and prominent caterers. Hampton, Va., Press of the Hampton Institute, 1912. 239 p.
TX715.B5

384
Bowers, Lessie. Plantation recipes. [New York] R. Speller, 1959. 194 p.
TX715.B76

385
Campbell, Tunis G. Hotel keepers, head waiters, and housekeepers' guide. Boston, Printed by Coolidge and Wiley, 1848. 192 p. illus.　TX925.C3

386
De Knight, Freda. The Ebony cookbook: a date with a dish; a cookbook of American Negro recipes. With a foreword by Gertrude Blair. Chicago, Johnson Pub. Co., 1962. 390 p. illus.　　　TX715.D326

387
Gaskins, Ruth L. A good heart and a light hand; Ruth L. Gaskins' collection of traditional Negro recipes. [Alexandria, Va., Fund for Alexandria, c1968] 110 p. illus.　　　　TX715.G243

388

Kaiser, Inez Y. Soul food cookery. New York, Pitman Pub. Co., 1968. 90 p.   DHU

389

Kaufman, William I., *and* Mary U. Cooper. The art of Creole cookery. Illustrated by Margot Tomes. Garden City, N.Y., Doubleday, 1962. 227 p. illus.   TX725.K333

390

[Mahammitt, Sarah H. T.] Recipes and domestic service; the Mahammitt School of Cookery. [Omaha, c1939] 160 p.   TX715.M246

"Copyright . . . by Mrs. T. P. Mahammitt."

391

National Council of Negro Women. The historical cookbook of the American Negro. Published under the auspices of the Council's Archives and Museum Dept. Compiled and edited by Sue Bailey Thurman, chairman. [Washington] Corporate Press, c1958. 144 p. illus.   TX715.N326

392

Negro Culinary Art Club of Los Angeles. Eliza's cook book; favorite recipes. Los Angeles, Wetzel Pub. Co. [c1936] 101 p.   TX715.N387

393

Ott, Eleanore. Plantation cookery of old Louisiana. With decorations by Mary Evans Isom. New Orleans, Harmanson [c1938] 96 p. illus., facsim.   TX715.O85

394

Porter, *Mrs.* M. E. Mrs. Porter's new southern cookery book, and companion for frugal and economical housekeepers; containing carefully prepared and practically tested recipes for all kinds of plain and fancy cooking. Philadelphia, J. E. Potter [c1871] 416 p.   TX715.P844

395

Smith, Myrtle E. A Civil War cook book; typical of the times but timely for today. Harrogate, Tenn., Priv. print., Lincoln Memorial University [1961] 268 p. illus.   TX715.S666

Bibliography: p. 267-268.

ECONOMIC CONDITIONS

396
Bell, William K. Fifteen million Negroes and fifteen billion dollars. New
York, W. K. Bell Publications [1956] 147 p.   E185.8.B46

397
Blair, Lewis H. A Southern prophecy: The prosperity of the South
dependent upon the elevation of the Negro (1889). Edited, with an
introduction by C. Vann Woodward. Boston, Little, Brown [1964]
xlvi, 201 p. facsim., port.   E185.61.B66 1964
   Bibliographical footnotes.

398
Bradford, Amory. Oakland's not for burning. New York, D. McKay Co.
[1968] 248 p.   HD5726.O22B7

399
Bullock, Henry A. Pathways to the Houston Negro market. [Ann Arbor,
Mich., Distributed by J. W. Edwards, 1957] 232 p. illus.   F394.H8B9

400
Davis, Robert E. The American Negro's dilemma; the Negro's self-imposed
predicament. New York, Philosophical Library [1954] 147 p.
          E185.6.D35

401

De Mond, Albert L. Certain aspects of the economic development of the American Negro, 1865-1900. Washington, Catholic University of America Press, 1945. 187 p. (Catholic University of America. Studies in economics, v. 18)   E185.8.D4

>   Thesis (Ph. D.)—Catholic University of America, 1945.
>   Bibliography: p. 163-183.

402

District of Columbia. *Dept. of Public Welfare.* The improving economic status of the Negro in the District of Columbia. Rev. Washington, Division of Research and Statistics, Dept. of Public Welfare, 1954. 1 v. (unpaged) illus.   E185.93.D6A5 1954c

403

DuBois, William E. B., *ed.* Economic co-operation among Negro Americans. Report of a social study made by Atlanta University under the patronage of the Carnegie Institution of Washington, D.C., together with the proceedings of the 12th Conference for the Study of the Negro Problems, held at Atlanta University, on Tuesday, May the 28th, 1907. Atlanta, Atlanta University Press, 1907. 184 p. diagrs. (Atlanta University publications, no. 12)   E185.5.A88 no. 12
                                                          HD3446.Z5N3

>   "Select bibliography of economic co-operation among Negro Americans": p. [6]-9.

404

Edwards, Paul K. The southern urban Negro as a consumer. New York, Prentice-Hall, 1932. xxiv, 323 p. illus., diagrs., maps.   E185.6.E38

>   Bibliography: p. [309]-315.

405

Fein, Rashi. An economic and social profile of the Negro American. Washington, Brookings Institution, 1966 [c1965] 815-846 p. (Brookings Institution reprints, 110)   E185.8.F4

>   "Reprinted January 1966 . . . from *Daedalus,* fall, 1965."
>   Includes bibliographical references.

406

Fleming, Walter L. The Freedmen's Savings Bank; a chapter in the economic history of the Negro race. Chapel Hill, University of North Carolina Press, 1927. 170 p. (Vanderbilt University publications)
                                                          HG2613.W34F6 1927

"An expansion of a paper . . . published in the *Yale Review* in 1906."

Bibliography: p. 17-18, 162-163.

407

Ginzberg, Eli, ed. The Negro challenge to the business community. New York, McGraw-Hill [1964] 111 p.   E185.8.G57

"Highlights of a conference held at Arden House on January 15 to 17, 1964 under the auspices of the executive program of the Graduate School of Business, Columbia University."

408

Harris, Abram L. The Negro as capitalist; a study of banking and business among American Negroes. Gloucester, Mass., P. Smith, 1968 [c1936] 205 p. illus.   E185.8.H26 1968

Bibliographical footnotes.

409

Henry, Waights G. The Negro as an economic factor in Alabama. Nashville, Printed for the author, Publishing House M. E. Church, South, Smith & Lamar, agents, 1919. 111 p.   E185.93.A3H5

Thesis (Ph. D.)—Boston University.
"Reference books": p. [107]-111.

410

Hill, Timothy A. The Negro and economic reconstruction. Washington, Associates in Negro Folk Education, 1937. 78 p. (Bronze booklet no. 5)   E185.5.B85 no. 5

"Selected readings" at end of each chapter.

411

Holmes, Samuel J. The Negro's struggle for survival; a study in human ecology. Port Washington, N.Y., Kennikat Press [1966, c1965] 296 p.   E185.88.H65 1966

First published in 1937.
Bibliography: p. 263-290.

412

Johnson, Joseph T. The potential Negro market. New York, Pageant Press [1952] 185 p.   HF3031.J6

413

Miller, Herman P. Poverty and the Negro. [Los Angeles, Institute of Government and Public Affairs, University of California, 1965?] 30 leaves. ([California. University. University at Los Angeles. Institute of Government and Public Affairs] MR-37)   AS36.C2A35 no. 37

"Paper presented at University of West Virginia Conference on Poverty, May 3, 1965."
Bibliographical footnotes.

414

National Urban League. Economic and social status of the Negro in the United States. [New York, 1961] 32 p.   E185.6.N257

Bibliography: p. 31-32.

415

The Negro and the city. New York, Time-Life Books [1968] 159 p. col. illus.   E185.8.N4 1968

"Adapted from a special issue [Jan. 1968] of *Fortune* on: 'Business and the Urban Crisis.'"
Contents.—Introduction, by R. C. Weaver.—The deeper shame of the cities, by M. Ways.—The new Negro mood, by R. Beardwood.—Business reclaims human resources, by G. Burck.—More dollars and more diplomas, by E. K. Faltermayer.—The St. Louis economic blues, by W. S. Rukeyser.—The case against unions, by T. O'Hanlon.—"Our war was with the police department," by E. Carruth.—Systems engineering invades the city, by L. Lessing.—Mortgages for the slums, by W. McQuade.—What business can do for the cities, by the editors of *Fortune.*

416

Newman, Dorothy K. The Negroes in the United States, their economic and social situation. Washington, U.S. Dept. of Labor, Bureau of Labor Statistics; for sale by the Supt. of Docs., U.S. Govt. Print. Off., 1966. 241 p. illus. (U.S. Bureau of Labor Statistics. Bulletin no. 1511)
          HD8051.A62 no. 1511
          E185.8.N47

Bibliography: p. 49-53.

417

Phillips, Ulrich B. The slave economy of the Old South; selected essays in economic and social history. Edited and with an introduction by Eugene D. Genovese. Baton Rouge, Louisiana State University Press [1968] xiv, 304 p.   HC107.A13P66

"A bibliography of the printed writings of Ulrich Bonnell Phillips, compiled by David M. Potter": p. 291-300.

Includes bibliographical references.

418

Pitts, Nathan A. The cooperative movement in Negro communities of North Carolina. Washington, Catholic University of America Press, 1950. 201 p. maps. (The Catholic University of America. Studies in sociology, v. 33)   HD3446.A3N85

Thesis—Catholic University of America.

Bibliography: p. [193]-196.

419

Schuchter, Arnold. White power, black freedom; planning the future of urban America. Boston, Beacon Press [1968] xvii, 650 p.   HT123.S38

Includes bibliographical references.

420

Sterner, Richard M., *and others.* The Negro's share; a study of income, consumption, housing and public assistance [by] Richard Sterner in collaboration with Lenore A. Epstein, Ellen Winston and others. New York, Harper [1943] 433 p.   E185.8.S8

421

Stuart, Merah S. An economic detour; a history of insurance in the lives of American Negroes. New York, W. Malliet, 1940. xxv, 339 p. facsims., plates, ports.   HG8799.S75

Bibliography: p. 337-338.

422

U.S. *Bureau of Labor Statistics.* The economic situation of Negroes in the United States. Rev. [Washington] U.S. Dept. of Labor; [for sale by the Supt. of Docs., U.S. Govt. Print. Off.] 1962. 32 p. tables. ([U.S. Dept. of Labor] Bulletin S-3)   E185.8.U529

423

U.S. *Bureau of Labor Statistics.* Notes on the economic situation of Negroes in the United States. 1957+ [Washington] tables.

E185.8.U527

424

U.S. *Dept. of Health, Education, and Welfare.* The Negro family's search for economic security, by Joseph H. Douglass, assistant to the Assistant

Secretary for Program Analysis. [Washington] 1956. 1 v. (various pagings) diagrs., tables.   E185.8.U558

Bibliography: p. [1]-11.

425

Washington, Booker T., *and* William E. B. DuBois. The Negro in the South, his economic progress in relation to his moral and religious development; being the William Levi Bull lectures for the year 1907. Philadelphia, G. W. Jacobs [1907] 222 p.   E185.6.W316

Contents.—1. The economic development of the Negro race in slavery, by B. T. Washington.—2. The economic development of the Negro race since its emancipation, by B. T. Washington.—3. The economic revolution in the South, by W. E. B. DuBois.—4. Religion in the South, by W. E. B. DuBois.—Notes to chapters 3 and 4 (Bibliography: p. 220-222).

426

Whiting, Helen A. J. Climbing the economic ladder. [Atlanta, 1948] 100 p. illus.   E185.8.W48

"Selected references for understanding and improving Southern life": p. 99-100.

Business

427

Association for the Study of Negro Life and History. The Negro as a business man, by J. H. Harmon, Jr., Arnett G. Lindsay, and Carter G. Woodson. Washington [c1929] 111 p.   E185.8.A84

Contents.—The Negro as a local business man.—The Negro in banking.—Insurance among Negroes.

428

Business leadership and the Negro crisis. Edited by Eli Ginzberg. New York, McGraw-Hill [1968] 175 p.   E185.8.B8

Papers presented at a conference conducted by the Graduate School of Business of Columbia University at Arden House in 1968.

429
Carter, Wilmoth A. The urban Negro in the South. New York, Vantage
Press [1962] 272 p. illus.   F264.R1C3
  Bibliography: p. 269-272.

430
DuBois, William E. B., *ed.* The Negro in business; report of a social study
made under the direction of Atlanta University; together with the Proceedings of the Fourth Conference for the Study of the Negro Problems, held at Atlanta University, May 30-31, 1899. Atlanta [Atlanta
University] 1899. 77 p. (Atlanta University publications, no. 4)
                                                    E185.5.A88 no. 4
                                                          E185.8.D83
431
Kinzer, Robert H., *and* Edward Sagarin. The Negro in American business;
the conflict between separatism and integration. New York, Greenberg
[1950] 220 p.   E185.8.K5
  "An expansion of a thesis written by Robert H. Kinzer and sub-
mitted [under title: *Separatism or Integration: the Dilemma of the
Negro in American Business*] to the Graduate School of Business
Administration of New York University . . . [for] the degree of master
of arts."
  Bibliography: p. 203-210.

432
National Conference on Small Business, *Washington, D.C., 1961.* Problems
and opportunities confronting Negroes in the field of business; report.
Chairman: Charles C. Diggs, Jr. Editor: H. Naylor Fitzhugh. [Washing-
ton] U.S. Dept. of Commerce, for sale by the Supt. of Docs., U.S.
Govt. Print. Off., 1962. 102 p.   E185.8.N23 1961c
  "Sponsored by an independent committee composed mainly of
Negroes engaged in business and related activities in Government and
education and some national organizations."

433
Pierce, Joseph A. Negro business and business education, their present and
prospective development. New York, Harper [1947] xiv, 338 p. tables.
(Atlanta University publications, no. 24)   E185.5.A88 no. 24
                                                          E185.8.P5
  "References" at end of most of the chapters.

434
Washington, Booker T. The Negro in business. Boston, Hertel, Jenkins
[c1907] 379 p. plates, ports.   E185.8.W31

Employment

435

Alexander, Richard D., *and others*. The management of racial integration in business; special report to management. Prepared under the supervision of Georges F. Doriot. New York, McGraw-Hill [1964] 147 p.

E185.8.A55

Bibliography: p. 139-147.

436

Becker, Gary S. The economics of discrimination. [Chicago] University of Chicago Press [1957] 137 p. diagrs. (Studies in economics of the Economics Research Center of the University of Chicago)

HD4903.5.U58B4

Bibliographical footnotes.

437

Blood, Robert O. Northern breakthrough. Belmont, Calif., Wadsworth Pub. Co. [1968] 157 p.   F614.M6B55

Bibliography: p. 151-152.

438

Cayton, Horace R., *and* George S. Mitchell. Black workers and the new unions. Chapel Hill, University of North Carolina Press, 1939. xviii, 473 p.   E185.8.C39

"Three industries have been chosen for examination: iron and steel, meat packing, and railroad car shops."

Bibliography: p. [458]-467.

439

Conference of Community Leaders on Equal Employment Opportunity, *Washington, D.C., 1962.* The American dream—equal opportunity; report on the Community Leaders' Conference, sponsored by President's Committee on Equal Opportunity, Washington, D.C., May 19, 1962. [Washington, U.S. Govt. Print. Off., 1962] 56 p. illus.

HD4903.5.U58C6 1962c

440

Connecticut. *Commission on Civil Rights.* Training of Negroes in the skilled trades, prepared by Henry G. Stetler, supervisor, Research Division. Hartford, 1954. 62 p.   LC2802.C8A52

441
Daykin, Jon J. A study of southern Negro police officers in eleven selected major mid-south cities. [University, Miss.] 1965. 137 leaves.

HV8145.A13D3

Thesis (M.A.)–University of Mississippi.
Bibliography: leaves [128]-137.

442
Donald, Henderson H. The Negro migration of 1916-1918. Washington, Association for the Study of Negro Life and History, 1921. 116 p.

E185.6.D67

"Reprinted from the *Journal of Negro History*, v. 6, no. 4, October 1921."

443
Durham, Philip, *and* Everett L. Jones. The Negro cowboys. New York, Dodd, Mead [1965] 278 p. illus., maps, ports.

F596.D8

444
Edwards, Gilbert Franklin. The Negro professional class. With a foreword by Otis Dudley Duncan. Glencoe, Ill., Free Press [1959] 224 p.

E185.82.E23

"A development of the author's doctoral dissertation at the University of Chicago."
Bibliography: p. 215-219.

445
Ferman, Louis A. The Negro and equal employment opportunities; a review of management experiences in twenty companies. New York, Praeger [1968] xv, 195 p. (Praeger special studies in U.S. economic and social development)

E185.8.F44

446
Ferman, Louis A., Joyce L. Kornbluh, *and* Joe A. Miller, *comps.* Negroes and jobs; a book of readings. Foreword by A. Philip Randolph. Ann Arbor, University of Michigan Press [1968] xv, 591 p.

E185.8.F45

Includes bibliographies.

447
Foley, Eugene P. The achieving ghetto. [Washington, National Press, 1968] 156 p.

E185.8.F6

Bibliographical references included in "Source notes" (p. 153-156).

448

Franklin, Charles L. The Negro labor unionist of New York; problems and conditions among Negroes in the labor unions in Manhattan with special reference to the N.R.A. and post-N.R.A. situations. New York, 1936. 417 p.   E185.8.F732

Thesis (Ph. D.)–Columbia University, 1936.

Published also as Studies in History, Economics and Public Law, edited by the Faculty of Political Science of Columbia University, no. 420.

Bibliography: p. 398-402.

449

Garfinkel, Herbert. When Negroes march; the March on Washington Movement in the organizational politics for FEPC. Glencoe, Ill., Free Press [1959] 224 p.   E185.61.G23

Bibliographical references included in "Notes" (p. 194-220).

450

Ginzberg, Eli. The Negro potential, by Eli Ginzberg assisted by James K. Anderson, Douglas W. Bray [and] Robert W. Smuts. New York, Columbia University Press, 1956. xvi, 144 p. tables.   E185.8.G58

Bibliographical references included in "Notes" (p. [139]-144).

451

Gourlay, Jack G. The Negro salaried worker. [New York] American Management Association [1965] 103 p. illus. (AMA research study 70)

HD21.A6 no. 70

Bibliographical footnotes.

452

Greene, Lorenzo J., *and* Myra C. Callis. The employment of Negroes in the District of Columbia. Washington, Association for the Study of Negro Life and History [1931] 89 p.   E185.8.G78

453

Greene, Lorenzo, J., *and* Carter G. Woodson. The Negro wage earner. Washington, Association for the Study of Negro Life and History [c1930] 388 p. diagrs., tables.   E185.8.G79

Bibliography: p. [369]-380.

454

Hayes, Laurence J. W. The Negro Federal Government worker; a study of his classification status in the District of Columbia, 1883-1938.

Washington, Graduate School, Howard University, 1941. 156 p. diagr., tables. (The Howard University studies in the social sciences, v. 3, no. 1)   E185.8.H38

Thesis (M.A.)–Howard University, 1941.

Bibliographical footnotes.

455

Haynes, George E. The Negro at work in New York City; a study in economic progress. New York, 1912. 159 p. diagrs., tables.

E185.93.N56H41

Thesis (Ph. D.)–Columbia University, 1912.

Published also as Studies in History, Economics and Public Law, edited by the Faculty of Political Science of Columbia University, v. 49, no. 3, whole no. 124.

"Select bibliography": p. 154-156.

456

Hiestand, Dale L. Economic growth and employment opportunities for minorities. Foreword by John F. Henning. Introduction by Eli Ginzberg. New York, Columbia University Press, 1964. xx, 127 p.

HD4903.5.U58H5 1964

"Another version of this study [is titled] *Economic Growth and the Opportunities of Minorities: an Analysis of Changes in the Employment of Negroes and Women.*"

Bibliography: p. [125]-127.

457

Huson, Carolyn F., *and* Michael E. Schiltz. College, color, and employment; racial differentials in postgraduate employment among 1964 graduates of Louisiana colleges. Chicago, National Opinion Research Center, 1966. xx, 124 p. (National Opinion Research Center. Report no. 116)   HM261.A1N3 no. 116

"Research . . . supported by the Office of Manpower Policy, Evaluation, and Research, U.S. Department of Labor, under grant no. 91-15-66-01."

458

Jackson, Luther P. Free Negro labor and property holding in Virginia, 1830-1860. New York, D. Appleton-Century Co. [1942] xix, 270 p. tables.   E185.93.V8J18

At head of title: The American Historical Association.

Bibliography: p. 230-238.

459
Jackson, Luther P. Negro office-holders in Virginia, 1865-1895. Norfolk, Va., Guide Quality Press, 1945, c1946. 88 p. port.   E185.93.V8J19

460
Jacobson, Julius, *ed.* The Negro and the American labor movement. Garden City, N.Y., Anchor Books, 1968. 430 p.   E185.8.J3

> Bibliographical references included in "Notes" (p. 401-426).

461
Krislov, Samuel. The Negro in Federal employment: the quest for equal opportunity. Minneapolis, University of Minnesota Press [1967] 157 p.
JK723.N4K7 1967
> Bibliographical footnotes.

462
Marshall, F. Ray, *and* Vernon M. Briggs. The Negro and apprenticeship. Baltimore, Johns Hopkins Press [1967] 283 p.   E185.8.M24

> "Based on a report prepared under a contract with the Office of Manpower Policy, Evaluation and Research, U.S. Department of Labor."
> Bibliographical footnotes.

463
Marshall, F. Ray. The Negro and organized labor. New York, Wiley [1965] 327 p.   E185.8.M25

> Bibliographical footnotes.

464
Marshall, F. Ray. The Negro worker. New York, Random House [1967] 180 p. (Studies in labor)   E185.8.M27

> "SLE5."
> Bibliography: p. [171]-174.

465
Mayhew, Leon H. Law and equal opportunity; a study of the Massachusetts Commission Against Discrimination. Cambridge, Harvard University Press, 1968. 313 p. (A Publication of the Joint Center for Urban Studies of the Massachusetts Institute of Technology and Harvard University)   KFM2811.5.N4M3

> Bibliographical references included in "Notes" (p. 297-308).

466
National Association for the Advancement of Colored People. *Labor Dept.*
The Negro wage-earner and apprenticeship training programs; a critical
analysis with recommendations. New York [1961] 59 p.   E185.8.N2
Bibliographical references included in "Notes" (p. 51-59).

467
National Conference on Equal Employment Opportunity, *Washington,
D.C., 1962.* A time for action; proceedings. [Washington, U.S. Govt.
Print. Off., 1963] 70 p. ports.   JK765.N32 1962
Sponsored by the Dept. of the Army.

468
National Industrial Conference Board. Company experience with Negro
employment. [New York, 1966] 2 v. illus., forms, maps. (*Its* Studies in
personnel policy, no. 201)   HF5549.A2N27 no. 201
"A research report from the Conference Board."
Bibliography: v. l, p. 172.

469
National Planning Association. *Committee of the South.* Selected studies
of Negro employment in the South, prepared for the NPA Committee
of the South. Washington, National Planning Association [1953-54]
5 v. (483 p.) illus. (*Its* Reports, no. 6)   HN79.A2N35 no. 6 1953
                                                 E185.8.N29
Bibliographical footnotes.
Contents.—1. Negro employment in 3 southern plants of International Harvester Company, by J. Hope, II.—2. 4 studies of Negro
employment in the Upper South, by D. Dewey.—3. Negro employment
in the Birmingham metropolitan area, by L. T. Hawley.—4. 2 plants:
Little Rock, by E. W. Eckard and B. U. Ratchford. 3 companies: New
Orleans area, by H. W. Wissner.—5. Negro employment practices in the
Chattanooga area, by W. H. Wesson, Jr.

——— ——— Another issue. [1955] 483 p. illus. (*Its* Report no. 6)
                                                 HN79.A2N35 no. 6 1955

470
National Urban League. *Dept. of Research and Community Projects.*
Negro membership in American labor unions. New York [1930] 175 p.
                                                 E185.8.N337
Issued by the agency under a variant name: Department of Research
and Investigations.

471

New York *(State) State Commission for Human Rights. Research Division.*
Apprentices, skilled craftsmen, and the Negro: an analysis. [New York,
New York State Commission Against Discrimination, 1960] 137 p.
tables.   HD4885.U52N42
   Bibliography: p. 135-137.

472

Nicol, Helen O. Negro women workers in 1960 [by Helen O. Nicol with
the assistance of Merci L. Drake. Washington] U. S. Dept. of Labor,
Women's Bureau; [for sale by the Supt. of Docs., U.S. Govt. Print. Off.,
1964] 55 p. illus., maps. (U.S. Women's Bureau. Bulletin 287)
                                                     HD6093.A35 no. 287
   "Supersedes Women's Bureau publication [Leaflet no. 19] *Negro*
Women and Their Jobs, dated 1954." By Miriam Keeler.

473

Norgren, Paul H., *and others.* Employing the Negro in American industry;
a study of management practices. New York, Industrial Relations Counselors, 1959. xiv, 171 p. (Industrial relations monographs, no. 17)
                                                     E185.8.N64

474

Norgren, Paul H., *and* Samuel E. Hill. Toward fair employment. With the
assistance of F. Ray Marshall. New York, Columbia University Press
1964. xiv, 296 p.   HD4903.5.U58N6
   Bibliography: p. [281]-283.

475

Northrup, Herbert R., *and* Richard L. Rowan, *eds.* The Negro and employ-
ment opportunity; problems and practices. Ann Arbor, Bureau of
Industrial Relations, Graduate School of Business Administration,
University of Michigan [1965] 411 p. illus., map.   E185.8.N649

   Papers presented at a conference held on November 13, 1964, and
sponsored by the Labor Relations Council of the Wharton School of
Finance and Commerce, University of Pennsylvania.
   Includes bibliographical references.

476

Northrup, Herbert R. The Negro in the aerospace industry. Philadelphia
Industrial Research Unit, Wharton School of Finance and Commerce
University of Pennsylvania; distributed by University of Pennsylvania

Press [1968] 90 p. illus. (The Racial policies of American industry.
Report no. 2)   E185.5.R3 no. 2
Bibliographical footnotes.

477
Northrup, Herbert R. The Negro in the automobile industry. Philadelphia,
Industrial Research Unit, Wharton School of Finance and Commerce,
University of Pennsylvania; distributed by University of Pennsylvania
Press [1968] 75 p. (The Racial policies of American industry. Report
no. 1)   E185.5.R3 no. 1
University of Pennsylvania. Wharton School of Finance and Com-
merce. Industrial Research Unit. Research report series.
Bibliographical footnotes.

477a
Northrup, Herbert R. Organized labor and the Negro. Foreword by Sum-
ner H. Slichter. New York, Harper [1944] xviii, 312 p. tables.
                                                     E185.8.N65
Bibliographical references included in "Notes" (p. [259]-288).
"Selected bibliography": p. 289-302.

478
Paynter, John H. Horse and buggy days with Uncle Sam. New York,
Margent Press, 1943. 190 p. ports.   E185.8.P38
Employment of Negroes under Civil Service.

479
Ringe, Helen H. Negroes in the United States: their employment and
economic status. Washington, U.S. Govt. Print. Off., 1952 [i.e. 1953]
58 p. diagrs., maps. (U.S. Bureau of Labor Statistics. Bulletin no. 1119)
                                                     HD8051.A62 no. 1119
                                                     E185.8.R55
Bibliography: p. 53-55.

480
Ross, Arthur M., *and* Herbert Hill, *eds.* Employment, race, and poverty.
[New York, Harcourt, Brace & World, 1967] 598 p.   E185.8.R6
One of a series of books from the four-year program of research and
conferences on the subject of unemployment and the American economy supported by a Ford Foundation grant to the Institute of Industrial Relations at the Berkeley campus of the University of California.

481
Ross, Malcolm H. All manner of men. New York, Reynal & Hitchcock
[1948] 314 p.   HD4903.R63
A study of racial prejudice in employment. The author served as
chairman of the Fair Employment Practices Committee during the
Second World War.

482
Rowan, Richard L. The Negro in the steel industry. Philadelphia, Industrial Research Unit, Wharton School of Finance and Commerce, University of Pennsylvania; distributed by University of Pennsylvania Press
[1968] 148 p. (The Racial policies of American industry. Report no. 3)
E185.5.R3 no. 3
Bibliographical footnotes.

483
Ruchames, Louis. Race, jobs & politics; the story of FEPC. New York,
Columbia University Press, 1953. 255 p.   HD4903.5.U58R8
Bibliographical references included in "Notes" (p. [215]-240).

484
Rutledge, Aaron L., *and* Gertrude D. Z. Gass. Nineteen Negro men; personality & manpower retraining. San Francisco, Jossey-Bass, 1967. xv,
109 p.   E185.8.R8

485
Sovern, Michael I. Legal restraints on racial discrimination in employment.
New York, Twentieth Century Fund, 1966. 270 p.   DLC-LL
"Notes" (54 p.) in pocket.
Bibliography: p. 259-264.

486
Spero, Sterling D., *and* Abram L. Harris. The black worker; the Negro and
the labor movement. Port Washington, N.Y., Kennikat Press [1966,
c1959] 509 p.   E185.8.S74 1966
First published in 1931.
Bibliography: p. 485-496.

487
Staupers, Mabel K. No time for prejudice; a story of the integration of
Negroes in nursing in the United States. New York, Macmillan [1961]
206 p. illus.   RT83.5.S75

488
U.S. *Commission on Civil Rights. State Advisory Committees Division.*
Reports on apprenticeship by the Advisory Committees to the United
States Commission on Civil Rights in California, Connecticut, District
of Columbia, Florida, Maryland, New Jersey, New York, Tennessee,
and Wisconsin. [Washington] 1964. 158 p.   E185.8.U553

Bibliographical footnotes.

489
U.S. *Dept. of Labor. Division of Negro Economics.* The Negro at work
during the world war and during reconstruction; statistics, problems,
and policies relating to the greater inclusion of Negro wage earners in
American industry and agriculture. Second study on Negro labor. Washington, Govt. Print. Off., 1921. 144 p. diagrs., plates, tables.
                                                  E185.8.U57

490
Wachtel, Dawn. The Negro and discrimination in employment. Ann Arbor,
Institute of Labor and Industrial Relations, University of Michigan-
Wayne State University [c1965] 96, [16] p.   E185.8.W2

Bibliography: p. [97]-[122].

491
Wesley, Charles H. Negro labor in the United States, 1850-1925; a study in
American economic history. New York, Russell & Russell [1967,
c1927] 343 p. map.   E185.8.W4 1967

Bibliography: p. 321-330.

492
Woodson, Carter G. The Negro professional man and the community, with
special emphasis on the physician and the lawyer. Washington, Association for the Study of Negro Life and History [c1934] xviii, 365 p.
                                                  E185.82.W88

Housing

493
Abrams, Charles. Forbidden neighbors; a study of prejudice in housing.
New York, Harper [1955] 404 p.   HD7293.A616

494

Abrams, Charles. Race bias in housing. [New York? 1947] 31 p.

E185.89.H6A2

"Sponsored jointly by the American Civil Liberties Union, National Association for the Advancement of Colored People [and] American Council on Race Relations."

495

Arter, Rhetta M. WINS pilot preview; report of an action-research, demonstration project on the process of achieving equal housing opportunities, Women's Integrating Neighborhood Services, sponsored by the Educational Foundation of National Council of Negro Women. [New York, Research and Action Associates, c1961] 202 p. illus.

E185.89.H6A7

496

Avins, Alfred, *ed.* Open occupancy vs. forced housing under the Fourteenth amendment; a symposium on anti-discrimination legislation, freedom of choice, and property rights in housing. New York, Bookmailer [c1963] 316 p. maps.   DLC-LL

Bibliographical footnotes.

497

Chicago. *Mayor's Commission on Human Relations.* The Trumbull Park Homes disturbances; a chronological report, August 4, 1953, to June 30, 1955. [Chicago, 1955?] 63 p.   E185.89.H6C5

498

Clark, Henry. The church and residential desegregation; a case study of an open housing covenant campaign. New Haven, College & University Press [1965] 254 p.   E185.89.H6C55

Bibliographical references included in "Notes" (p. 234-254).

499

Commission on Race and Housing. Where shall we live? Report. Berkeley, University of California Press, 1958. 77 p.   HD7293.C6427

500

Connecticut. *Commission on Civil Rights.* Racial integration in private residential neighborhoods in Connecticut, by Henry G. Stetler, supervisor, Research Division. Hartford, 1957. 55 p.   E185.89.H6C6

501

Connecticut. *Commission on Civil Rights.* Racial integration in public housing projects in Connecticut, prepared by Henry G. Stetler, supervisor, Research Division. Hartford, 1955 [i.e. 1956] 72 p.

E185.89.H6C63

502

Deutsch, Morton, *and* Mary E. Collins. Interracial housing; a psychological evaluation of a social experiment. Minneapolis, University of Minnesota Press [1951] xv, 173 p.   E185.89.H6D4

Reprint issued by Russell & Russell, 1968.

Bibliography: p. 149.

503

Duncan, Otis D., *and* Beverly Duncan. The Negro population of Chicago; a study of residential succession. [Chicago] University of Chicago Press [1957] xxiv, 367 p. diagrs., maps (part fold.), tables. (Monograph series of the Chicago Community Inventory of the University of Chicago)

F548.9.N3D8

Bibliography: p. 355-358.

504

Foote, Nelson N., *and others.* Housing choices and housing constraints. New York, McGraw-Hill, 1960. 450 p. illus. (ACTION series in housing and community development)   HD7293.F62

Includes bibliography.

505

Glazer, Nathan, *and* Davis McEntire, *eds.* Studies in housing & minority groups. With an introduction by Nathan Glazer. Special research report to the Commission on Race and Housing. Berkeley, University of California Press, 1960. xvii, 228 p. maps, tables. (Publications of the Commission on Race and Housing)   E185.89.H6G55

506

Goldblatt, Harold S. Westchester real estate brokers, builders, bankers & Negro home-buyers; a report to the Housing Council of the Urban League of Westchester County, Inc. on opportunities for private open-occupancy housing in Westchester. [n.p.] 1954. 51 leaves.

E185.89.H6G6

507

Grier, Eunice S., *and* George W. Grier. Discrimination in housing; a handbook of fact. [New York, Anti-defamation League of B'nai B'rith, 1960] 67 p. (Freedom pamphlets)   HD7293.G7

508
Grier, Eunice S., *and* George W. Grier. Privately developed interracial housing; an analysis of experience. Special research report to the Commission on Race and Housing. Berkeley, University of California Press, 1960. 264 p.   E185.89.H6G69

Bibliography: p. [251]-257.

509
Grier, George W., *and* Eunice S. Grier. Equality and beyond; housing segregation and the goals of the Great Society. Chicago, Quadrangle Books, 1966. 115 p. maps.   HD7293.G72

"Published in cooperation with the Anti-defamation League of B'nai B'rith."

Based on the authors' *Discrimination in Housing*.

Bibliographical references included in "Notes" (p. 101-109).

510
Johnson, Philip A. Call me neighbor, call me friend: the case history of the integration of a neighborhood on Chicago's south side. Garden City, N. Y., Doubleday, 1965. 184 p. illus.   F548.9.N3J6

Bibliography: p. [177]-183.

511
Jones, William H. The housing of Negroes in Washington, D.C.; a study in human ecology. Washington, Howard University Press, 1929. 191 p diagrs., form, maps, plates, port.   E185.93.D6J6

"An investigation made under the auspices of the Interracial Committee of the Washington Federation of Churches."

Bibliography: p. [157]-158.

512
Knight, Charles L. Negro housing in certain Virginia cities. Richmond, Va. William Byrd Press, 1927. 158 p. illus. (Publications of the University of Virginia. Phelps-Stokes fellowship papers, no. 8)   E185.93.V8K6

513
Kraus, Henry. In the city was a garden; a housing project chronicle. New York, Renaissance Press, 1951. 255 p.   F869.S38K7

Housing of Negroes in San Pedro, California.

514
Laurenti, Luigi. Property values and race; studies in seven cities. Special research report to the Commission on Race and Housing [prepared

under the direction of Davis McEntire] Berkeley, University of California Press, 1960. xix, 256 p. diagrs., maps, tables.   E185.89.H6L3

Bibliography: p. [249]-252.

515

Leaman, Samuel H. A study of housing decisions by Negro home owners and Negro renters. Chapel Hill [N.C.] 1967. 136 leaves. (Environmental policies and urban development thesis series, no. 8)   E185.89.H6L4

Thesis (Master of Regional Planning)–University of North Carolina. Bibliography: leaves [132]-136.

516

Long, Herman H., *and* Charles S. Johnson. People vs. property; race restrictive covenants in housing. Nashville, Fisk University Press, 1947. 107 p. diagrs., maps.   E185.89.H6L7

Bibliographical footnotes.

517

Messner, Stephen D. Minority groups and housing; a selected bibliography, 1950-67. Selected and edited under the direction of Stephen D. Messner. [Storrs, Center for Real Estate and Urban Economic Studies, University of Connecticut, 1968] 60 p. (University of Connecticut. Center for Real Estate and Urban Economic Studies. General series, no. 1)   HD251.C745 no. 1

518

Meyerson, Martin, *and* Edward C. Banfield. Politics, planning, and the public interest; the case of public housing in Chicago. Glencoe, Ill., Free Press [1955] 353 p. illus.   HD7304.C4M4

519

Needham, Maurice D. Negro Orleanian: status and stake in a city's economy and housing. New Orleans, Tulane Publications [1962] 278 p. illus.   F379.N5N33

520

New York *(State) State Commission for Human Rights.* In search of housing; a study of experiences of Negro professional and technical personnel in New York State, by Eunice and George Grier. [New York] State Commission Against Discrimination, 1958. 52 p.   E185.93.N56N44

521

Northwood, Lawrence K., *and* Ernest A. T. Barth. Urban desegregation; Negro pioneers and their white neighbors. Seattle, University of Washington Press, 1965. xv, 131 p. map.   E185.89.H6N6

Bibliography: p. 121-131.

522

Potomac Institute, *Washington, D.C.* The Federal role in equal housing opportunity; an affirmative program to implement Executive Order 11063. [Prepared by Arthur J. Levin, staff director. Washington, 1964] 28 p.   HD7293.P626

523

President's Conference on Home Building and Home Ownership, *Washington, D.C., 1931.* Negro housing; report of the Committee on Negro Housing, Nannie H. Burroughs, chairman; prepared for the committee by Charles S. Johnson; edited by John M. Gries and James Ford. Washington [c1932] xiv, 282 p. plates.   E185.86.P87

On cover: *Physical Aspects; Social and Economic Factors; Home Ownership and Financing.*
Bibliography: p. 260-271.

524

Rapkin, Chester, *and* William G. Grigsby. The demand for housing in racially mixed areas; a study of the nature of neighborhood change. Special research report to the Commission on Race and Housing and the Philadelphia Redevelopment Authority. Berkeley, University of California Press, 1960. xx, 177 p. illus., maps, tables. (Publications of the Commission on Race and Housing)   F158.9.N3R3

Bibliographical footnotes.

525

Reid, Margaret G. Housing and income. [Chicago] University of Chicago Press [1962] xx, 415 p. diagrs., tables.   HD7293.A3R4

Bibliography: p. 406-409. Bibliographical footnotes.

526

Schorr, Alvin L. Slums and social insecurity, an appraisal of the effectiveness of housing policies in helping to eliminate poverty in the United States. Washington, U.S. Govt. Print. Off. [1963] 168 p. (U.S. Social Security Administration. Division of Research and Statistics. Research report no. 1)   HD7123.A39 no. 1

Bibliography: p. 151-168.

527
Sternlieb, George. The tenement landlord. New Brunswick, N.J., Urban Studies Center, Rutgers, State University [c1966] xvii, 269 p. illus., plates. HD7304.N6S7

Includes bibliographies.

528
Taeuber, Karl E., *and* Alma F. Taeuber. Negroes in cities; residential segregation and neighborhood change. Chicago, Aldine Pub. Co. [1965] xvii, 284 p. illus., maps. (Population Research and Training Center monographs) E185.89.H6T3

Bibliography: p. 267-277.

529
Tillman, James A. Not by prayer alone; a report on the Greater Minneapolis Interfaith Fair Housing Program. Philadelphia, United Church Press [1964] 223 p. E185.89.H6T5

530
Tilly, Charles, Wagner D. Jackson, *and* Barry Kay. Race and residence in Wilmington, Delaware. [New York] Bureau of Publications, Teachers College, Columbia University, 1965. 145 p. illus., maps. E185.89.H6T56

Bibliography: p. 135-140.

531
Tucker, Sterling. Why the ghetto must go. [New York, Public Affairs Committee, 1968] 28 p. illus. (Public affairs pamphlet, no. 423) E185.615.T83

Abstracted from the author's *Beyond the Burning: Life and Death of the Ghetto.*

532
U.S. *Commission on Civil Rights.* Civil rights U.S.A.; housing in Washington, D.C. [Washington, 1962] 45 p. tables. E185.89.H6U47

Bibliographical footnotes.

533
U.S. *Commission on Civil Rights.* Family housing and the Negro serviceman; 1963 staff report. Submitted to the United States Commission on Civil Rights, October 1963. [Washington, 1964] 48 p. E185.89.H6U47 1964

Bibliographical footnotes.

534

U.S. *Housing and Home Finance Agency. Office of Program Policy.* Our nonwhite population and its housing: the changes between 1950 and 1960. Washington [U.S. Govt. Print. Off.] 1963. 104 p. tables.

E185.89.H6U5 1963a

535

Vose, Clement E. Caucasians only: the Supreme Court, the NAACP, and the restrictive covenant cases. Berkeley, University of California Press, 1959. 296 p. illus., maps, ports.   DLC-LL

Bibliographical references included in "Notes" (p. [253]-286).

536

Weaver, Robert C. The Negro ghetto. New York, Russell & Russell [1967, c1948] xviii, 404 p. illus., maps.   E185.89.H6W4 1967

Bibliography: p. 371-375.

537

West Virginia. *Bureau of Negro Welfare and Statistics.* Negro housing survey of Charleston, Keystone, Kimball, Wheeling and Williamson. Prepared and issued by Bureau of Negro Welfare and Statistics of the State of West Virginia, 1938. Isaac M. Carpenter, director. [Charleston, Jarrett Print. Co., 1938] 35 p. illus., diagrs., maps, tables. E185.6.W42

538

Wolff, Reinhold P., *and* David K. Gillogly. Negro housing in the Miami area; effects of the postwar building boom. [Coral Gables, Fla.] c1951. 22 p. illus. (Bureau of Business and Economic Research, University of Miami. Area development series, no. 1)   HC107.F62D52 no. 1

539

Woofter, Thomas J., *and* Madge H. Priest. Negro housing in Philadelphia, a study made for the Institute of Social and Religious Research and the Interracial Commission. [Philadelphia] 1927. 30 p. maps.

E185.86.W905

"Published for distribution in Philadelphia by the Friends' Committee on Interests of the Colored Race, Whittier Center Housing Company, Philadelphia Housing Association."

EDUCATION

540
Alabama. University. *Bureau of Educational Research.* A study of Stillman
Institute, a junior college for Negroes, conducted by the Bureau of
Educational Research, College of Education, University of Alabama;
edited by Paul W. Terry, director [and] L. Tennent Lee, associate
director. University, University of Alabama Press [1947] xxx, 304 p.
illus., plates, ports. (*Its* Studies in education, no. 8 [i.e. 9])
LC2852.T8652A6

541
Anderson, Margaret. The children of the South. With a foreword by Ralph
McGill. New York, Farrar, Straus and Giroux [1966] xiv, 208 p.
LC2801.A83

542
Ashmore, Harry S. The Negro and the schools. Foreword by Owen J.
Roberts. [2d ed.] Chapel Hill, University of North Carolina Press
[1954] xv, 239 p. illus., maps.   NcU

"This edition contains the full text of the Court decision (except for
technical footnotes) and has been revised to bring the legal history of
segregation up to date."
    Bibliography: p. 218-220.

543
Badger, Henry G. Statistics of Negro colleges and universities: students,
staff, and finances, 1900-1950. Washington, Federal Security Agency,

Office of Education, 1951. 16 p. tables. ([U.S. Office of Education]
Circular no. 293)   L111.A72 no. 293
                                                                        LC2781.B3
Also designated *Statistical Circular.*

——— ——— [Supplement] Statistics of Negro colleges and universities,
1951-52 and fall of 1954. [Washington] U.S. Dept. of Health, Education, and Welfare, Office of Education [1955] 16 p. tables. ([U.S.
Office of Education] Circular no. 448)   L111.A72 no. 448

544
Bates, Daisy G. The long shadow of Little Rock, a memoir. New York, D.
McKay Co. [1962] 234 p. illus.   F419.L7B3

The Little Rock school crisis.

545
Beam, Lura. He called them by the lightning; a teacher's odyssey in the
Negro South, 1908-1919. Indianapolis, Bobbs-Merrill [1967] 230 p.
                                                         E185.93.S8B4
546
Bede, *Brother.* A study of the development of Negro education under
Catholic auspices in Maryland and the District of Columbia, by Michael
Francis Rouse (Brother Bede, C.F.X.). Baltimore, Johns Hopkins Press,
1935. 125 p. (The Johns Hopkins University studies in education,
no. 22)   LB5.J6 no. 22
                                                    LC2802.M3B4 1935
Thesis (Ph.D.)—Johns Hopkins University.
"A selected and annotated bibliography": p. 115-121.

547
Berman, Daniel M. It is so ordered: the Supreme Court rules on school
segregation. New York, Norton [1966] 161 p. facsims.   DLC-LL

Appendixes (p. [131]-149): The texts of the Supreme Court opinions: Brown *v.* Board of Education of Topeka (1945); Bolling *v.* Sharpe
(1945).—The implementation decision: Brown *v.* Board of Education of
Topeka (1955).
Bibliographical footnotes.

548
Bernstein, Abraham A. The education of urban population. Consulting
editor, Paul Nash. New York, Random House [1967] xvi, 398 p.
                                                            LC5119.B4
Bibliography: p. [379]-386.

549
Blaustein, Albert P. Civil rights U.S.A.: public schools; cities in the North and West, 1963: Camden and environs. Staff report submitted to the U.S. Commission on Civil Rights. [Washington, 1964] 55 p. maps, tables. LA332.C3B55

Bibliographical references included in "Footnotes" (p. 46-48).

550
Blaustein, Albert P., *and* Clarence C. Ferguson. Desegregation and the law; the meaning and effect of the school segregation cases. [2d ed. rev.] New York, Vintage Books [1962] 359 p. (Caravelle editions) DLC-LL

Bibliographical references included in "Table of authorities" (p. 313-345).

551
Blossom, Virgil T. It has happened here. New York, Harper [1959] 209 p. F419.L7B53

Concerns desegregation of public schools in Little Rock.

552
Bond, Horace M. The education of the Negro in the American social order. With a new preface and an additional chapter by the author. New York, Octagon Books, 1966. xxvi, 531 p. illus. LC2801.B65 1966

First published in 1934.
Bibliography: p. 491-511.

553
Bond, Horace M. Negro education in Alabama; a study in cotton and steel. Washington, Associated Publishers, 1939. 358 p. illus., diagrs., maps. LC2802.A2B6 1939

"The Susan Colver Rosenberger prize essay, 1937, the University of Chicago."

Issued also as thesis (Ph.D.), University of Chicago, under title: *Social and Economic Influences on the Public Education of Negroes in Alabama, 1865-1930.*

Bibliography: p. 293-304.

554
Bouma, Donald H., *and* James Hoffman. The dynamics of school integration; problems and approaches in a northern city. Grand Rapids, W. B. Erdmans Pub. Co. [1968] 158 p. LB3062.B6

Bibliography: p. 149-154.

555
Brickman, William W., *and* Stanley Lehrer, *eds.* The countdown on segregated education. New York, Society for the Advancement of Education, 1960. 175 p.   LB3062.B7

556
Brown, Charles A. The origin and development of secondary education for Negroes in the metropolitan area of Birmingham, Alabama. [Birmingham, Commercial Print. Co., c1959] 98 p. illus.   LC2803.B5B7

557
Brown, Hugh V. E-qual-ity education in North Carolina among Negroes. [Raleigh, N.C., Irving-Swain Press, 1964] 198 p. illus., ports.
                                                              LC2802.N8B69
    Bibliographical footnotes.

558
Brown, Hugh V. A history of the education of Negroes in North Carolina. [Raleigh, Irving Swain Press, 1961] 167 p. illus.   LC2802.N8B7

559
Brown, Robert R. Bigger than Little Rock. Greenwich, Conn., Seabury Press, 1958. 150 p.   F419.L7B7

559a
Brownlee, Frederick L. Heritage of freedom, a centenary story of ten schools offering education in freedom. Philadelphia, United Church Press [1963] 108 p. illus.   LC2801.B85

560
Bullock, Henry A. A history of Negro education in the South; from 1619 to the present. Cambridge, Harvard University Press, 1967. 399 p. illus.
                                                              LC2801.B9
    Bibliographical references included in "Notes" (p. 291-314).

561
Caldwell, Dista H. The education of the Negro child. New York, Carlton Press, 1961. 51 p. (A Reflection book)   LC2731.C3

562
Caliver, Ambrose. A background study of Negro college students, by Ambrose Caliver, senior specialist in the education of Negroes, Office of

Education. Washington, U.S. Govt. Print. Off., 1933. 132 p. diagrs., tables. (U.S. Office of Education. Bulletin, 1933, no. 8)

L111.A6 1933 no. 8
LC2801.C28

At head of title: United States Department of the Interior. Harold L. Ickes, Secretary. Office of Education. William John Cooper, Commissioner.

Bibliography: p. 116-117.

563
Caliver, Ambrose. A personnel study of Negro college students; a study of the relations between certain background factors of Negro college students and their subsequent careers in college. New York, Teachers College, Columbia University, 1931. 146 p. diagrs., forms. (Teachers College, Columbia University. Contributions to education, no. 484)

LC2801.C8 1931
LB5.C8 no. 484

"The study includes 450 cases, comprising the entering students at Fisk University for the years 1926, 1927, and 1928."–p. 9.

Issued also as thesis (Ph.D.)–Columbia University.

Bibliography: p. 124-128.

564
Campbell, Ernest Q. When a city closes its schools, by Ernest Q. Campbell, with the assistance of Charles E. Bowerman [and] Daniel O. Price. Chapel Hill, Institute for Research in Social Science, University of North Carolina, 1960. 195 p. tables. (University of North Carolina, Institute for Research in Social Science. Monographs)   LA381.N8C3

565
Clark, Kenneth B., *and* Lawrence Plotkin. The Negro student at integrated colleges. [New York] National Scholarship Service and Fund for Negro Students, 1963. 59 p.   LC2801.C55

Bibliography: p. 53-54.

566
Clift, Virgil A., Archibald W. Anderson, *and* Henry Gordon Hullfish, *eds.* Negro education in America; its adequacy, problems, and needs. New York, Harper [1962] xxiii, 315 p. (Yearbook of the John Dewey Society, 16th)   L101.U6J6 16th, 1962

Bibliographical footnotes.

567

[Coleman, James S.] Equality of educational opportunity; [summary report. Washington] U.S. Dept. of Health, Education, and Welfare, Office of Education; [for sale by the Supt. of Docs., U.S. Govt. Print. Off., 1966] 33 p. illus.   LA209.2.C58

"OE-38000."

A slightly different version of the summary included, as section 1, in the main report of the survey.

"The survey was carried out by the National Center for Educational Statistics of the U.S. Office of Education."

568

Coles, Robert. The desegregation of southern schools: a psychiatric study. New York, Anti-defamation League of B'nai B'rith, 1963. 25 p.

LB3062.C6

Bibliographical footnotes.

569

Conant, James B. Slums and suburbs; a commentary on schools in metropolitan areas. New York, McGraw-Hill [1961] 147 p.   LC5115.C6

570

Crain, Robert L. The politics of school desegregation; comparative case studies of community structure and policy-making. With the assistance of Morton Inger, Gerald A. McWorter [and] James J. Vanecko. Chicago, Aldine Pub. Co. [1968] xviii, 390 p. (National Opinion Research Center. Monographs in social research, 14)   LA209.2.C7

Bibliography: p. 373-377.

571

Cuthbert, Marion V. Education and marginality; a study of the Negro woman college graduate. New York, 1942. xviii, 167 p. tables.

LC2781.C8

Thesis (Ph.D.)–Columbia University, 1942.
Bibliography: p. 161-166.

572

Dabney, Lillian G. The history of schools for Negroes in the District of Columbia, 1807-1947. Washington, Catholic University of America Press, 1949. 287 p.   LC2802.D65D3

Thesis–Catholic University of America.
Bibliography: p. 255-277.

573
Damerell, Reginald G. Triumph in a white suburb; the dramatic story of Teaneck, N.J., the first town in the Nation to vote for integrated schools. Introductions by Robert J. Havighurst and Neil V. Sullivan. New York, W. Morrow, 1968. 351 p. maps. LA333.T4D3

574
Davis, William R. The development and present status of Negro education in east Texas. New York, Teachers College, Columbia University, 1934. 150 p. illus., diagrs., maps. (Teachers College, Columbia University. Contributions to education, no. 626) LC2802.T4D3 1934a
LB5.C8 no. 626
Issued also as thesis (Ph.D.)–Columbia University.
Bibliography: p. 139-150.

575
Day, Richard E. Civil rights, U.S.A.; public schools, Southern States, 1963: North Carolina. Staff report submitted to the United States Commission on Civil Rights [Washington? 1963?] 60 p. maps.
LA340.D3
Bibliographical references included in "Notes" (p. 42-48).

576
Derbigny, Irving A. General education in the Negro college. Stanford University, Stanford University Press [1947] 255 p. LC2781.D4

Bibliography: p. 245-249.

577
DuBois, William E. B., *ed.* The college-bred Negro; report of a social study made under the direction of Atlanta University; together with the Proceedings of the Fifth Conference for the Study of the Negro Problems, held at Atlanta University, May 29-30, 1900. Atlanta, Atlanta University Press, 1900. 115 p. (Atlanta University publications, no. 5)
E185.5.A88 no. 5
LC2781.D8 1900
"A select bibliography of the American Negro for general readers": p. 6-9.

578
DuBois, William E. B., *and* Augustus G. Dill, *eds.* The common school and the Negro American; report of a social study made by Atlanta University under the patronage of the trustees of the John F. Slater Fund, with the Proceedings of the 16th Annual Conference for the Study of

the Negro Problems, held at Atlanta University, on Tuesday, May 30th, 1911. Atlanta, Atlanta University Press, 1911. 140 p. (The Atlanta University publications, no. 16)   LC2771.D7

"A select bibliography of common school education for Negro Americans": p. [9]-12.

579
Florida. *Attorney General.* Oliver Brown, et al., appellants, *v.* Board of Education of Topeka, Shawnee County, Kansas, et al. Harry Briggs, Jr., et al., appellants, *v.* R. W. Elliott, et al. Dorothy E. Davis, et al., appellants, *v.* County School Board of Prince Edward County, Virginia, et al. Frances B. Gebhart, et al., petitioners, *v.* Ethel Louise Belton, et al. Amicus curiae brief of the attorney general of Florida. Richard W. Ervin, attorney general of the State of Florida. Ralph E. Odum, assistant attorney general, State of Florida. [Tallahassee, 1954] 243 p.   FU

At head of title: In the Supreme Court of the United States. October term, 1954. No. _____ .

580
Forten, Charlotte L. Journal; with an introduction and notes by Ray Allen Billington. New York, Dryden Press [1953] 248 p. maps.

LA2317.F67A3
Bibliographical references included in "Notes" (p. [205]-244).
The life of the Sea Islands Negroes is described in this diary of a Negro teacher during 1854-64.

581
Gallagher, Buell G. American caste and the Negro college. With a foreword by William H. Kilpatrick. New York, Gordian Press, 1966 [c1938] 463 p. illus.   LC2781.G3 1966

Issued also as thesis, Columbia University.
Bibliography: p. [419]-443.

582
Gates, Robbins L. The making of massive resistance; Virginia's politics of public school desegregation, 1954-1956. Chapel Hill, University of North Carolina Press [1964] xx, 222 p. illus., maps.   LA379.G3

Bibliography: p. 215-218.

583
Ginzberg, Eli, *and others.* The middle-class Negro in the white man's world. New York, Columbia University Press, 1967. 182 p. E185.82.G5

Findings from case studies initiated in 1964 by the Conservation of Human Resources Project, Columbia University.

584

Gordon, Edmund W., *and* Doxey A. Wilkerson. Compensatory education for the disadvantaged; programs and practices, preschool through college. New York, College Entrance Examination Board, 1966. 209 p.

LC4091.G57
Bibliography: p. 194-198.

585

Green, Donald R., *and* Warren E. Gauerke. If the schools are closed: a critical analysis of the private school plan. Atlanta, Southern Regional Council, 1959. 40 p.   LB3062.G73

586

Green, Robert L., *and others.* The educational status of children during the first school year following four years of little or no schooling. [East Lansing] School for Advanced Studies, College of Education, Michigan State University, 1966. 126 leaves. forms.   LC2802.V8G7

Cooperative research project no. 2498 supported by the Cooperative Research Program of the Office of Education, U.S. Dept. of Health, Education, and Welfare.

Includes bibliographies.

587

Greene, Harry W. Holders of doctorates among American Negroes: an educational and social study of Negroes who have earned doctoral degrees in course, 1876-1943. Boston, Meador Pub. Co. [1946] 275 p.

LC2781.G7
Bibliography: p. 247-254.

588

Greene, Mary F., *and* Orletta Ryan. The schoolchildren growing up in the slums. New York, Pantheon Books [1966, c1965] 227 p.

LC5133.N4G7
589

Group for the Advancement of Psychiatry. *Committee on Social Issues.* Emotional aspects of school desegregation; a report by psychiatrists. [New York, Group for the Advancement of Psychiatry, 1960] 47 p.

LB3062.G75 1960
"An abbreviated and less technical version of Report no. 37, *Psychiatric Aspects of School Desegregation, May, 1957.*"
Includes bibliographical references.

590

Gurin, Patricia, *and* Daniel Katz. Motivation and aspiration in the Negro college. Ann Arbor, Mich., Survey Research Center, Institute for Social Research, University of Michigan, 1966. xvi, 346 p.   LC2781.G8

Final report.
Project no. 5-0787. Contract no. OE-4-10-095. Research performed under contract with the U.S. Office of Education.
Bibliography: p. 341-346.

591

Guzman, Jessie P. Some achievements of the Negro through education. 2d rev. ed. Tuskegee Institute, Ala., Dept. of Records and Research, 1951. 41 leaves. (Records and research pamphlet, no. 1)   E185.96.G8 1951

Bibliography: p. 39-40.

592

Guzman, Jessie P. Twenty years of court decisions affecting higher education in the South, 1938-1958. [Tuskegee Institute, Ala.] 1960. 36 p.
DLC-LL

593

Hansen, Carl F. Miracle of social adjustment: desegregation in the Washington, D.C. schools. [New York, Anti-defamation League of B'nai B'rith, 1957] 70 p. illus. (Freedom pamphlets)   LB3062.H3

––– Addendum: a five year report. [New York, Anti-defamation League of B'nai B'rith, 1960] 31 p.   LB3062.H3 Suppl.

594

Hayes, Rutherford B., *Pres. U.S.* Teach the freeman; the correspondence of Rutherford B. Hayes and the Slater Fund for Negro Education, 1881-1887. Edited by Louis D. Rubin. [Baton Rouge] Louisiana State University Press [1959] 2 v.   LC2707.J6

595

Hill, Herbert, *and* Jack Greenberg. Citizen's guide to desegregation; a study of social and legal change in American life. Boston, Beacon Press [1955] 185 p.   DLC-LL

596

Holley, Joseph W. Education and the segregation issue; a program of education for the economic and social regeneration of the southern Negro. New York, William-Frederick Press, 1955. 62 p. illus.   E185.97.H714

597
Holley, Joseph W. You can't build a chimney from the top; the South through the life of a Negro educator. New York, William-Frederick Press, 1948. 226 p. illus., ports. E185.97.H715

598
Holmes, Dwight O. W. The evolution of the Negro college. New York, Teachers College, Columbia University, 1934. 221 p. (Teachers College, Columbia University. Contributions to education, no. 609)
LC2801.H57 1934a
LB5.C8 no. 609
Thesis (Ph.D.)—Columbia University.
Bibliography: p. 211-221.

599
Humphrey, Hubert H., *ed.* School desegregation: documents and commentaries. New York, Crowell [1964] 314 p. LB3062.H8 1964
"Also published under the title *Integration vs. Segregation.*"
Bibliography: p. 305-308.

600
Hundley, Mary G. The Dunbar story, 1870-1955. With an introduction by Robert C. Weaver. New York, Vantage Press [1965] 179 p. [4] plates.
LD7501.W3D8
About Dunbar High School, Washington, D. C.
"Alma mater. Words by Dr. A. J. Cooper. Music by Miss M. L. Europe": (close score, for chorus SATB): plate [4].
Includes bibliographies.

601
In their own words; a student appraisal of what happened after school desegregation. Analysis by Mark A. Chesler. Atlanta, Southern Regional Council [1967] 76 p. LB3062.I45

602
Integrated Education. Learning together; a book on integrated education. Edited by Meyer Weinberg. Chicago, Integrated Education Associates, 1964. 222 p. LB3062.I5
Contains all the articles published in the first six numbers of *Integrated Education,* which started publication in January 1963.
Bibliography: p. 211-222.

603
International Research Associates. Access to public libraries; a research project prepared for the Library Administration Division, American Library Association. Chicago, American Library Association, 1963. xxiii, 160 p. map, tables.   Z711.9.I5
    Bibliography: p. 154-156.

604
Jaffe, Abram J., Walter Adams, *and* Sandra G. Meyers. Negro higher education in the 1960's. New York, Praeger [1968] xxvii, 290 p. illus. (Praeger special studies in U.S. economic and social development)
                                                            LC2781.J3
    Bibliography: p. [285]-290.

605
Johnson, Charles S. The Negro college graduate. Chapel Hill, University of North Carolina Press, 1938. xvii, 399 p. diagrs., maps (part fold.), tables.   LC2781.J6
    Bibliography: p. 378-384.

606
Kendall, Robert. White teacher in a black school. New York, Devin-Adair [1964] 241 p.   LC2803.L6K4

607
Kilpatrick, James J. The Southern case for school segregation. [New York] Crowell-Collier Press [1962] 220 p.   E185.61.K5
    "A bibliographical note": p. 213-220.

608
Knapp, Robert B. Social integration in urban communities; a guide for educational planning. New York, Bureau of Publications, Teachers College, Columbia University, 1960. 196 p. (Teachers College studies in education)   LB3062.K55
    Bibliography: p. 192-196. Bibliographical footnotes.

609
Kohl, Herbert R. Teaching the unteachable; the story of an experiment in children's writing. Introduction by John Holt. [New York, New York Review, 1967] 63 p. illus. (A New York review book)
                                                    LC2803.N5K6 1967

610

Konl, Herbert R. 36 children. Illustrations by Robert George Jackson. [New York] New American Library [1967] 227 p. illus.

LC2803.H3K6 1967

Includes letters, stories, etc., by the author's students in an East Harlem elementary school.

611

Kornhauser, Stanley H. Planning for the achievement of quality integrated education in desegregated schools; a composite report on the recommendations of workshop participants. Report writer and coordinator: Stanley H. Kornhauser. Editor: Martin Silverman. [New York, Board of Education, City of New York, Office of Intergroup Education] 1968. 100 p.   HT1506.K65

Report of a workshop for teachers held May 6, 13, and 20, 1967, and sponsored by the Board of Education's Office of Integration and Human Relations.

612

Kozol, Jonathan. Death at an early age; the destruction of the hearts and minds of Negro children in the Boston public schools. Boston, Houghton Mifflin, 1967. 240 p.   LC2803.B7K6

Bibliographical references included in "Notes" (p. [235]-240).

613

McGinnis, Frederick A. The education of Negroes in Ohio. Wilberforce, Ohio, 1962. 104 p.   LC2802.O5M2

614

McGinnis, Frederick A. A history and an interpretation of Wilberforce University. Wilberforce, Ohio [Blanchester, Ohio, Printed at the Brown Pub. Co.] 1941. 215 p. plates, ports.   LC2851.W62M2

Bibliography: p. 203-208.

615

McGrath, Earl J. The predominantly Negro colleges and universities in transition. [New York] Published for the Institute of Higher Education by the Bureau of Publications, Teachers College, Columbia University [1965] xv, 204 p. map. (Publications of the Institute of Higher Education)   LC2801.M28

Bibliography: p. 194-204.

616

McMillan, Lewis K. Negro higher education in the State of South Carolina. [Orangeburg? S.C., 1953, c1952] 296 p. facsims.   LC2802.S6M25

617

Mallery, David. Negro students in independent schools. Boston, National Association of Independent Schools [1963] 93 p.   LC2731.M25

   "This monograph is no. 8 in a series of studies initiated by the Committee on Educational Practices of the National Council of Independent Schools and . . . continued under the direction of its successor, the Committee on Research [later Committee on Educational Practices] of the National Association of Independent Schools."

618

Maryland. *Commission on Interracial Problems and Relations.* Desegregation in the Baltimore city schools. [Study sponsored by the Maryland Commission on Interracial Problems and Relations and the Baltimore Commission on Human Relations. Baltimore, 1955] 32 p.

LB3062.M32

619

Maryland. *Commission on Interracial Problems and Relations.* The report of a study on desegregation in the Baltimore city schools, by Elinor Pancoast and others. [Baltimore, 1956] 114 p.   LB3062.M34

   Prepared under the direction of a joint committee representing the Maryland Commission on Interracial Problems and Relations and the Baltimore Commission on Human Relations.

   Bibliographical footnotes.

620

Meece, Leonard E. Negro education in Kentucky; a comparative study of white and Negro education on the elementary and secondary school levels. Lexington, Ky., University of Kentucky [1938] 180 p. diagrs., maps. (Bulletin of the Bureau of School Service, College of Education, University of Kentucky. v. 10, no. 3)   LC2802.K4M4

   Bibliography: p. [176]-178.

621

Meredith, James H. Three years in Mississippi. Bloomington, Indiana University Press [1966] 328 p.   LD3412.9.M4A3

   Autobiographical.

   An account of the experiences of the first Negro to gain admission to the University of Mississippi.

622

Meyer, Gladys E. Parent action in school integration; a New York experience. New York, United Parents Associations of New York City [1961] 46 p.   LB3062.M4

623

Morgan, John W. The origin and distribution of the graduates of the Negro colleges of Georgia. Milledgeville, Ga., Priv. print., 1940. 118 p. map, tables.   E185.82.M84

  Bibliography: p. 117-118.

624

Muse, Benjamin. Ten years of prelude: the story of integration since the Supreme Court's 1954 decision. New York, Viking Press [1964] 308 p.
                    E185.61.M989
  Bibliography: p. 289-291. "Reference notes": p. 292-297.

625

National Education Association of the United States. *Research Division.* Studies of educational problems involved in school integration. [Washington, 1960] 31 p.   LB3062.N3

626

National Scholarship Service and Fund for Negro Students. Opportunities in interracial colleges, edited by Richard L. Plaut, executive vice-chairman. New York, 1951. 240 p.   LC2801.N3

627

Noble, Jeanne L. The Negro woman's college education. New York, Teachers College, Columbia University, 1956. 163 p. tables. (TC studies in education)   LC1605.N6

  Bibliography: p. 145-150.

628

Norfleet, Marvin B. Forced school integration in the U.S.A. New York, Carlton Press, 1961. 248 p.   LB3062.N57

629

North Carolina. *Division of Negro Education.* Some tasks of union school principals in North Carolina, by S. E. Duncan, Division of Negro Education. Raleigh [1955] 141 p.   LC2802.N8A52 1955

630

Pennington, Edgar L. Thomas Bray's Associates and their work among the Negroes. Worcester, Mass., The Society, 1939. 95 p.   LC2801.P45

At head of title: American Antiquarian Society.
"Reprinted from the Proceedings of the American Antiquarian Society for Oct., 1938."

631

Phelps-Stokes Fund. Ladders to improvement; report of a project for the improvement of instruction in secondary schools. Aaron Brown, editor. New York, 1960. 249 p. illus., diagrs., maps.   LC2707.P45

Bibliography: p. 231-249.

632

Plaut, Richard L. Blueprint for talent searching; America's hidden manpower. [New York] National Scholarship Service and Fund for Negro Students [1957] 41 p.   LB2338.P56

633

Poverty, education, and race relations; studies and proposals. [By] William C. Kvaraceus, John S. Gibson [and] Thomas J. Curtin. With contributions by Minna K. Barnett [and others] Boston [Published for the Lincoln Filene Center, Tufts University, Medford, Mass. by] Allyn and Bacon [1967] 226 p.   LC2801.P63

"Most of these selected papers were drawn from the educational television course, Education and Race Relations."
Bibliographical footnotes. Bibliography: p. 201-210.

634

Range, Willard. The rise and progress of Negro colleges in Georgia, 1865-1949. Athens, University of Georgia Press [1951] 254 p. [Phelps-Stokes fellowship studies, no. 15]   E185.5.G35 no. 15
                                                                    LC2802.G4R35
Bibliography: p. 236-248.

635

Record, Wilson, *and* Jane C. Record, *eds.* Little Rock, U.S.A. San Francisco, Chandler Pub. Co. [1960] 338 p. illus. (Materials for analysis)
                                                                    LA242.L5R4
A chronological account of the integration of Central High School, Little Rock, Arkansas.

636
Sexton, Patricia C. Education and income; inequalities of opportunity in our public schools. Foreword by Kenneth B. Clark. New York, Viking Press, 1961. 298 p. illus. LA210.S4

637
Smith, Robert C. They closed their schools; Prince Edward County, Virginia, 1951-1964. Chapel Hill, University of North Carolina Press [1965] 281 p. LA380.P74S6

Bibliographical references included in "Notes" (p. [267]-281).

638
Southern Education Reporting Service. Southern schools: progress and problems, prepared by staff members and associates of Southern Education Reporting Service. Edited by Patrick McCauley and Edward D. Ball. Data collection directed by Bennie Carmichael. Chapters contributed by Tom Flake [and others] With introductions by Relman Morin [and] John A. Griffin. Nashville [1959] 174 p. illus., tables. LA201.S6

639
Southern Education Reporting Service. A statistical summary, State by State, of segregation-desegregation activity affecting southern schools from 1954 to present, together with pertinent data on enrollment, teachers, colleges, litigation and legislation. Rev. Nashville, 1961. 49 p. LB3062.S58 1961

640
Southern Education Reporting Service. With all deliberate speed; segregation-desegregation in southern schools. Prepared by staff members and associates of Southern Education Reporting Service: Bert Collier [and others] Edited by Don Shoemaker. New York, Harper [1957] 239 p. LB3062.S6

Bibliography: p. 218-224.

641
Spellman, Cecil L. Rough steps on my stairway; the life history of a Negro educator. New York, Exposition Press [1953] 273 p. LC2731.S65

642
Swint, Henry L. The northern teacher in the South, 1862-1870. New York, Octagon Books, 1967. 221 p. map. LC2801.S9 1967

Reprint of the 1941 ed.
Bibliography: p. 201-207.

643

Trillin, Calvin. An education in Georgia; the integration of Charlayne Hunter and Hamilton Holmes. New York, Viking Press [1964] 180 p.

LB3062.T7

644

Trubowitz, Sidney. A handbook for teaching in the ghetto school. Chicago, Quadrangle Books [1968] 175 p.   LC4091.T7

Bibliography: p. 147-168.

645

U.S. *Commission on Civil Rights.* Civil rights U.S.A.: public schools, cities in the North and West, 1962; staff reports. [Washington, For sale by the Supt. of Docs., U.S. Govt. Print. Off., 1962] 309 p. illus., maps (part fold.)   LB3062.U63

646

U.S. *Commission on Civil Rights.* Civil rights U.S.A.: public schools, Southern States, 1962; staff reports. [Washington, For sale by the Supt. of Docs., U.S. Govt. Print. Off., 1962] 217 p.   LA209.2.A47

Includes bibliographical notes.

647

U.S. *Commission on Civil Rights.* Equal protection of the laws in public higher education, 1960. [Washington, 1961] xv, 355 p. diagrs., maps, tables.   DLC-LL

Bibliography: p. 329-332.

648

U.S. *Commission on Civil Rights.* Racial isolation in the public schools; a report. Washington, For sale by the Supt. of Docs., U.S. Govt. Print. Off. [1967] 2 v.   LA210.A45

Bibliographical footnotes.

649

U.S. *Commission on Civil Rights.* Southern school segregation, 1966-67; a report. [Washington] 1967. 163 p.   LA210.A46

Bibliographical footnotes.

650

U.S. *Congress. House. Committee on Education and Labor.* Integration in public education programs. Hearings before the Subcommittee on

Integration in Federally Assisted Public Education Programs of the Committee on Education and Labor, House of Representatives, Eighty-seventh Congress, second session, on H.R. 6890 [and others]. Washington, U.S. Govt. Print. Off., 1962. 2 pts. (720 p.) illus.   LB3062.U635

Hearings held Feb. 27-June 15, 1962.

651

U.S. *Congress. House. Committee on Education and Labor.* Integration in public education programs. Report of the Subcommittee on Integration in Federally Assisted Public Education Programs. Washington, U.S. Govt. Print. Off., 1962. 138 p. illus.   LB3062.U636

At head of title: 87th Cong., 2d sess. Committee print.
Bibliography: p. 98.

651a

U.S. *Office of Education.* Negro education; a study of the private and higher schools for colored people in the United States. Prepared in cooperation with the Phelps-Stokes Fund under the direction of Thomas Jesse Jones, specialist in the education of racial groups, Bureau of Education. Washington, Govt. Print. Off., 1917. 2 v. illus., maps (1 fold.), plates, tables (part fold.) (Bulletin, 1916, no. 38-39)

L111.A6 1916 no. 38-39
LC2801.U64
LC2801.A5 1917

At head of title: Department of the Interior. Bureau of Education.

652

U.S. *Office of Education.* Survey of Negro colleges and universities, prepared in the Division of Higher Education, Arthur J. Klein, chief. Washington, U.S. Govt. Print. Off., 1929. 964 p. tables. (*Its* Bulletin, 1928, no. 7)

L111.A6 1928 no. 7
LC2801.A38

At head of title: Department of the Interior. Bureau of Education.
Each chapter also issued separately in 1928.
Contents.—1, 2, and 3. Introduction, control and finance, education service.—4. Alabama.—5. Arkansas.—6. Delaware and Maryland. —7. District of Columbia.—8. Florida.—9. Georgia.—10. Kentucky. —11. Louisiana.—12. Mississippi and Oklahoma.—13. Missouri. —14. North Carolina.—15. Ohio and West Virginia.—16. Pennsylvania. —17. South Carolina.—18. Tennessee.—19. Texas.—20. Virginia.

653

U.S. *Office of Education. Division of Vocational Education.* Negro farm families can feed themselves; a handbook for teachers. Federal Security

Agency, Paul V. McNutt, administrator. U.S. Office of Education, John W. Studebaker, commissioner. Washington, U.S. Govt. Print. Off., 1942. 52 p. illus., diagrs., tables. [*Its* Leaflet no. 8] LC1045.A27 no. 8

Text continued on p. [3] of cover.

"Prepared jointly by the Agricultural Education Service and Home Economics Education Service."

"Prepared in the interest of the national nutrition program by the Vocational Division of the U.S. Office of Education. Issued by the Office of Defense Health and Welfare Services."—Verso of title page.

Revision of U.S. Office of Education. Vocational Division. Misc[ellany] 2563, "Negro Farm Familes Can Feed Themselves."

"Suggested references on teaching units": p. 49-[53].

654

Virginia. *Commission on Constitutional Government.* Did the Court interpret or amend? The meaning of the Fourteenth amendment, in terms of a State's power to operate racially separate public schools, as defined by the courts. [Richmond, 1960] 43 p. (Historic statements and papers expounding the role of the States in their relation to the central government, 5)   Vi

655

Washington, Booker T. My larger education; being chapters from my experience. Illustrated from photographs. Garden City, N.Y., Doubleday, Page, 1911. 313 p. plates, ports.   E185.97.W28

656

Washington, Booker T., *ed.* Tuskegee & its people: their ideals and achievements. New York, Appleton, 1905. xiv, 354 p. illus.   LC2851.T82W2

Reprint issued by Negro Universities Press, 1969.

Contents.—1. The school and its purposes.—2. Autobiographies by graduates of the school.

657

Washington Center for Metropolitan Studies, *Washington, D.C.* In search of a future; a pilot study of career-seeking experiences of selected high school graduates in Washington, D.C. Washington [196-] 117 leaves.

LC2803.W3W35

658

Weinberg, Meyer, *comp.* Integrated education, a reader. Beverly Hills, Calif., Glencoe Press [1968] 376 p. illus., maps.   LB3062.W42

Consists of selections from the magazine, *Integrated Education.* Includes bibliographies.

659

Wiggins, Samuel P. The desegregation era in higher education [by] Sam P. Wiggins, director, Southern Study in Higher Education. Berkeley, Calif., McCutchan Pub. Corp. [1966] 106 p. illus.　　　　LB2341.W54

Includes bibliographical references.

660

Wilkerson, Doxey A. Special problems of Negro education. Prepared for the Advisory Committee on Education. Washington, U.S. Govt. Print. Off., 1939. xvi, 171 p. tables. ([U.S.] Advisory Committee on Education. Staff study no. 12)　　　　L111.A93 no. 12
　　　　　　　　　　　　　　　　　　　　　　　　LC2801.W5

"Publications of the committee": p. 171.

661

Wilson, Charles H. Education for Negroes in Mississippi since 1910. Boston, Meador Pub. Co. [1947] 641 p. illus., ports.　　　　LC2802.M7W5

Bibliography: p. 595-607.

662

Woodson, Carter G. The education of the Negro prior to 1861. New York, Arno Press, 1968. 454 p. (The American Negro, his history and literature)　　　　LC2741.W7 1968

Reprint of the 2d ed., 1919.
Bibliography: p. 399-434.

663

Work Conference on Curriculum and Teaching in Depressed Urban Areas, *Columbia University, 1962.* Education in depressed areas; [papers] . A. Harry Passow, editor. New York, Bureau of Publications, Teachers College, Columbia University, 1963. 359 p. tables.　　　　LC5105.W6 1962

Includes bibliographies.

664

Wright, Marion M. T. The education of Negroes in New Jersey. New York, Teachers College, Columbia University, 1941. 227 p. (Teachers College, Columbia University. Contributions to education, no. 815)
　　　　　　　　　　　　　　　　　　　　　　　LC2802.N5W7 1941

Thesis (Ph.D.)–Columbia University.
Bibliography: p. 212-227.

ENTERTAINMENT

665

Bond, Frederick W. The Negro and the drama; the direct and indirect contribution which the American Negro has made to drama and the legitimate stage, with the underlying conditions responsible. Washington, Associated Publishers [c1940] 213 p.   PS3338.N4B6

   Bibliography: p. 202-208.

666

Fletcher, Tom. 100 years of the Negro in show business; the Tom Fletcher story. New York, Burdge [1954] 337 p. illus.   ML3561.N4F5

667

Hughes, Langston, *and* Milton Meltzer. Black magic; a pictorial history of the Negro in American entertainment. Englewood Cliffs, N.J., Prentice-Hall [1967] 375 p. illus., ports.   PN2286.H75

668

Isaacs, Edith J. R. The Negro in the American theatre. New York, Theatre Arts, 1947. 143 p. illus., ports.   PN2286.I8

669

Jerome, Victor J. The Negro in Hollywood films. New York, Masses & Mainstream [1950] 64 p.   PN1995.9.N4J4

"An expansion of a lecture . . . delivered at a public forum held under the auspices of the Marxist cultural magazine, *Masses & Mainstream* . . . New York, on February 3, 1950."
Bibliographical footnotes.

670
Mitchell, Loften. Black drama; the story of the American Negro in the theatre. New York, Hawthorn Books [1967] 248 p. illus., ports.
PS338.N4M5

671
Patterson, Lindsay, *comp.* Anthology of the American Negro in the theatre; a critical approach. New York, Publishers Co. [1967] xiv, 306 p. illus., facsims., ports. (International library of Negro life and history)
PN2226.P3
Published under the auspices of the Association for the Study of Negro Life and History.
Bibliography: p. [293]-294.

672
Sandle, Floyd L. The Negro in the American educational theatre: an organizational development, 1911-1964. [Grambling? La.] 1964. xviii, 202 p. illus., ports.
PN3182.S3
Bibliography: p. 199-202.

FOLK-LORE AND FOLK-TALES

673

Abrahams, Roger D. Deep down in the jungle . . .; Negro narrative folklore from the streets of Philadelphia. Hatboro, Pa., Folklore Associates, 1964. 287 p. illus.   GR103.A2

Bibliography: p. 269-275.

674

Adams, Edward C. L. Congaree sketches; scenes from Negro life in the swamps of the Congaree and tales by Tad and Scip of heaven and hell with other miscellany. With an introduction by Paul Green. Chapel Hill, University of North Carolina Press, 1927. xvii, 116 p.   PZ3.A2114Co

675

Ballowe, Hewitt L. The Lawd sayin' the same; Negro folk tales of the Creole country. Introduction by Donald Joseph. [Baton Rouge] Louisiana State University Press [1947] xvi, 254 p. illus.   PZ3.B2162Law

676

Bennett, John. The doctor to the dead; grotesque legends & folk tales of old Charleston. New York, Rinehart [1946] xv, 260 p. illus.

GR103.B4

677

Botkin, Benjamin A., ed. A treasury of Mississippi River folklore; stories, ballads, traditions, and folkways of the mid-American river country.

Foreword by Carl Carmer. New York, Crown Publishers [1955] xx, 620 p. illus. GR109.B58

Includes melodies with words.

Bibliographical footnotes.

677a

Bradford, Roark. Ol' man Adam and his chillun; being the tales they tell about the time when the Lord walked the earth like a natural man. With drawings by A. B. Walker. New York, Harper, 1928. xxiv, 264 p. illus. PS3503.R221506 1928

678

Bradford, Roark. This side of Jordan. With drawings by Erich Berry. New York, Harper, 1929. 255 p. illus. PZ3.B7254Th

679

Brewer, John Mason, *comp.* American Negro folklore. Illustrations by Richard Lowe. Chicago, Quadrangle Books, 1968. xviii, 386 p. illus., music. GR103.B66

680

Brewer, John Mason. Aunt Dicy tales; snuff-dipping tales of the Texas Negro. Foreword by Roy Bedichek. Illustrations by John T. Biggers. [Austin? Tex.] 1956. 80 p. illus. GR103.B67

681

Brewer, John Mason. Dog ghosts, and other Texas Negro folk tales. Drawings by John T. Biggers. Foreword by Chapman J. Milling. Austin, University of Texas Press [1958] 124 p. illus. GR103.B68

682

Brewer, John Mason. The Word on the Brazos; Negro preacher tales from the Brazos bottoms of Texas. Foreword by J. Frank Dobie; illustrations by Ralph White, Jr. Austin, University of Texas Press, 1953. 109 p. illus. GR103.B7

683

Brewer, John Mason. Worser days and better times; the folklore of the North Carolina Negro. With preface & notes by Warren E. Roberts. Drawings by R. L. Toben. Chicago, Quadrangle Books [1965] 192 p. illus. GR103.B72

Bibliography: p. 17-18.

684

Carmer, Carl L. Stars fell on Alabama. New York, Hill and Wang [1961, c1934] 291 p. illus. (American century series, AC37)

F326.C275 1961

685

Chappell, Louis W. John Henry; a folk-lore study. Port Washington, N.Y., Kennikat Press [1968] 144 p. (Kennikat Press series in Negro culture and history)   PS461.J6C5 1968

Reprint of the 1933 ed.
Bibliography: p. [144]. Bibliographical footnotes.

686

Christensen, *Mrs.* A. M. H. Afro-American folk lore; told round cabin fires on the Sea Islands of South Carolina. Boston, J. G. Cupples Co. [1892] xiv, 116 p. plates.   PZ8.1.C462A

687

Courlander, Harold. Terrapin's pot of sense. Illustrated by Elton Fax. New York, Holt [1957] 125 p. illus.   PZ8.1.C8Te

Short stories.

688

Dobie, James Frank, *ed.* Follow de drinkin' gou'd. Austin, Texas Folk-Lore Society, c1928. 201 p. music. (Publications of the Texas Folk-Lore Society. no. 7)   ICN

"Proceedings of the thirteenth annual session (1927) of the Texas Folk-Lore Society": p. [181]-182.
Bibliographical footnotes.

689

Dobie, James Frank, *ed.* Tone the bell easy. [Facsim. ed.] Dallas, Southern Methodist University Press [1965, c1932] 199 p. illus., music. (Texas Folklore Society. Publication no. 10) GR108.D55 1965a

"Proceedings of the Texas Folk-Lore Society, 1932": p. [186]-187.

690

Dorson, Richard M., *comp.* American Negro folktales, collected with introduction and notes by Richard M. Dorson. Greenwich, Conn., Fawcett Publications [1967] 378 p. (A Fawcett premier book, t357)

GR103.D58

Selected primarily from the compiler's *Negro Folktales in Michigan,* 1956, and *Negro Tales from Pine Bluff, Arkansas, and Calvin, Michigan,* 1958.

Bibliography: p. [379]-[381].

691

Dorson, Richard M., *ed.* Negro folktales in Michigan. Cambridge, Harvard University Press, 1956. 245 p. illus.   GR103.D6

692

Dorson, Richard M., *ed.* Negro tales from Pine Bluff, Arkansas, and Calvin, Michigan. Bloomington, Indiana University Press, 1958. xviii, 292 p. (Indiana University publication. Folklore series, no. 12)   GR108.D6

In 2 pts.; pt. 1 consists of tales by various informants; pt. 2, tales by James Douglas Suggs.

Bibliography: p. 289-292. Includes bibliographical references.

693

Duncan, Eula G. Big Road Walker. Based on stories told by Alice Cannon; illustrated by Fritz Eichenberg. New York, F. A. Stokes Co., 1940. 121 p. illus.   PZ8.1.D87Bi

694

Gonzales, Ambrose E. The black border; Gullah stories of the Carolina coast (with a glossary). Columbia, S.C., State Co., 1922. 348 p.

E185.93.S7G6

GR103.G6

694a

Gonzales, Ambrose E. With Aesop along the black border. Columbia, S.C., State Co., 1924. xiv, 298 p.   GR103.G65

"The fables contained in this volume were . . . published in the *State* between August 1923 and February 1924."

695

Harris, Joel Chandler. Uncle Remus: his songs and his sayings. With a foreword by Marc Connelly and woodcuts by Seong Moy. New York, For the members of the Limited Editions Club, 1957. xviii, 158 p. illus.

PZ7.H242Un45

696

Hughes, Langston, *and* Arna W. Bontemps, *eds.* The book of Negro folk-lore. New York, Dodd, Mead, 1958. 624 p. illus.   GR103.H74

697

Hurston, Zora N. Mules and men; with an introduction by Frank Boas. 1(
illustrations by Miguel Covarrubias. Philadelphia, Lippincott, 1935
342 p. illus., plates.   GR103.H&

    Contents.–pt. 1. Folk tales.–pt. 2. Hoodoo.–Appendix. 1. Negr<
songs with music (p. 309-[331]). 2. Formulae of hoodoo doctors
3. Paraphernalia of conjure. 4. Prescriptions of root doctors.

698

Jackson, Bruce, *comp*. The Negro and his folklore in nineteenth-century
periodicals, edited, with an introduction, by Bruce Jackson. Austin
Published for the American Folklore Society by the University of Texa
Press [1967] xxiii, 374 p. (Publications of the American Folklor<
Society. Bibliographical and special series, v. 18)   GR103.J:

    Includes spirituals (principally unaccompanied).
Bibliography: p. 353-367.

699

Johnson, Guy B. Folk culture on St. Helena Island, South Carolina. Fore
word by Don Yoder. Hatboro, Pa., Folklore Associates, 1968 [c1930]
xxi, 183 p.   E185.93.S7J67 196&

    Includes music.
Bibliography: p. 174-179.

700

Johnson, Guy B. John Henry; tracking down a Negro legend. Chapel Hill
University of North Carolina Press, 1929. 155 p. facsim. (University o<
North Carolina. Social study series)   PS461.J6J<
                                                    ML3556.J7J:

    Includes music.
"Bibliography of John Henry": p. [152]-155.

701

Jones, Charles C. Negro myths from the Georgia coast told in the vernacu
lar. Boston, Houghton, Mifflin, 1888. 171 p.   GR103.J<

702

Love, Rose L., *ed*. A collection of folklore for children in elementary
school and at home. New York, Vantage Press [1964] 83 p. illus.
                                                        GR105.L<
    Includes music.

702a

Owen, Mary A. Voodoo tales, as told among the Negroes of the Southwest; collected from original sources by Mary Alicia Owen; introduction by Charles Godfrey Leland; illustrated by Juliette A. Owen and Louis Wain. New York, G. P. Putnam, 1893. xv, 310 p. illus.

GR103.O82

Published in London the same year under title: *Old Rabbit, the Voodoo, and Other Sorcerers.*

703

Parsons, Elsie W. C., *ed.* Folklore of the Sea Islands, South Carolina. Cambridge, Mass., American Folk-Lore Society, 1923. xxx, 219 p. map. (Memoirs of the American Folk-Lore Society, v. 16) GR1.A5 v. 16

Contains music.
"List of informants or writers of the tales": p. xxiii-xxvi.
"Bibliography and abbreviations": p. xxvii-xxx.

704

Puckett, Newbell N. Folk beliefs of the southern Negro. Montclair, N.J., Patterson Smith, 1968 [c1926] xiv, 644 p. illus. (Patterson Smith reprint series in criminology, law enforcement, and social problems, publication no. 22) GR103.P8 1968

Bibliography: p. [583]-598.

705

Robb, Bernard. Welcum hinges, with a foreword by Alexander William Armour and an introduction by Thomas Lomax Hunter; gravure illustrations by Woodi Ishmael. New York, E. P. Dutton, 1942. 215 p. illus., plates. GR103.R6

Plantation folk tales and sayings, in the Negro dialect and idiom of "Uncle Woodson," at Gay Mont, the Robb estate in Caroline County, Va.

706

Sale, John B. The tree named John. With twenty-two silhouettes by Joseph Cranston Jones. Chapel Hill, University of North Carolina Press, 1929. 151 p. illus., plates. GR103.S3

707

Stoney, Samuel G., *and* Gertrude M. Shelby. Black Genesis; a chronicle. Illustrations by Martha Bensley Bruére. New York, Macmillan, 1930. xxix, 192 p. illus. GR103.S8

"Tales of the Gullah Negroes of the Carolina low country [told in the Gullah dialect]"—Foreword.

"The family tree of Gullah folk speech and folk tales": p. ix-xxv.

708

Writers' Program. *Georgia.* Drums and shadows; survival studies among the Georgia coastal Negroes [by the] Savannah unit, Georgia Writers' Project, Work Projects Administration; foreword by Guy B. Johnson photographs by Muriel and Malcolm Bell, Jr. Athens, University of Georgia Press, 1940. xx, 274 p. plates, ports.   E185.93.G4W7

Bibliography: p. 259-263.

709

Writers' Program. *South Carolina.* South Carolina folk tales; stories of animals and supernatural beings, compiled by workers of the Writers' Program of the Works Projects Administration in the State of South Carolina. Sponsored by the University of South Carolina. Columbia S.C. [1941] 122 p. (Bulletin of the University of South Carolina October 1941)   GR110.S6W7

"Bibliography for South Carolina folk tales": p. 118-122.

710

Writers' Program. *Tennessee.* God bless the devil! Liars' bench tales [by] James R. Aswell, Julia Willhoit, Jennette Edwards [and others] of the Tennessee Writers' Project; with illustrations by Ann Kelley of the Tennessee Art Project. Chapel Hill, University of North Carolina Press 1940. 254 p. illus.   GR110.T4W7

"Arranged and edited by James R. Aswell."—Preface.

711

Aplin, Norita, Shirley Seaton, *and* Juanita Storey. The Negro American: his role, his quest. Clyde F. Varner, editor. Cleveland, Cleveland Public Schools, 1968. 246 p. map.   E185.A56

     Bibliography: p. 220-238.

712

Aptheker, Herbert, *ed.* A documentary history of the Negro people in the United States. Preface by W. E. B. DuBois. New York, Citadel Press [1951] xvi, 942 p.   E185.A58

713

Aptheker, Herbert. Essays in the history of the American Negro. New York, International Publishers [1964] 216 p.   E185.A6 1964

     Bibliography: p. 211-216.

714

Aptheker, Herbert. To be free; studies in American Negro history. New York, International Publishers [1948] 256 p.   E185.A63

     "Reference notes": p. 193-248.

715

Bennett, Lerone. Before the Mayflower; a history of the Negro in America 1619-1966. 3d ed. Chicago, Johnson Pub. Co., 1966. 449 p. illus. maps, ports.   E185.B4 1966

Bibliography: p. [428]-442.

716

Bennett, Lerone. Black Power, U.S.A., the human side of Reconstruction 1867-1877. Chicago, Johnson Pub. Co., 1967. 401 p. illus., ports.
                                                                    E185.2.B38

Bibliography: p. 390-393.

717

Bittle, William E., *and* Gilbert Geis. The longest way home; Chief Alfred C Sam's back-to-Africa movement. With the research assistance of Donald F. Parker. Detroit, Wayne State University Press, 1964. 229 p.
                                                                    E448.B615

Includes bibliographical "Notes" (p. 213-221).

718

Bontemps, Arna W. Story of the Negro; illustrated by Raymond Lufkin 2d ed., enl. New York, Knopf, 1955. 243 p. illus.   E29.N3B6 1955

719

Boykin, James H. The Negro in North Carolina prior to 1861; an historical monograph. New York, Pageant Press [1958] 84 p.   E185.93.N6B6

Bibliographical references included in "Notes" (p. 77-84).

720

Broderick, Francis L., *and* August Meier, *eds.* Negro protest thought in the twentieth century. Indianapolis, Bobbs-Merrill Co. [1966, c1965] xliii 444 p. (The American heritage series)   E185.B87

721

Broom, Leonard, *and* Norval D. Glenn. Transformation of the Negro American. New York, Harper & Row [1965] 207 p.   E185.6.B84

Bibliography: p. 193-199.

722

Brown, Ina C. The story of the American Negro. Decorations by Aaron Douglas. Rev. ed. New York, Friendship Press [1950] 212 p. illus.
                                                                    E185.6.B85 1950

Bibliography: p. 191-200.

723
Brown, William W. The rising sun; or, The antecedents and advancement of the colored race. Boston, A. G. Brown, 1874. 552 p. port.   E185.B884

"Representative men and women": p. 418-552.

724
Cain, Alfred E., ed. The winding road to freedom; a documentary survey of Negro experiences in America. Drawings: Horace Varela. Yonkers [N.Y.] Educational Heritage [1965] 384 p. illus., facsims., maps, ports. (Negro heritage library)   E185.C14

Bibliography: p. 374-377.

725
Caughey, John W., John H. Franklin, and Ernest R. May. Land of the free; a history of the United States. Educational advisers: Richard M. Clowes [and] Alfred T. Clark, Jr. [Rev.] New York, Benziger Bros., 1966. 658 p. illus. (part col.), ports.   E178.1.C36 1966

Includes bibliographies.

726
Chambers, Lucille A., ed. America's tenth man; a pictorial review of one-tenth of a nation, presenting the Negro contribution to American life today. Foreword by Henry Cabot Lodge, Jr. New York, Twayne Publishers [1957] 351 p. illus.   E185.6.C46

727
Christian, Kathryn. The history of the Negro American; resource material. [Des Moines] Des Moines Public Schools, 1968. 43 p.   E185.C52

Bibliography: p. 43.

728
Cincinnati. *Public Schools.* The Negro in American life [by] Mabel Morsbach. New York, Harcourt, Brace & World [1967] 273 p. illus., maps, ports.   E185.C56 1967

Bibliography: p. 255-260.

729
Conrad, Earl. The invention of the Negro. New York, P. S. Eriksson [1967, c1966] 244 p.   E185.C74

Bibliography: p. [232]-236.

730

Coulter, Ellis M. The Civil War and readjustment in Kentucky. Gloucester, Mass., P. Smith, 1966 [c1926] 468 p. maps.   E509.C83 1966

Bibliography: p. 449-458.

731

Cromwell, John W. The Negro in American history; men and women eminent in the evolution of the American of African descent. Washington, American Negro Academy, 1914. 284 p. plates, ports.   E185.C92

Bibliography: p. 257-262.

Reprint issued by Johnson Reprint Corp., 1969.

732

Davie, Maurice R. Negroes in American society. New York, Whittlesey House [1949] 542 p. maps.   E185.6.D3

Includes "References."

733

Delany, Martin R. The condition, elevation, emigration, and destiny of the colored people of the United States. New York, Arno Press, 1968. 214 p. (The American Negro, his history and literature)

E185.D33 1968

Reprint of the 1852 ed., with a new introduction.

734

Drotning, Phillip T. A guide to Negro history in America. Garden City, N.Y., Doubleday, 1968. xiv, 247 p.   E185.D72

735

Eisenstadt, Murray. The Negro in American life. New York, Oxford Book Co. [1968] 380 p. (Oxford readings in social studies)   E184.6.E35

Includes bibliographies.

736

Eppse, Merl R. A guide to the study of the Negro in American history. Nashville, National Publication Co. [1943] 181 p.   E185.E69 1943

"First printing, June, 1937 . . . Third printing, revised and enlarged, September, 1943."

Bibliography: p. 180-181.

737

Eppse, Merl R. The Negro, too, in American history. Nashville, National Publication Co., 1949. xxii, 644 p. illus., maps, ports.

E185.E696 1949

Bibliographical references included in introduction. "Reading material": p. 551-572.

738
Ferris, William H. The African abroad; or, His evolution in western civilization, tracing his development under Caucasian milieu. New Haven, Tuttle, Morehouse & Taylor Press, 1913. 2 v. illus., plates, ports.

E185.F39

739
Fishel, Leslie H., *and* Benjamin Quarles. The Negro American; a documentary history. Glenview, Ill., Scott, Foresman [1967] 536 p. illus., facsims., maps, ports. E185.F5

Bibliographical footnotes.

740
Foster, William Z. The Negro people in American history. New York, International Publishers [1954] 608 p. E185.F6

Bibliography: p. 567-592.

741
Franklin, John H. The free Negro in North Carolina, 1790-1860. Chapel Hill, University of North Carolina Press, 1943. 271 p. maps, tables.

E185.93.N6F7

Bibliography: p. [247]-258.

742
Franklin, John H. From slavery to freedom; a history of Negro Americans. 3d ed. [rev. and enl.] New York, Knopf, 1967. xxii, 686, xliii p. illus., ports. E185.F825 1967

"Bibliographical notes": p. [653]-686.

743
Franklin, John H. The militant South, 1800-1861. Cambridge, Belknap Press of Harvard University Press, 1956. 317 p. F213.F75

Includes bibliography.

744
Frazier, Edward Franklin. The Negro in the United States. Rev. ed. New York, Macmillan [1957] xxxiii, 769 p. diagrs., maps, tables.

E185.F833 1957

Bibliography: p. 707-752.

745

Freidel, Frank B. The Negro and Puerto Rican in American history. Boston, Heath [1964] 27 p. illus., ports.   E185.F85

746

Fuller, Thomas O. Pictorial history of the American Negro; a story of progress and development along social, political, economic, educational and spiritual lines. Memphis, Tenn., Pictorial History, 1933. xxiii, 375 p. illus. (part col.), maps, ports.   E185.F97

   Bibliography: p. 361-363.

747

Goldston, Robert C. The Negro revolution. New York, Macmillan [1968] 247 p. illus., ports.   E185.G6

748

Greene, Lorenzo J. The Negro in colonial New England, 1620-1776. Port Washington, N.Y., Kennikat Press [1966, c1942] 404 p.

                    E445.N5G7 1966
   Reprint of a thesis, Columbia University, 1942.
   Bibliography: p. [361]-384.

749

Harlan, Louis R. The Negro in American history. Washington, American Historical Association [1965] 29 p. (Service Center for Teachers of History. Publication no. 61)   E175.1.H3

   Bibliography: p. 26-29.

750

Hartshorn, William N., *ed.* An era of progress and promise, 1863-1910; the religious, moral, and educational development of the American Negro since his emancipation. George W. Penniman, associate editor. Boston, Priscilla Pub. Co., 1910. 576 p. illus., ports.   E185.6.H33

751

Hesseltine, William B., *ed.* The tragic conflict; the Civil War and Reconstruction. Selected and edited with introduction and notes by William B. Hesseltine. New York, G. Braziller, 1962. 528 p. (The American epochs series)   E464.H4

   Bibliography: p. [527]-528.

752

Hodges, Carl G., *and* Helene H. Levene, *comps.* Illinois Negro history-makers. Compiled with the assistance of Helen Horney, Julia Wanless and the Illinois State Historical Library staff. Chicago, Illinois Emancipation Centennial Commission, 1964. 91 p. illus., ports. E185.93.I2H6

753

Hughes, Langston, *and* Milton Meltzer. A pictorial history of the Negro in America. 3d rev. ed. New York, Crown Publishers [1968] 380 p. illus., maps, ports. E185.H83 1968

"Third revision by C. Eric Lincoln and Milton Meltzer." Bibliography: p. 375.

754

Jordan, Winthrop D. White over black: American attitudes toward the Negro, 1550-1812. Chapel Hill, Published for the Institute of Early American History and Culture at Williamsburg, Va., by the University of North Carolina Press [1968] xx, 651 p. map. E185.J69

Bibliography: p. 610-614. Bibliographical footnotes.

755

Katz, William L., *comp.* Eyewitness; the Negro in American history. New York, Pitman Pub. Corp. [1967] xix, 554 p. illus., facsims., ports. E185.K28

756

Katz, William L. Teachers' guide to American Negro history. Chicago, Quadrangle Books [1968] 192 p. illus., ports. E185.K285

Includes bibliographies.

757

Lincoln, Charles Eric. The Negro pilgrimage in America. New York, Bantam Books [1967] 184 p. illus., facsims., ports. (Bantam pathfinder editions) E185.L47

758

Little, Malcolm. Malcolm X on Afro-American history. [New York, Merit Publishers, 1967] 48 p. E185.L5

"Speech . . . from . . . a public meeting on January 24, 1965."

759

Litwack, Leon F. North of slavery; the Negro in the free States, 1790-1860. [Chicago] University of Chicago Press [1961] 318 p. E185.9.L5

"Bibliographical essay": p. 280-303.

760

Logan, Rayford W., *and* Irving S. Cohen. The American Negro; old world background and new world experience. With the editorial assistance of Howard R. Anderson. Boston, Houghton Mifflin [1967] 278 p. illus., maps, ports. (Houghton Mifflin social studies program; history)

                                                      E185.L84

Bibliography: p. 266-268.

761

Logan, Rayford W. The betrayal of the Negro, from Rutherford B. Hayes to Woodrow Wilson. New enl. ed. New York, Collier Books [1965] 447 p.   E185.61.L64 1965

"Originally published as *The Negro in American Life and Thought: the Nadir, 1877-1901.*"
Bibliographical references included in "Notes" (p. 397-430).

762

Logan, Rayford W. The Negro in the United States, a brief history. Princeton, D. Van Nostrand [1957] 191 p. (An Anvil original, no. 19)

                                                     E185.L85

Includes bibliography.

763

McPherson, James M. The Negro's Civil War; how American Negroes felt and acted during the war for the Union. New York, Pantheon Books [1965] 358 p. illus., ports.   E540.N3M25

"A note on sources": p. [343]-347.

764

McPherson, James M. The struggle for equality; abolitionists and the Negro in the Civil War and Reconstruction. Princeton, Princeton University Press, 1964. 474 p. illus.   E449.M476

"Bibliographical essay": p. 433-450.

765

Mazyck, Walter H. George Washington and the Negro. Washington, Associated Publishers [c1932] 180 p.   E312.17.M38

766

Meier, August, *and* Elliott M. Rudwick. From plantation to ghetto; an interpretive history of American Negroes. New York, Hill and Wang [1966] 280 p. map.   E185.M4

767
Meier, August. Negro thought in America, 1880-1915; racial ideologies in the age of Booker T. Washington. Ann Arbor, University of Michigan Press [1963] 336 p.   E185.6.M5

"Bibliographical note": p. 280-282. Bibliographical references included in "Notes" (p. 283-316).

768
Meltzer, Milton. In their own words; a history of the American Negro. New York, Crowell [1964-67] 3 v. illus., facsims., ports.   E185.M54

Includes bibliographies.
Contents.–[1.] 1619-1865.–[2.] 1865-1916.–[3.] 1916-1966.

769
Meltzer, Milton, *and* August Meier. Time of trial, time of hope; the Negro in America, 1919-1941. Illustrated by Moneta Barnett. Garden City, N.Y., Doubleday, 1966. 120 p. illus., ports. (Zenith books)
E185.6.M54

770
The Negro in American history. [Mortimer J. Adler, general editor; Charles Van Doren, editor; George Ducas, executive editor] With an introduction by Saunders Redding. [Chicago] Encyclopaedia Britannica Educational Corp. [1969] 3 v. illus.   E185.N4

Contents.–1. Black Americans, 1928-1968.–2. A taste of freedom, 1854-1927.–3 Slaves and masters, 1567-1854.

771
New York *(City) Board of Education*. The Negro in American history. Albany, Reprinted by the University of the State of New York, Bureau of Secondary Curriculum Development, 1965. 158 p.   E185.N56

Bibliography: p. 151-158.
A curriculum guide which includes the African heritage.

772
Ottley, Roi. Black odyssey, the story of the Negro in America. New York, C. Scribner's Sons, 1948. 340 p.   E185.O85

Bibliography: p. 315-322.

773
Pease, Frederick H. Found wanting. [Richmond, Va., 1968] 214 p.
E185.P35

774

Pease, William H., *and* Jane H. Pease. Black Utopia; Negro communal experiments in America. Madison, State Historical Society of Wisconsin, 1963. 204 p.   E448.P36

Bibliography: p. [191]-200.

775

Pennington, James W. C. Text book of the origin and history, &c. &c. of the colored people. Hartford, L. Skinner, Printer, 1841. 96 p.

E185.P41

Earliest attempt to write the history of the Negro.

776

Pinkney, Alphonso. Black Americans. Englewood Cliffs, N.J., Prentice-Hall [1959] xvii, 226 p. (Ethnic groups in American life series)   E185.P5

Includes bibliographies.

777

Powell, Adam Clayton. Marching blacks, an interpretive history of the rise of the black common man. New York, Dial Press, 1945. 218 p.

E185.6.P8

Bibliography: p. 215-218.

778

Quarles, Benjamin. Black abolitionists. New York, Oxford University Press [1969] 310 p.   E449.Q17

"Note on bibliographical literature": p. 251-252. Bibliographical references included in "Notes" (p. 253-292).

779

Quarles, Benjamin. The Negro in the making of America. New York, Collier Books [1964] 288 p. (A Collier books original)   E185.Q2

"AS 534."
Bibliography: p. 267-271.

780

Redding, Jay Saunders. The Negro. Washington, Potomac Books, 1967. 101 p. illus. (The U.S.A. survey series)   E185.R42

Bibliography: p. 91-94.

781

Redding, Jay Saunders. On being Negro in America. Indianapolis, Bobbs-Merrill [1951] 156 p.   E185.61.R3

782

Redding, Jay Saunders. They came in chains; Americans from Africa. Philadelphia, Lippincott [1950] 320 p. (The Peoples of America series)

E185.R4

Bibliography: p. 304-308.

783

Rogers, Joel A. Africa's gift to America; the Afro-American in the making and saving of the United States. New York [1959] 254 p. illus.

E185.R74

784

Rogers, Joel A. 100 amazing facts about the Negro, with complete proof; a short cut to the world history of the Negro. [24th rev. ed.] New York [1963] 58 p. illus., ports.   HT1581.R62 1963

Stamped on t.p.: Distributed by Sportshelf, New Rochelle, N.Y.

785

Rose, Arnold M., *ed.* Assuring freedom to the free; a century of emancipation in the USA. With an introduction by Lyndon B. Johnson. Detroit, Wayne State University Press, 1964. 306 p.   E185.6.R74

Bibliographical footnotes.

786

Sloan, Irving J. The American Negro; a chronology and fact book. 2d ed. Dobbs Ferry, N.Y., Oceana Publications, 1968. 112 p.

E185.S57 1968

Bibliography: p. 71-[74].

787

Staudenraus, P. J. The African colonization movement, 1816-1865. New York, Columbia University Press, 1961. 323 p.   E448.S78

Bibliographical references included in "Notes" (p. [252]-304). "Bibliographical essay": p. [305]-310.

788

Tannenbaum, Frank. Slave and citizen, the Negro in the Americas. New York, Knopf, 1947 [i.e. 1946] 128 p. double table.   E29.N3T3

Bibliographical footnotes.

789

Thorpe, Earl E. The mind of the Negro; an intellectual history of Afro-Americans. Baton Rouge, La., Printed by Ortlieb Press [1961] 562 p.

E185.82.T5

Bibliographical references included in "Footnotes" (p. [496]-548).

790

Thorpe, Earl E. Negro historians in the United States. Baton Rouge, La., Fraternal Press [1958] 188 p.   E175.T5

Bibliography: p. 169-180.

791

Townsend, William H. Lincoln and the Bluegrass; slavery and civil war in Kentucky. [Lexington] University of Kentucky Press [1955] xiv, 392 p. illus., facsims., ports.   E457.T78

"Bibliographical notes": p. [359]-385.

792

U.S. *Congress. House. Committee on Education and Labor. Select Subcommittee on Labor.* To establish a National Commission on Negro History and Culture. Hearing, Ninetieth Congress, second session, on H.R. 12962. March 18, 1968. Washington, U.S. Govt. Print. Off., 1968. 127 p. illus.   KF27.E345 1968b

Bibliographical footnotes.

793

Van Deusen, John G. The black man in white America. Washington, Associated Publishers, 1938. 338 p.   E185.6.V28

Bibliography: p. 301-318.

794

Voegeli, V. Jacque. Free but not equal; the Midwest and the Negro during the Civil War. Chicago, University of Chicago Press [1967] 215 p.

E185.9.V6

Includes bibliographical references.

795

Wade, Richard C., *ed.* The Negro in American life; selected readings, edited and annotated by Richard C. Wade with the editorial assistance of Howard R. Anderson. Boston, Houghton Mifflin [1965] 182 p. illus., ports. (Life in America series)   E185.W17

Houghton Mifflin social studies program; history.

796

Wagandt, Charles L. The mighty revolution; Negro emancipation in Maryland, 1862-1864. Baltimore, Johns Hopkins Press [1964] 299 p. illus., maps.   E512.W2

Bibliography: p. 269-284.

797

Washington, Booker T. The story of the Negro; the rise of the race from slavery. New York, P. Smith, 1940. 2 v. port.   E185.W316 1940

"Published, November, 1909. Reprinted 1940."
Bibliographical footnotes.
Contents.–v. 1. pt. 1. The Negro in Africa. pt. 2. The Negro as a slave.–v. 2. pt. 3. The Negro as a freeman.

798

Wesley, Charles H. Neglected history; essays in Negro history by a college president: Charles H. Wesley. Wilberforce, Ohio, Central State College Press, 1965. 200 p.   E185.W46

Bibliographical references included in "Historical notes" (p. 164-187).

799

Wesley, Charles H., *ed.* The Negro in the Americas. Washington, Graduate School, Howard University [1940] 86 p. (Public lectures of the Division of the Social Sciences of the Graduate School, Howard University. v. 1)   H31.H65 v. 1
E29.N3W5

Contents.–The Negro in the British West Indies, by Eric Williams.–Notes on the Negro in the French West Indies, by L.T. Achille.–The Negro in Spanish America, by R. W. Logan.–The Negro in Brazil, by Richard Pattee.–The Haitian nation, by Dantes Bellegarde.–Race, migration and citizenship, by Ira De A. Reid.–The Negro in the United States and Canada, by C. H. Wesley.

800

Weyl, Nathaniel. The Negro in American civilization. Washington, Public Affairs Press [1960] 360 p.   E185.W5

"References": p. 322-351.

801

Williams, George W. History of the Negro race in America. New York, Bergman Publishers [1968] 2 v. port.   E185.W7 1968

Reprint of the 1883 ed.
Bibliographical footnotes.

802

Woodson, Carter G. Free Negro heads of families in the United States in 1830, together with a brief treatment of the free Negro. Washington,

Association for the Study of Negro Life and History [c1925] lviii, 296 p.   E185.W887

"Second of a series of documentary studies of the free Negro provided for by a grant . . . from the Laura Spelman Rockefeller memorial in 1921."–Foreword.
Bibliographical footnotes.

803

Woodson, Carter G., *ed.* The mind of the Negro as reflected in letters written during the crisis, 1800-1860. New York, Russell & Russell [1969] xxxii, 672 p.   E185.W8877 1969

Reprint of the 1926 ed.
Bibliographical footnotes.

804

Woodson, Carter G., *and* Charles H. Wesley. The Negro in our history. 10th ed., further rev. and enl. Washington, Associated Publishers [1962] 833 p. illus.   E185.W89 1962

Bibliography: p. 775-803.

805

Woodson, Carter G. Negro makers of history. Washington, Associated Publishers [c1928] 362 p. illus., facsims., map, ports.   E185.W895

"An adaptation of [the author's] *The Negro in Our History* to the capacity of children in the elementary schools."–Preface.

806

Woodward, Comer Vann. The burden of southern history. Baton Rouge, Louisiana State University Press [1960] 205 p.   F209.W6

Essays.

807

Wynes, Charles E., *ed.* The Negro in the South since 1865; selected essays in American Negro history. University, University of Alabama Press [1965] 253 p. (Southern historical publications, no. 10)   E185.6.W97

Bibliographical footnotes.

Slavery

808

Aptheker, Herbert. American Negro slave revolts. New York, International Publishers [1963] 409 p.   E447.A67 1963

Issued also as thesis (Ph.D.), Columbia University.

Includes bibliography.

809

Aptheker, Herbert. Nat Turner's slave rebellion. Together with the full text of the so-called "confessions" of Nat Turner made in prison in 1831. New York, Published for A.I.M.S. by Humanities Press [1966] 152 p. facsim.   F232.S7A8

Thesis (M.A.)–Columbia University.

Bibliography: p. 111-125.

810

Aptheker, Herbert. One continual cry; David Walker's Appeal to the colored citizens of the world, 1829-1830, its setting & its meaning, together with the full text of the third, and last, edition of the Appeal. New York, Published for A.I.M.S. by Humanities Press [1965] 150 p.

Bibliography: p. 149-150.   E446.W2A6

811

Bancroft, Frederic. Slave-trading in the Old South. Baltimore, J. H. Furst Co., 1931. 415 p. facsims., plates, table.   E442.B21

812

Barnes, Gilbert H. The antislavery impulse, 1830-1844. With a new introduction by William G. McLoughlin. New York, Harcourt, Brace & World [1964] xxxv, 298 p.   E449.B264 1964

First published in 1933.

Includes bibliographical references.

813

Brackett, Jeffrey R. The Negro in Maryland; a study of the institution of slavery. Baltimore, N. Murray, publication agent, Johns Hopkins University, 1889. 268 p. (Johns Hopkins University studies in historical and political science. Extra v. 6)   H31.J62 v. 6
                                                          E445.M3B7

814

Bruce, Kathleen. Virginia iron manufacture in the slave era. New York, A. M. Kelley, 1968. 482 p. illus., facsim., map, port. (Library of early American business and industry, 22)   HD9517.V52B7 1968

Reprints of economic classics.

Reprint of the 1930 ed.

Bibliography: p. 431-451.

815
Buckmaster, Henrietta, *pseud.* Let my people go; the story of the under ground railroad and the growth of the abolition movement. New York Harper [c1941] 398 p. map, plates, ports.   E450.B89 1941

London edition (V. Gollancz) has title: *Out of the House of Bond- age.*
Bibliography: p. 375-388.

816
Coffin, Levi. Reminiscences of Levi Coffin, the reputed president of the underground railroad. New York, A. M. Kelley, 1968. 712 p. ports (Reprints of economic classics)   E450.C64 1968

Reprint of the 1876 ed.

817
Coleman, John Winston. Slavery times in Kentucky. Chapel Hill, Univer sity of North Carolina Press, 1940. xiv, 351 p. facsims., plates, ports.
                                                                      E445.K5C7
"Selected bibliography": p. 327-332.

818
Davis, David B. The problem of slavery in Western culture. Ithaca, N.Y. Cornell University Press [1966] xiv, 505 p.   HT871.D2

Bibliographical footnotes.

819
Dillon, Merton L. Benjamin Lundy and the struggle for Negro freedom Urbana, University of Illinois Press, 1966. 285 p. port.   E446.D5

Bibliography: p. [263]-267.

820
Donnan, Elizabeth, *ed.* Documents illustrative of the history of the slave trade to America. Washington, Carnegie Institution of Washington 1930-35. 4 v. map, tables. (Carnegie Institution of Washington. Publica tion no. 409)   E441.D68
                                                                      AS32.A5 no. 409

On verso of t.p.: Division of Historical Research, Carnegie Institu tion of Washington.
Contents.—1. 1441-1700.—2. The eighteenth century.—3. New England and the middle colonies.—4. The border colonies and th southern colonies.

821

Donovan, Frank R. Mr. Lincoln's proclamation; the story of the Emancipation Proclamation. New York, Dodd, Mead [1964] 146 p. illus., ports.   E457.2.D68

822

Douglas, William O. Mr. Lincoln & the Negroes; the long road to equality. New York, Atheneum, 1963. 237 p.   E457.2.D7

    Appendix (p. 117-232) contains texts of documents from 1776 to 1963.

823

Drewry, William S. The Southampton Insurrection. Murfreesboro, N.C., Johnson Pub. Co., 1968. 240 p. illus., maps, ports. (A Virginia heritage book)   F232.S7D7 1968

    Reprint of the 1900 ed., with biographical notes on the author and an index.
    Bibliography: p. 198-201.

824

Duberman, Martin B., *ed.* The antislavery vanguard: new essays on the abolitionists. Princeton, Princeton University Press, 1965. 508 p.
      E449.D84
    Bibliographical footnotes.

825

DuBois, William E. B. The suppression of the African slave-trade to the United States of America, 1638-1870. New York, Longmans, Green, 1896. 335 p. diagrs. (Harvard historical studies, v. 1)   E441.D81

    Appendixes.—A. A chronological conspectus of colonial and State legislation restricting the African slave-trade, 1641-1787.—B. A chronological conspectus of State, national, and international legislation, 1788-1871.—C. Typical cases of vessels engaged in the American slave-trade, 1619-1864.—D. Bibliography (p. [299]-325).

826

Dumond, Dwight L. Antislavery origins of the Civil War in the United States. Ann Arbor, University of Michigan Press, 1939. 143 p.
      E449.D87
    "Commonwealth Foundation lectures, University College, London, second term, 1938-39."
    "List of additional readings": p. 131-134. "Selected bibliography of proslavery and antislavery publications": p. 135-139.

827

Dumond, Dwight L. Antislavery; the crusade for freedom in America. Ann Arbor, University of Michigan Press [1961] 422 p. illus., facsims., maps, ports.   E441.D84

Bibliographical references included in "Notes" (p. [373]-413).

828

Elkins, Stanley M. Slavery; a problem in American institutional and intellectual life. 2d ed. Chicago, University of Chicago Press [1968] 263 p.
E443.E4 1968

Bibliographical footnotes.

829

Federal Writers' Project. Lay my burden down; a folk history of slavery, edited by B. A. Botkin. Chicago, University of Chicago Press [1945] xxi, 285 p. plates.   E444.F26

"A selection and integration of excerpts and complete narratives from the Slave Narrative Collection of the Federal Writers' Project."

830

Filler, Louis. The crusade against slavery, 1830-1860. New York, Harper [1960] 318 p. illus. (The New American nation series)   E449.F49

Bibliography: p. 281-303.

831

Fisk University, *Nashville. Social Science Institute.* Unwritten history of slavery, autobiographical account of Negro ex-slaves. Nashville, 1945. 322 (i.e. 323) leaves. (*Its* Social science source documents, no. 1)
E444.F5

"The interviews with these ex-slaves were conducted during 1929 and 1930 by Mrs. Ophelia Settle Egypt."—Introductory note.

832

Fitzhugh, George. Cannibals all! or, Slaves without masters. Edited by C. Vann Woodward. Cambridge, Belknap Press of Harvard University Press, 1960. 264 p. (The John Harvard library)   E449.F555 1960

833

Foner, Philip S. Business & slavery: the New York merchants & the irrepressible conflict. New York, Russell & Russell [1968] 356 p.
F128.44.F67 1968

Reprint of the 1941 ed.
Bibliography: p. 323-336.

834

Gara, Larry. The liberty line; the legend of the underground railroad. Lexington, University of Kentucky Press [1961] 201 p.   E450.G22

    Bibliographical footnotes.

835

Genovese, Eugene D. The political economy of slavery; studies in the economy & society of the slave South. New York, Pantheon Books [1965] xiv, 304 p.   E442.G45

    Includes bibliographies.

836

Halasz, Nicholas. The rattling chains; slave unrest and revolt in the antebellum South. New York, D. McKay Co. [1966] 274 p.   E447.H3

    Bibliography: p. 257-266.

837

Helper, Hinton R. The impending crisis of the South; how to meet it. Edited by George M. Fredrickson. Cambridge, Mass., Belknap Press of Harvard University Press, 1968. lxiii, 429 p. (The John Harvard library)
     E449.H483 1968

    Reprint of the 1857 ed. with a new introduction by the editor.
    Bibliographical footnotes.

838

Hollander, Barnett. Slavery in America. New York, Barnes & Noble [1963] 212 p.   DLC-LL

839

Jenkins, William S. Pro-slavery thought in the Old South. Gloucester, Mass., P. Smith, 1960 [c1935] 381 p.   E441.J46 1960

    Bibliography: p. 309-358.

839a

Jernegan, Marcus W. Laboring and dependent classes in colonial America, 1607-1783; studies of the economic, educational, and social significance of slaves, servants, apprentices, and poor folk. Chicago, University of Chicago Press [c1931] 256 p. (Social service monographs, no. 17)   E188.J57

    "Bibliographical note": p. 211-212. "Notes": p. 213-248.

840

Johnson, Frank R. The Nat Turner slave insurrection. Murfreesboro, N.C.
Johnson Pub. Co. [1966] 248 p. illus., maps.   F232.S7J6

"The confessions of Nat Turner": p. 225-248.
Bibliographical references included in "Notes" (p. 187-210).

841

Kemble, Frances A. Journal of a residence on a Georgian plantation in
1838-1839. Edited, with an introduction, by John A. Scott. New York
Knopf, 1961. lxx, 415 p. facsim., maps, port.   F290.K332 1961

"Bibliographical notes": p. 406-415. Bibliographical footnotes.

842

Korn, Bertram W. Jews and Negro slavery in the Old South, 1789-1865.
Elkins Park, Pa., Reform Congregation Keneseth Israel, 1961. 68 p.
illus.   E441.K6:

"Delivered as the presidential address at the fifty-ninth annual meet
ing of the American Jewish Historical Society, February 18, 1961, and
reprinted from the March, 1961, issue of its quarterly *Publication.*"
Bibliographical footnotes.

843

Lader, Lawrence. The bold Brahmins; New England's war against slavery
1831-1863. New York, Dutton, 1961. 318 p. illus.   E449.L1

Bibliography: p. 293-312.

844

Latham, Frank B. The Dred Scott decision, March 6, 1857; slavery and th
Supreme Court's self-inflicted wound. New York, F. Watts [1968]
54 p. illus., facsims., ports. (A Focus book)   KF4545.S5L

Bibliography: p. 52.

845

Lester, Julius, *comp.* To be a slave. Illustrated by Tom Feelings. New
York, Dial Press [1968] 160 p. illus.   E444.L4

A compilation, selected from various sources and arranged chrono
logically, of the reminiscences of slaves and ex-slaves about their experi
ences from the leaving of Africa through the Civil War and into th
early twentieth century.
Bibliography: p. 159-160.

846

Lloyd, Arthur Y. The slavery controversy, 1831-1860. Chapel Hill, University of North Carolina Press, 1939. 337 p.   E449.L76

"Selected bibliography": p. [287]-322.

847

Lofton, John. Insurrection in South Carolina: the turbulent world of Denmark Vesey. Yellow Springs, Ohio, Antioch Press [1964] 294 p. maps.
                                                                    F279.C4L6
Bibliography: p. [274]-286.

848

Loguen, Jermain W. The Rev. J. W. Loguen as a slave and as a freeman. A narrative of real life. Syracuse, N.Y., J. G. K. Truair, Printers, 1859. 454 p. port.   E444.L83

Written in the third person, but apparently the work of Loguen.
"Testimony of Rev. E. P. Rogers," including a poem "Loguen's Position": p. 445-450.

849

McKitrick, Eric L., *ed.* Slavery defended: the views of the Old South. Englewood Cliffs, N.J., Prentice-Hall [1963] 180 p. (A Spectrum book)
                                                                    E449.M16
"Suggestions for further reading, and acknowledgments": p. 179-180.

850

McManus, Edgar J. A history of Negro slavery in New York. Foreword by Richard B. Morris. [Syracuse, N.Y.] Syracuse University Press [1966] 219 p.   E445.N56M3

"Bibliographical note": p. 201-212.

851

May, Samuel J. Some recollections of our antislavery conflict. New York, Arno Press, 1968. 408 p. (The American Negro, his history and literature)   E449.M461 1968

Reprint of the 1869 ed., with a new introduction.

852

Moore, George H. Notes on the history of slavery in Massachusetts. New York, Negro Universities Press [1968] 256 p.   E445.M4M8 1968

Reprint of the 1866 ed.
Bibliographical footnotes.

853

Olmsted, Frederick L. Journey through Texas; a saddle-trip on the south-western frontier. Edited by James Howard. Austin, Tex., Von Boeckmann-Jones Press [distributed by University Cooperative Bookstore] 1962. 299 p. illus.   F391.O512 1962

Bibliography: p. 291-295.

854

Owens, William A. Slave mutiny; the revolt on the schooner Amistad. New York, J. Day Co. [1953] 312 p. illus.   E447.O9

855

Phillips, Ulrich B. American Negro slavery; a survey of the supply, employment and control of Negro labor as determined by the plantation regime. New York, Appleton, 1918. 529 p.   E441.P549

Bibliographical footnotes.

856

Phillips, Ulrich B. Life and labor in the Old South. Boston, Little, Brown [1963] 375 p. illus.   F209.P563

Bibliographical footnotes.

857

Pickard, Kate E. R. The kidnapped and the ransomed. [New York] Negro Publication Society of America, 1941. 315 p. ([Negro Publication Society of America. Publications] Series 1, History. no. 1)   E444.S855

"The first edition . . . appeared in 1856."—Editor's note.
"Appendix. Seth Conklin [by W. H. Furness]": p. 293-315.

858

Postell, William D. The health of slaves on southern plantations. Baton Rouge, Louisiana State University Press [1951] 231 p. illus. (Louisiana State University studies. Social science series, no. 1)   E443.P7

Bibliography: p. 214-226.

859

Rozwenc, Edwin C., *ed.* Slavery as a cause of the Civil War. Rev. ed. Boston, Heath [1963] 120 p. (Problems in American civilization; readings selected by the Dept. of American Studies, Amherst College)
                    E459.R6 196

"Suggestions for additional reading": p. 103-104.

860
Ruchames, Louis, *ed.* The abolitionists; a collection of their writings. New York, Putnam [1963] 259 p. E449.R88

861
Sanborn, Franklin B. Recollections of seventy years. Boston, R. G. Badger, 1909. Detroit, Gale Research Co., 1967. 2 v. (607 p.) illus., facsims., ports. (The Gale library of lives and letters: American writers series)
E449.S21 1967
Contents.—v. 1. Political life.—v. 2. Literary life.

862
Scarborough, Ruth. The opposition to slavery in Georgia prior to 1860. New York, Negro Universities Press [1968, c1933] 257 p.
E445.G3S25 1968
Bibliography: p. 252-257.

863
Sellers, James B. Slavery in Alabama. University, University of Alabama Press, 1950. 426 p. illus., ports. E445.A3S4
Bibliography: p. [399]-409.

864
Sherrard, Owen A. Freedom from fear; the slave and his emancipation. New York, St. Martin's Press [1961, c1959] 200 p. HT1162.S45 1961
Bibliography: p. [191]-193.

865
Shugg, Roger W. Origins of class struggle in Louisiana; a social history of white farmers and laborers during slavery and after, 1840-1875. [Baton Rouge] Louisiana State University Press [1968] xiv, 372 p. (Louisiana paperbacks, L-36) F374.S58 1968
Bibliography: p. 332-363.

866
Siebert, Wilbur H. The underground railroad from slavery to freedom. With an introduction by Albert Bushnell Hart. New York, Russell & Russell [1967] xxv, 478 p. illus., facsim., maps (part fold.), ports.
E450.S57 1967
Reprint of the 1898 ed.
Bibliography: p. 380-402.

867

Spears, John R. The American slave trade; an account of its origin, growth, and suppression. Abridged ed. New York, Ballantine Books [1960] 158 p. illus. (Ballantine books, 392K)   E441.S736

868

Stampp, Kenneth M. The peculiar institution: slavery in the ante-bellum South. New York, Knopf, 1956. 435 p.   E441.S8

"Manuscripts consulted, and their locations": p. 431-[436]. Bibliographical footnotes.

869

Starkey, Marion L. Striving to make it my home; the story of Americans from Africa. New York, Norton [1964] 256 p.   E441.S82

Bibliographical references included in "Notes" (p. 251-256).

870

Starling, Marion W. The slave narrative; its place in American literary history. New York, New York University, 1949. 19 p.   E444.S8

Abridgement of thesis—New York University.
Bibliographical footnotes.

871

Stephenson, Clarence D. The impact of the slavery issue on Indiana County. Marion Center, Pa., Mahoning Mimeograph & Pamphlet Service [1964] 155 p. illus., facsims., ports. (Indiana County historical series, no. 2)   F157.I3S78

Bibliography: p. 151-155.

872

Still, William. The underground rail road. A record of facts, authentic narratives, letters &c., narrating the hardships, hair-breadth escapes and death struggles of the slaves in their efforts for freedom, as related by themselves and others, or witnessed by the author; together with sketches of some of the largest stockholders, and most liberal aiders and advisers, of the road. Philadelphia, Porter & Coates, 1872. 780 p. illus., plates, ports.   E450.S85

Reprint issued by Arno Press, 1968.

873

Strother, Horatio T. The underground railroad in Connecticut. Middletown, Conn., Wesleyan University Press [1962] 262 p. illus.   E450.S93

874

The Suppressed book about slavery. New York, Arno Press, 1968. 432 p.
illus. (The American Negro; his history and literature)

E449.S9592 1968

Reprint of the 1864 ed.

875

Sydnor, Charles S. Slavery in Mississippi. Gloucester, Mass., P. Smith, 1965
[c1933] 270 p. map. E445.M6S92 1965

At head of title: The American Historical Association.
Bibliography: p. 255-262.

876

Taylor, Joe G. Negro slavery in Louisiana. [Baton Rouge] Louisiana Historical Association [1963] 260 p. E445.L8T3

Bibliography: p. 239-252.

877

Trefousse, Hans L. The radical Republicans; Lincoln's vanguard for racial
justice. New York, Knopf, 1969 [c1968] xiv, 492, xvii p. illus., ports.

E449.T79

Bibliography: p. 471-492.

877a

Turner, Edward R. The Negro in Pennsylvania, slavery—servitude—
freedom, 1639-1861. Washington, American Historical Association,
1911. 314 p. (Prize essays of the American Historical Association,
1910) E185.93.P41T9

To this essay was awarded the Justin Winsor Prize in American
History for 1910.
Bibliography: p. 255-294.

878

Turner, Nat. The confessions of Nat Turner, the leader of the late insurrection in Southampton, Va., as fully and voluntarily made to Thomas
R. Gray, in the prison where he was confined. Richmond, T. R. Gray,
1832. 24 p. F232.S7T9

879

Wade, Richard C. Slavery in the cities; the South, 1820-1860. New York,
Oxford University Press, 1964. 340 p. E443.W3

Bibliographical references included in "Notes" (p. [287]-323).

880

Walker, David. David Walker's appeal, in four articles, together with a preamble, to the coloured citizens of the world, but in particular, and very expressly, to those of the United States of America. Edited and with an introduction by Charles M. Wiltse. New York, Hill and Wang [1965] 78 p. (American century series, AC73)   E446.W178

Reprint of the 1929 ed.
Bibliographical footnotes.

881

Wish, Harvey, *ed.* Slavery in the South; first-hand accounts of the antebellum American Southland from northern & southern whites, Negroes, & foreign observers. New York, Farrar, Straus [1964] xxi, 290 p. facsim. (Materials of American history series)   E441.W78

Bibliography: p. [xxiii].

882

Zilversmit, Arthur. The first emancipation; the abolition of slavery in the North. Chicago, University of Chicago Press [1967] 262 p.   E446.Z5

"Bibliography essay": p. [245]-250.

Reconstruction

883

Abbott, Martin. The Freedmen's Bureau in South Carolina, 1865-1872. Chapel Hill, University of North Carolina Press [1967] 162 p.

F274.A23

Bibliography: p. [145]-158.

884

Allen, James S. Reconstruction; the battle for democracy (1865-1876). New York, International Publishers [c1937] 256 p. illus. [A history of the American people]   E668.A45

"Selected bibliography": p. 249-252.

884a

Andrews, Sidney. The South since the war, as shown by fourteen weeks of travel and observation in Georgia and the Carolinas. Boston, Ticknor and Fields, 1866. 400 p.   F216.A56

885

Bentley, George R. A history of the Freedmen's Bureau. Philadelphia, University of Pennsylvania, 1955. 298 p.   E185.2.B4

> Thesis—University of Wisconsin.
> Bibliography: p. 266-279.

886

Botume, Elizabeth H. First days amongst the contrabands. New York, Arno Press, 1968. 286 p. (The American Negro, his history and literature)   E185.93.S7B7 1968

> Reprint of the 1893 ed., with a new introduction.

887

Brock, William R. An American crisis: Congress and Reconstruction, 1865-1867. [New York] St. Martin's Press [1963] 312 p.   E668.B85

> "Bibliographical note": p. 305.

888

Bruce, Philip A. The plantation Negro as a freeman; observations on his character, condition, and prospects in Virginia. New York, G. P. Putnam's Sons, 1889. 262 p. (Questions of the day, no. 57)

    E185.6.B88

889

Buckmaster, Henrietta, *pseud.* Freedom bound. New York, Macmillan [1965] 185 p.   E185.2.B9

> Bibliography: p. 183-184.

890

Carter, Hodding. The angry scar; the story of Reconstruction. Garden City, N.Y., Doubleday, 1959. 425 p. (Mainstream of America series)

    E668.C3

> Bibliography: p. [411]-414.

891

Coulter, Ellis M. The South during Reconstruction, 1865-1877. [Baton Rouge] Louisiana State University Press, 1947. 426 p. illus., maps (1 fold.) (A History of the South, v. 8)   F216.C6

> "Critical essay on authorities": p. 392-407.

892

Craven, Avery O. Reconstruction: the ending of the Civil War. New York, Holt, Rinehart and Winston [1969] 330 p.   E668.C9

> Bibliography: p. 308-315.

893

Crowe, Charles R., *ed.* The age of Civil War and Reconstruction, 1830-1900; a book of interpretative essays. Homewood, Ill., Dorsey Press, 1966. 479 p. (The Dorsey series in American history)   F209.C7

Includes bibliographies.

894

Current, Richard N., *ed.* Reconstruction, 1865-1877. Englewood Cliffs, N.J., Prentice-Hall [1965] 183 p. (A Spectrum book, S-114: Eyewitness accounts of American history)   E668.C98

895

Dennett, John R. The South as it is: 1865-1866. Edited and with an introduction by Henry M. Christman. New York, Viking Press [1965] 370 p.   F216.D4 1965

A series of articles written for *The Nation,* July 1865-Apr. 1866.

896

Donald, Henderson H. The Negro freedman; life conditions of the American Negro in the early years after emancipation. New York, H. Schuman, 1952. 270 p.   E185.2.D63

Bibliography: p. [255]-258.

897

Drisko, Carol F., *and* Edgar A. Toppin. The unfinished march; the Negro in the United States, Reconstruction to World War I. Illustrated by Tracy Sugarman. Garden City, N.Y., Doubleday, 1967. 118 p. col. illus. (Zenith books)   E185.6.D7

898

DuBois, William E. B. Black Reconstruction in America; an essay toward a history of the part which black folk played in the attempt to reconstruct democracy in America, 1860-1880. New York, Russell & Russell [1966, c1935] 746 p.   E668.D83 1966

Bibliography: p. 731-737.

899

Dunning, William A. Reconstruction, political and economic, 1865-1877. New York, Harper, 1907. xvi, 378 p. maps, port. (The American nation; a history, v. 22)   E178.A54 v. 22

"Critical essay on authorities": p. [342]-357.

900

Evans, William McKee. Ballots and fence rails; Reconstruction on the lower Cape Fear. Chapel Hill, University of North Carolina Press [1967] 314 p. maps.   F262.C2E9 1967

   Bibliography: p. [291]-301.

901

Ficklen, John R. History of Reconstruction in Louisiana, through 1868. Gloucester, Mass., P. Smith, 1966 [c1910] 234 p. (Johns Hopkins University. Studies in historical and political science, ser. 28, no. 1)

                    H31.J6 ser. 28, no. 1 1966

   Bibliographical footnotes.

902

Fleming, Walter L., *ed.* Documentary history of Reconstruction, political, military, social, religious, educational & industrial, 1865 to the present time. Cleveland, A. H. Clark Co., 1906-7. 2 v. facsims., plates, port.

                    E668.F58

903

Fleming, Walter L., *ed.* Documents relating to Reconstruction. Morgantown, W. Va., 1904. [269] p.   E668.F59

   Contents.—no. 1. The constitution and the ritual of the Knights of the White Camelia.—no. 2. Revised and amended prescript of Ku Klux Klan.—no. 3. Union League documents.—no. 4-5. Public frauds in South Carolina. The constitution of the Council of Safety. Local Ku Klux constitution. The '76 Association.—no. 6-7. Freedmen's Bureau documents. The Freedmen's Savings Bank.—no. 8. Laws relating to freedmen, 1865-6.

904

Franklin, John H. The Emancipation Proclamation. Garden City, N.Y., Doubleday, 1963. 181 p. illus.   E453.F8

   "Sources": p. 157-162. Bibliographical references included in "Notes" (p. [163]-173).

905

Franklin, John H. Reconstruction: after the Civil War. [Chicago] University of Chicago Press [1961] 258 p. illus. (The Chicago history of American civilization)   E668.F7

   "Suggested reading": p. 232-242.

906

Henry, Robert S. The story of Reconstruction. Indianapolis, Bobbs-Merril
Co. [c1938] 633 p. map (on lining papers), plates.   E668.H51(

Bibliography included in "Acknowledgments."

907

Hyman, Harold M., *ed.* New frontiers of the American Reconstruction
Urbana, University of Illinois Press, 1966. 156 p.   E668.H9£

Papers presented at a conference held at the University of Illinois i
April 1965.
Includes bibliographical footnotes.

908

Hyman, Harold M., *comp.* The radical Republicans and Reconstruction
1861-1870. Indianapolis, Bobbs-Merrill [1967] lxxxvi, 538 p. (Th
American heritage series, 47)   E668.H98.

Bibliography: lxix-lxxxvi.

909

Lynch, John R. The facts of Reconstruction. New York, Neale Pub. Co.
1913. 325 p. ports.   E668.L9£

"The state of Mississippi is made the pivotal one in the presentatio
of the facts and historical points touched upon in this work."—Preface

910

McCarthy, Charles H. Lincoln's plan of reconstruction. New York
McClure, Phillips, 1901. xxiv, 504 p.   E456.M2.

911

McKitrick, Eric L. Andrew Johnson and Reconstruction. [Chicago] Uni
versity of Chicago Press [1960] 533 p.   E668.M15(

"Selected bibliography, with notes": p. 511-521.

912

McWhiney, Grady, *ed.* Reconstruction and the freedmen. Chicago, Ran
McNally [1963] 54 p. (The Berkeley series in American history)
E185.2.M.

Bibliography: p. 54.

913

Nunn, William C. Texas under the carpetbaggers. Austin, University o
Texas Press [1962] 304 p. illus.   F391.N96

Bibliography: p. 263-269.

914

Pollard, Edward A. The lost cause regained. New York, G. W. Carleton, 1868. 214 p.   E666.P77

915

Randall, James G. The Civil War and Reconstruction. Boston, D. C. Heath [c1937] xvii, 959 p. illus., diagrs., facsims., maps, ports.   E468.R26

"Bibliographical note": p. 881-883. Bibliography: p. 885-924.

916

Richardson, Joe M. The Negro in the reconstruction of Florida, 1865-1877. Tallahassee, Florida State University, 1965. 255 p. (Florida State University studies, no. 46)   AS36.F57 no. 46

Bibliography: p. 241-249.

917

Shenton, James P., *ed.* The Reconstruction; a documentary history of the South after the war: 1865-1877. New York, Putnam [1963] 314 p.

E668.S543

918

Sinclair, William A. The aftermath of slavery; a study of the condition and environment of the American Negro. With an introduction by Thomas Wentworth Higginson. Boston, Small, Maynard, 1905. 358 p.

E185.6.S61

919

Skaggs, William H. The southern oligarchy; an appeal in behalf of the silent masses of our country against the despotic rule of the few. New York, Devin-Adair Co., 1924. 472 p.   F209.S62

920

Stampp, Kenneth M. The era of Reconstruction, 1865-1877. New York, Knopf, 1965. 228 p.   E668.S79

"Bibliographical note": p. 217-[229].

921

Sterling, Dorothy. Forever free, the story of the Emancipation Proclamation. Illustrated by Ernest Crichlow. Garden City, N.Y., Doubleday [1963] 208 p. illus.   E453.S83 1963

Bibliographical references included in "Note to the reader" (p. [199]-204).

922

Straker, David Augustus. The new South investigated. Detroit, Ferguso
Print. Co., 1888. 230 p. port.   F215.S8

923

Swint, Henry L., *ed.* Dear ones at home; letters from contraband camp
Nashville, Vanderbilt University Press, 1966. 274 p. map.   E185.2.S9

   Letters written 1861-1870, chiefly by Lucy and Sarah Chase.
   Bibliography: p. 259-267.

924

Taylor, Alrutheus A. The Negro in South Carolina during the Reconstruc
tion. Washington, Association for the Study of Negro Life and Histor
[c1924] 341 p.   E185.93.S7T

   Bibliography: p. 314-322.

925

Taylor, Alrutheus A. The Negro in the reconstruction of Virginia. Washing
ton, Association for the Study of Negro Life and History [c1926
300 p.   E185.93.V8T

   Bibliography: p. 287-292.

926

Wallace, John. Carpet-bag rule in Florida; the inside workings of th
reconstruction of civil government in Florida after the close of the Civi
War. A facsimile reproduction of the 1888 ed., with introduction &
notes by Allan Nevins. Gainesville, University of Florida Press, 1964
xxxii, 444 p. col. coat of arms, ports. (Quadricentennial edition of th
Floridiana facsimile & reprint series)   F316.W19 1888

   Bibliographical references included in "Notes" (p. xxv-xxvi).

927

Whyte, James H. The uncivil war; Washington during the Reconstruction
1865-1878. New York, Twayne Publishers [1958] 316 p. illus.

                                                              F198.W4

   Bibliography: p. 296-305.

928

Williams, George W. 1862—emancipation day—1884. The Negro as a polit
ical problem. Oration . . . at the Asbury Church, Washington, D.C.
April 16, 1884. Boston, A. Mudge, Printers, 1884. 40 p.   E185.6.W7

929

Williamson, Joel. After slavery; the Negro in South Carolina during the Reconstruction, 1861-1877. Chapel Hill, University of North Carolina Press [1965] 442 p.   E185.93.S7W73

Bibliography: p. [419]-430.

930

Wilson, Joseph T. Emancipation: its course and progress; from 1481 B.C. to A.D. 1875, with a review of President Lincoln's proclamations, the XIII amendment, and the progress of the freed people since emancipation; with a history of the emancipation monument. Hampton, Va., Normal School Steam Power Press Print, 1882. 242 p. port. E453.W77

Revised and enlarged from a pamphlet published in 1881.

LEGAL STATUS

931

Avins, Alfred, comp. The Reconstruction amendments' debates: the legis
lative history and contemporary debates in Congress on the 13th, 14th
and 15th amendments. Richmond, Virginia Commission on Constitu
tional Government, 1967. xxxii, 764 p.   KF4756.A29A9

Selections from the *Congressional Globe* and the *Congressiona
Record*, covering the years 1849 to 1875.
Bibliography: p. i-ii.

932

Berger, Morroe. Equality by statute; the revolution in civil rights. Rev. ed
Garden City, N. Y., Doubleday, 1967. 253 p.   KF4757.B4 1967

Bibliography: p. [230]-236.

933

Catterall, Helen H. T., ed. Judicial cases concerning American slavery and
the Negro. New York, Octagon Books, 1968. 5 v.   KF4545.S5C3 1968

Reprint of the 1926 ed.
Vols. 4-5, "with additions by James J. Hayden."
Bibliographical footnotes.
Contents.—v. 1. Cases from the courts of England, Virginia, West
Virginia, and Kentucky.—v. 2. Cases from the courts of North Carolina
South Carolina, and Tennessee.—v. 3. Cases from the courts of Georgia

Florida, Alabama, Mississippi, and Louisiana.–v. 4. Cases from the courts of New England, the middle States, and the District of Columbia.–v. 5. Cases from the courts of States north of the Ohio and west of the Mississippi Rivers, Canada and Jamaica.

934
Collins, Charles W. The Fourteenth amendment and the States: a study of the operation of the restraint clauses of section one of the Fourteenth amendment to the Constitution of the United States. Boston, Little, Brown, 1912. xxi, 220 p. diagrs., tables.   JK169 14th 1912

Some of these studies "have within recent months appeared, in substantially their present form" in the *American Law Review,* the *Yale Law Journal,* the *Columbia Law Review,* and the *South Atlantic Quarterly.*–Preface.

935
Conference on Discrimination and the Law, *University of Chicago, 1963.* Discrimination and the law; [papers] edited by Vern Countryman. Chicago, University of Chicago Press [1965] xiv, 170 p.   DLC-LL

Sponsored by the University of Chicago Law School and others. Bibliography: p. 145-152.

936
Georgia. *Laws, statutes, etc.* Compilation of Georgia laws and opinions of the attorney general relating to segregation of the races. Compiled and edited by State Law Dept. [Atlanta, 1956] 93 p.   DLC-LL

937
Greenberg, Jack. Race relations and American law. New York, Columbia University Press, 1959. 481 p.   DLC-LL

Bibliography: p. [421]-437. Bibliographical footnotes.

938
Higbee, Jay A. Development and administration of the New York State law against discrimination. University, University of Alabama Press [1967, c1966] xxii, 396 p.   KFN5697.H5

Bibliography: p. [337]-354.

939
Mangum, Charles S. The legal status of the Negro. Chapel Hill, University of North Carolina Press, 1940. 436 p.   DLC-LL
                                                                    E185.6.M33

"Selected bibliography": p. [425]-426.

940

Miller, Loren. The petitioners; the story of the Supreme Court of th
United States and the Negro. New York, Pantheon Books [1966] xv
461 p.   DLC-LI
   Bibliographical references included in "Notes" (p. [435]-455).

941

Murray, Pauli, *ed.* States' laws on race and color, and appendices contain
ing international documents, Federal laws and regulations, local ordi
nances and charts. [Cincinnati, Woman's Division of Christian Service
Board of Missions and Church Extension, Methodist Church] 1950 [i.e
1951] 746 p. forms.   DLC-L

   ——— ——— 1955 supplement, compiled and edited by Verge Lake an
Pauli Murray. Cincinnati, Woman's Division of Christian Service, Boar
of Missions of the Methodist Church, 1955. 256 p.   DLC-L

942

Snethen, Worthington G., *comp.* The black code of the District of Colum
bia, in force September 1st, 1848. New York, Published for the A. & F
Anti-slavery Society, by W. Harned, 1848. 61 p.   DLC-L

   Contents.—The District of Columbia.—Ordinances of the corporatio
of Washington.—Ordinances of the corporation of Georgetown.

943

Stephenson, Gilbert T. Race distinctions in American law. New York, D
Appleton, 1910. xiv, 388 p.   JK1781.S

944

Styles, Fitzhugh L. Negroes and the law in the race's battle for liberty
equality and justice under the Constitution of the United States; witl
causes celebres. Boston, Christopher Pub. House [c1937] 320 p. port
                                                             DLC-L
                                                         E185.61.S9
   The manuscript of the author's address before the National Ba
Association at Baltimore, August 1934, on the battle of the Negro a
the bar of justice, is the basis of this book.
   Bibliography: p. 320.

945

Ten Broek, Jacobus. Equal under law. New, enl. ed. New York, Collie
Books [1965] 352 p.   E449.T4 196

First ed. published in 1951 under title: *The Antislavery Origins of the Fourteenth Amendment.*

"Source materials": p. 344-347.

946

U.S. *Supreme Court.* The Supreme Court on racial discrimination. Edited by Joseph Tussman. New York, Oxford University Press, 1963. 393 p.

DLC-LL

947

Wilson, Theodore B. The black codes of the South. University, University of Alabama Press [1965] 177 p. (Southern historical publications, no. 6)

DLC-LL

Bibliography: p. 167-174.

LITERATURE

History and Criticism

948

Abramson, Doris E. Negro playwrights in the American theatre, 1925-1959. New York, Columbia University Press, 1969. 335 p.   PS351.A2

    Bibliography: p. [307]-317.

949

Bone, Robert A. The Negro novel in America. [Rev. ed.] New Haven, Yale University Press [1965] 289 p.   PS153.N5B6 1965

    Bibliography: p. 255-270.

950

Brawley, Benjamin G., *ed.* Early Negro American writers; selections with biographical and critical introductions. Chapel Hill, University of North Carolina Press, 1935. 305 p.   PS508.N3B7

951

Brawley, Benjamin G. The Negro genius; a new appraisal of the achievement of the American Negro in literature and the fine arts. New York, Biblo and Tannen, 1966 [c1937] 366 p.   E185.82.B816 1966

    Bibliography: p. 331-350.

952

Brawley, Benjamin G. The Negro in literature and art in the United States. 3d ed. New York, Duffield, 1929. 231 p. plates, ports.   E185.82.B824

Bibliography: p. 213-228.

Contents.–The Negro genius.–Phillis Wheatley.–A hundred years of striving.–Orators. Douglass and Washington.–Paul Laurence Dunbar. –Charles W. Chesnutt.–W. E. Burghardt DuBois.–William Stanley Braithwaite.–James Weldon Johnson.–Other writers.–The new realists. –The stage.–Painters. Henry O. Tanner.–Sculptors. Meta Warrick Fuller.–Music.–Appendix: The Negro in American fiction. The Negro in American literature.–The Negro in contemporary literature.

953

Bronz, Stephen H. Roots of Negro racial consciousness; the 1920's: three Harlem Renaissance authors. New York, Libra [1964] 101 p.

PS508.N3B73

Bibliography: p. 95-101.

Contents.–Introduction.–James Weldon Johnson.–Countee Cullen. –Claude McKay.–Conclusion.–Notes.

954

Brown, Sterling A. The Negro in American fiction. Washington, Associates in Negro Folk Education, 1937. 209 p. (Bronze booklet no. 6)

E185.5.B85 no. 6
PS374.N4B7

"Selected reading list": p. 207-209.

955

Butcher, Margaret J. The Negro in American culture; based on materials left by Alain Locke. New York, Knopf, 1956. 294 p.   E185.82.B89

956

Dreer, Herman. American literature by Negro authors. New York, Macmillan, 1950. xvii, 334 p. ports.   PS508.N3D7

Bibliography: p. 327-332.

957

Ellison, Ralph. Shadow and act. New York, Random House [1964] xxii, 317 p.   PS153.N5E4 1964

958

Ferguson, Blanche E. Countee Cullen and the Negro renaissance. New York, Dodd, Mead [1966] 213 p. illus., ports.   PS3505.U287Z6

Bibliography: p. 205-206.

959

Ford, Nick A. The contemporary Negro novel; a study in race relations. College Park, Md., McGrath Pub. Co., 1968 [c1936] 108 p.

PS374.N4F6 1968

Bibliography: p. 107-108.

960

Gloster, Hugh M. Negro voices in American fiction. Chapel Hill, University of North Carolina Press, 1948. xiv, 295 p.   PS374.N4G5

Bibliography: p. 273-288.

961

Green, Elizabeth A. L. The Negro in contemporary American literature; an outline for individual and group study. College Park, Md., McGrath Pub. Co. [1968, c1928] 92 p.   PS153.N5G7 1968

Includes bibliographical references.

962

Gross, Seymour L., *and* John E. Hardy, *eds.* Images of the Negro in American literature. Chicago, University of Chicago Press [1966] 321 p. (Patterns of literary criticism)   PS173.N4G7

Bibliography: p. 289-315.

963

Hughes, John M. C. The Negro novelist; a discussion of the writings of American Negro novelists, 1940-1950, by Carl Milton Hughes [pseud.]. New York, Citadel Press [1953] 288 p.   PS374.N4H8

Bibliography: p. [279]-285.

964

Littlejohn, David. Black on white; a critical survey of writing by American Negroes. New York, Grossman, 1966. 180 p.   PS153.N5L5

965

Loggins, Vernon. The Negro author, his development in America to 1900. Port Washington, N. Y., Kennikat Press [1964, c1959] 480 p. (Columbia University studies in English and comparative literature)

PS153.N5L65 1964

Issued also as thesis, Columbia University, 1931.
"Bibliographies": p. [408]-457.

966

Margolies, Edward. Native sons; a critical study of twentieth-century Negro American authors. Philadelphia, Lippincott [1968] 210 p.

PS153.N5M26

Contents.—Perspectives.—The first forty years: 1900-1940; [W. E. B. DuBois and others] —Migration: William Attaway and *Blood on the Forge.*—Richard Wright: *Native Son* and three kinds of revolution. —Race and sex; the novels of Chester Himes.—The Negro church; James Baldwin and the Christian vision.—History as blues: Ralph Ellison's *Invisible Man.*—The new nationalism: Malcolm X.—The expatriate as novelist: William Demby.—Prospects: LeRoi Jones?—Bibliography (p. 201).

967

McCall, Dan. The example of Richard Wright. New York, Harcourt, Brace & World [c1969] 202 p.   PS3545.R815Z7

968

Mays, Benjamin E. The Negro's God as reflected in his literature. Lithographs by James L. Wells. Boston, Chapman & Grimes [c1938] 269 p.

PS153.N5M3

Bibliography: p. 257-263.

969

Nelson, John H. The Negro character in American literature. Lawrence, Kan., Dept. of Journalism Press, 1926. 146 p. (Bulletin of the University of Kansas. v. 27, no. 15. Humanistic studies. v. 4, no. 1)

PS173.N4N4 1926a

Issued also in bound form as *Humanistic Studies,* v. 4, no. 1, without the cover having series note, Bulletin of the University of Kansas, v. 27, no. 15.

970

Nilon, Charles H. Faulkner and the Negro. Boulder, University of Colorado Press, 1962. 111 p. (University of Colorado studies. Series in language and literature, no. 8)   P25.C64 no. 8

Bibliographical footnotes.

971

Redding, Jay Saunders. To make a poet black. Chapel Hill, University of North Carolina Press, 1939. 142 p.   PS153.N5R4

"Factual material and critical opinion on American Negro literature."—Preface.

Bibliography: p. [131]-136.

972
Turner, Darwin T., *and* Jean M. Bright, *eds.* Images of the Negro in America. Boston, D. C. Heath [1965] 113 p. (Selected source materials for college research papers)   PS508.N3T8

Bibliographical references included in "Suggestions for library work" (p. 112-113).

973
Turner, Lorenzo D. Anti-slavery sentiment in American literature prior to 1865. Port Washington, N. Y., Kennikat Press [1966] 188 p.
                                                                    PS169.S47T8 1966

Reprint of a thesis, University of Chicago, 1926.
Bibliography: p. 153-182.

974
Wagner, Jean. Les poètes nègres des États-Unis; le sentiment racial et religieux dans la poésie de P. L. Dunbar à L. Hughes (1890-1940). Paris, Librairie Istra, 1963 [c1962] 637 p.   PS153.N5W3

Bibliography: p. [601]-620.

Anthologies

975
Brown, Sterling A., Arthur P. Davis, *and* Ulysses G. Lee, *eds.* The Negro caravan, writings by American Negroes. New York, Dryden Press [c1941] xviii, 1082 p.   PS508.N3B75

Reprint issued by Arno Press, 1969.

976
Calverton, Victor F., *ed.* Anthology of American Negro literature, edited, with an introduction, by V. F. Calverton. New York, Modern Library [c1929] 535 p. (The Modern library of the world's best books)
                                                                         PS591.N4C3

Bibliography: p. 700-718.

977
Chapman, Abraham, *comp.* Black voices; an anthology of Afro-American literature. Edited, with an introduction and biographical notes, by

Abraham Chapman. New York, New American Library [1968] 718 p.
(A Mentor book)   PS508.N3C5
    Bibliography: p. 700-718.

978
Conference of Negro Writers. *1st, New York, 1959*. The American Negro
    writer and his roots; selected papers. New York, American Society of
    African Culture, 1960. 70 p. illus.   PS153.N5C6 1959ac

979
Cromwell, Otelia, Lorenzo D. Turner, *and* Eva B. Dykes, *eds.* Readings
    from Negro authors, for schools and colleges, with a bibliography of
    Negro literature. New York, Harcourt, Brace [c1931] 388 p.
                                                       PS508.N3C7
    "A bibliography of Negro literature": p. 371-383; contains "Collat-
    eral reading."

980
Culp, Daniel W., *ed.* Twentieth century Negro literature; or, A cyclopedia
    of thought on the vital topics relating to the American Negro, by one
    hundred of America's greatest Negroes. Naperville, Ill., J. L. Nichols
    [1902] 472 p. ports.   E185.5.C97

981
Cunard, Nancy, *comp.* Negro anthology, made by Nancy Cunard,
    1931-1933. London, Published by Nancy Cunard at Wishart, 1934.
    854 p. illus., facsims., maps, ports.   HT1581.C8

    Contains music.
    Contents.–America.–Negro stars.–Music.–Poetry.–West Indies and
    South America.–Europe.–Africa.

982
Emanuel, James A., *and* Theodore L. Gross, *comps.* Dark symphony:
    Negro literature in America. New York, Free Press [1968] xviii, 604 p.
                                                       PS508.N3E4
    Bibliography: p. 564-600.

983
Hill, Herbert, *ed.* Anger, and beyond: the Negro writer in the United
    States. New York, Harper & Row [1966] xxii, 227 p.   PS153.N5H5

984
Hill, Herbert, *ed.* Soon, one morning; new writing by American Negroes,
    1940-1962. Selected and edited, with an introduction and biographical
    notes, by Herbert Hill. New York, Knopf, 1963. 617 p.   PS508.N3H5

985

Hughes, Langston. The Langston Hughes reader. New York, G. Braziller, 1958. 501 p. PS3515.U274A6 1958

986

Johnson, Charles S., *ed.* Ebony and topaz, a collectanea. New York, Opportunity, National Urban League [c1927] 164 p. illus., facsims., plates, ports. PS508.N3J6

987

Jones, LeRoi, *and* Larry Neal, *comps.* Black fire; an anthology of Afro-American writing. New York, Morrow, 1968. xviii, 670 p. illus.

PS508.N3J64

988

Jones, LeRoi, *ed.* The moderns; an anthology of new writing in America. New York, Corinth Books, 1963. xvi, 351 p. PS536.J6

Bibliographical references included in "Acknowledgments" (p. [vii-viii]).

989

Locke, Alain L., *ed.* The new Negro; an interpretation. With a new introduction by Allan H. Spear. New York, Johnson Reprint Corp., 1968. xxii, xviii, 446 p. illus., music, ports. E185.82.L75 1968

The text is a reprint of the 1925 ed.
Includes bibliographies.

990

Moon, Bucklin, *ed.* Primer for white folks. Garden City, N.Y., Doubleday, Doran, 1945. xiv, 491 p. E185.5.M72

991

Plato, Ann. Essays; including biographies and miscellaneous pieces, in prose and poetry. Hartford, Printed for the author, 1841. xx, 122 p.

PS2593.P347 1841

992

Watkins, Sylvestre C., *ed.* Anthology of American Negro literature; with an introduction by John T. Frederick. New York, Modern Library [1944] xvii, 481 p. (The Modern library of the world's best books)

PS508.N3W3

"Biographical notes": p. [457]-481.

993

Watts Writers' Workshop. From the ashes; voices of Watts. Edited and with an introduction by Budd Schulberg. [New York] New American Library [1967] 277 p.   PS508.N3W33

994

Williams, John A., *comp.* Beyond the angry black. [2d ed.] New York, Cooper Square Publishers, 1966. xix, 198 p.   PS509.N4B4 1966

A reissue with new material of *The Angry Black,* published in 1962.

Essays and Addresses

995

Adoff, Arnold, *comp.* Black on black; commentaries by Negro Americans. Foreword by Roger Mae Johnson. New York, Macmillan [1968] 236 p.
                                                              E185.5.A24

996

Ahmann, Mathew H., *ed.* The new Negro. Contributors: Stephen J. Wright [and others]. In the symposium: James Baldwin [and others]. Notre Dame, Ind., Fides Publishers [1961] 145 p.   E185.6.A26

Includes papers presented at the lst convention of the National Catholic Conference for Interracial Justice, held in Detroit in 1961.

997

Baldwin, James. Nobody knows my name; more notes of a native son. New York, Dial Press, 1961. 241 p.   E185.61.B197

998

Bennett, Lerone. The Negro mood, and other essays. Chicago, Johnson Pub. Co., 1964. 104 p.   E185.61.B43

999

Bernstein, Barton J., *ed.* Towards a new past; dissenting essays in American history. New York, Pantheon Books [1968] 364 p.   E175.B46

Includes bibliographical references.

1000

Brotz, Howard, *ed.* Negro social and political thought, 1850-1920; representative texts. New York, Basic Books [1966] 593 p.   E185.B876

Includes bibliographies.

1001

Clark, Kenneth B. Social power and social change in contemporary America; an address [delivered on July 18, 1966, before an audience of summer interns working in the Dept. of State, the Agency for International Development, and the United States Information Agency. Washington, Dept. of State; for sale by the Supt. of Docs., U. S. Govt. Print. Off., 1966] 20 p. ([U.S.] Dept. of State. Publication 8125. Department and Foreign Service series, 134)   HN57.C55

"Prepared under the auspices of the U.S. Department of State's Equal Employment Opportunity Program, Office of the Deputy Under Secretary for Administration."

1002

Clarke, John H., *ed.* William Styron's Nat Turner; ten black writers respond. Boston, Beacon Press [1968] 120 p. illus.   PS3569.T9C633

Appendix (p. [93]-117): The text of *The Confessions of Nat Turner.*

1003

Crummell, Alexander. Africa and America; addresses and discourses. Springfield, Mass., Willey, 1891. 466 p. port.   E185.5.C95

1004

Crummell, Alexander. The relations and duties of free colored men in America to Africa. A letter to Charles B. Dunbar. Hartford, Press of Case, Lockwood, 1861. 54 p.   E448.C95

1005

Daedalus. The Negro American. Edited and with introductions by Talcott Parsons and Kenneth B. Clark, and with a foreword by Lyndon B. Johnson. Illustrated with a 32 page portfolio of photographs by Bruce Davidson, selected and introduced by Arthur D. Trottenberg. Boston, Houghton, Mifflin, 1966. xxix, 781 p. illus. (The Daedalus library [v. 7])   E185.6.D24

Most of the essays, some in slightly different form, appeared originally in the fall 1965 and winter 1966 issues of *Daedalus.*
Includes bibliographical references.

1006

Daniel, Bradford, *ed.* Black, white, and gray; twenty-one points of view on the race question. New York, Sheed and Ward [1964] 308 p.
E185.61.D26

1007

Douglass, Frederick. Three addresses on the relations subsisting between the white and colored people of the United States. Washington, Gibson Bros., Printers, 1886. 68 p.   E185.61.D734

1008

Drimmer, Melvin, *comp.* Black history; a reappraisal, edited with commentary by Melvin Drimmer. Garden City, N. Y., Doubleday, 1968. xx, 553 p.   E185.D7

     Essays which present the Negro's role in American history, each prefaced by an analysis of the historical events surrounding the period it covers.

     Bibliography: p. [531]-538.

1009

DuBois, William E. B. Darkwater; voices from within the veil. New York, Harcourt, Brace and Howe, 1920. 276 p.   E183.5.D8

     Reprinted in part from various periodicals.

1010

DuBois, William E. B. The souls of black folk; essays and sketches. New York, Blue Heron Press, 1953. 264 p. illus.   E185.5.D81 1953

     First printed in 1903.

1011

Ebony. White on black; the views of twenty-two white Americans on the Negro. Edited by Era Bell Thompson and Herbert Nipson, editors of Ebony magazine. Chicago, Johnson Pub. Co., 1963. 230 p.   E185.6.E26

1012

Franklin, John H. Lincoln and public morality; an address delivered at the Chicago Historical Society on February 12, 1959. [Chicago] Chicago Historical Society, 1959. 24 p.   JA79.F66

1013

Freedom of Information Conference, *8th, University of Missouri, 1965.* Race and the news media. Edited by Paul L. Fisher and Ralph Lowenstein. New York, Praeger [1967] 158 p.   E185.61.F84 1965aa

     Papers and summaries of discussion sessions of the conference sponsored by the Freedom of Information Center of the University of Missouri and the Anti-defamation League of B'nai B'rith.

1014

Goldwin, Robert A., *comp.* Civil disobedience; five essays by Martin Luther King, Jr. [and others]. Edited by Robert A. Goldwin. [Gambier, Ohio, Public Affairs Conference Center, Kenyon College, 1968] 1 v. (various pagings)   JC328.G58

Bibliographical footnotes.

Contents.—Letter from the Birmingham city jail, by M. L. King, Jr. —The case against civil disobedience, by H. J. Storing.—Reflections on civil disobedience and lawlessness, by P. Goodman.—Civil disobedience and beyond, by J. Farmer.—The American tradition of civil disobedience: a response to Henry David Thoreau, by H. V. Jaffa.

1015

Goldwin, Robert A., *ed.* 100 years of emancipation, essays by Harry V. Jaffa [and others]. Chicago, Rand McNally [1964] 217 p. (Rand McNally public affairs series)   E185.61.G62 1964a

Bibliographical footnotes.

1016

Grimke, Francis J. Christianity and race prejudice; two discourses delivered in the Fifteenth Street Presbyterian Church, Washington, D.C., May 29th, and June 5th, 1910. By the pastor Rev. Francis J. Grimke. [Washington, Press of W. E. Cobb, 1910] 29 p.   E185.61.G87
BX9178.G764C6 no. 4

1017

Grimke, Francis J. Equality of rights for all citizens, black and white, alike. A discourse delivered in the Fifteenth Street Presbyterian Church, Washington, D.C., Sunday, March 7th, 1909, by the pastor, Rev. Francis J. Grimke. [Washington, 1909] 19 p.   E185.61.G875

1018

Hill, Roy L. Rhetoric of racial revolt. Denver, Golden Bell Press, 1964. 378 p.   E185.6.H52

1019

Howard University, *Washington, D.C. Graduate School. Division of the Social Sciences.* The new Negro thirty years afterward; papers contributed to the sixteenth annual spring conference . . . April 20, 21, and 22, 1955. Edited by Rayford W. Logan, chairman, Eugene C. Holmes [and] G. Franklin Edwards. Washington, Howard University Press, 1955 [i.e. 1956] 96 p.   E185.5.H73 1955a

"Dedicated to the memory of Professor Alain Locke."

Includes bibliographies. "Bibliography of the writings of Alain Leroy Locke . . . by Robert E. Martin": p. 89-96.

1020

Johnson, Lyndon B., *Pres. U.S.* The one huge wrong: President Lyndon Johnson speaking at Howard University in Washington on June 4, 1965, analysing the Negro problem; [linocut illustrations by Paul Peter Piech]. Bushey (Herts.), Taurus Press [1968] [15] p. illus.   E185.J63

"Two hundred and eighty [numbered] copies have been printed plus a 30 special bound edition. This is copy number 216."

1021

Jones, LeRoi. Home; social essays. New York, Morrow, 1966. 252 p.

E185.6.J74

1022

King, Donald B., *and* Charles W. Quick, *eds.* Legal aspects of the civil rights movement. With an introduction by James M. Nabrit, Jr. Detroit, Wayne State University Press, 1965. 447 p.   DLC-LL

"Civil rights law of 1964": p. 333-375.
Bibliography: p. 431-446.

1023

King, Martin Luther. I have a dream; speech at the March on Washington. [n.p.] c1963. 6 p.   E185.61.K53

1024

King, Martin Luther. The trumpet of conscience. New York, Harper & Row [1968, c1967] 78 p. (Massey lectures, 1967)   E185.97.K5 1968

Canadian ed. (Canadian Broadcasting Co.) has title: *Conscience for Change.*

1025

Lincoln, Charles Eric. Sounds of the struggle; persons and perspectives in civil rights. New York, Morrow, 1967. 252 p.   E185.615.L5

Includes bibliographical references.

1026

Little, Malcolm. Malcom X speaks; selected speeches and statements. [Edited, with prefatory notes, by George Breitman] New York, Merit Publishers, 1965. 242 p. illus., ports.   E185.61.L58

1027

Little, Malcolm. The speeches of Malcolm X at Harvard. Edited, with an introductory essay, by Archie Epps. New York, W. Morrow, 1968. 191 p.   E185.61.L59 1968

Bibliographical references included in "Footnotes" (p. [183]-191).

1028

Mack, Raymond W. Race, class, and power. 2d ed. [New York] American Book Co. [1968] 468 p.   E184.A1M145 1968

Includes bibliographical references.

1029

Meier, August, *and* Elliott M. Rudwick, *comps.* The making of black America; essays in Negro life & history. New York, Atheneum, 1969. xvi, 377, 507 p. (Studies in American Negro life)   E185.M43

Includes bibliographical references.
Contents.—The origins of black Americans.—The black community in modern America.

1030

Miller, Kelly. Race adjustment [and] The everlasting stain. New York, Arno Press, 1968. 306, 352 p. (The American Negro, his history and literature)   E185.M66 1968

Reprint of the 1908 ed. of *Race Adjustment* and of the 1924 ed. of *The Everlasting Stain.*

1031

Murphy, Raymond J., *and* Howard Elinson, *eds.* Problems & prospects of the Negro movement. Belmont, Calif., Wadsworth Pub. Co. [1966] 440 p. illus., (Wadsworth continuing education series)   E185.615.M8

Bibliography: p. 437-440. Includes bibliographical references.

1032

Nelson, Alice R. M. D., *ed.* Masterpieces of Negro eloquence; the best speeches delivered by the Negro from the days of slavery to the present time. New York, Bookery Pub. Co. [c1914] 512 p. port.   PS663.N4N4

1033

Pipes, William H. Death of an "Uncle Tom." New York, Carlton Press [1967] 118 p. (A Hearthstone book)   E185.61.P6

Bibliographical footnotes.

1034

Redding, Jay Saunders. No day of triumph. With an introduction by Richard Wright. New York, Harper [1942] 342 p.   E185.6.R42

1035

Rousseve, Ronald J. Discord in brown and white; nine essays on intergroup relations in the United States by a Negro American. New York, Vantage Press [1961] 89 p.   E185.61.R82

"Selected references": p. 87-89.

1036

Stone, Chuck. Tell it like it is. New York, Trident Press, 1967 [c1968] 211 p.   E185.61.S872 1968

1037

Theobald, Robert. An alternative future for America; essays and speeches. Edited by Kendall College. [Chicago, Swallow Press, 1968] 186 p. illus.   HN65.T44

1038

Truman, Harry S., *Pres. U.S.* Freedom and equality, addresses. David S. Horton, editor. Columbia, University of Missouri Press [1960] 85 p.   JC599.U5T7

1039

Washington, Booker T. Character building; being addresses delivered on Sunday evenings to the students of Tuskegee Institute. New York, Doubleday, Page, 1902. 291 p. front.   BJ1581.W15

1040

Washington, Booker T. Selected speeches. Edited by E. Davidson Washington. Garden City, N.Y., Doubleday, Doran, 1932. xvi, 283 p. port.   E185.6.W319

1041

Westin, Alan F., *ed.* Freedom now! The civil-rights struggle in America. New York, Basic Books [1964] xv, 346 p.   E185.61.W54

Bibliography: p.[329]-341.

1042

Why I believe there is a God; sixteen essays by Negro clergymen. With an introduction by Howard Thurman. Chicago, Johnson Pub. Co., 1965. 120 p.   BT102.W5

1043
Wish, Harvey, *ed.* The Negro since emancipation. Englewood Cliffs, N.J., Prentice-Hall [1964] 184 p. (A Spectrum book)   E185.61.W79
   Bibliography: p. 183-184.

1044
Woodson, Carter G., *ed.* Negro orators and their orations. New York, Russell & Russell [1969] 711 p.   PS663.N4W6 1969
   Reprint of the 1925 ed.
   Bibliographical footnotes.

Fiction

1044a
Ashby, William M. Redder blood; a novel. New York, Cosmopolitan Press, 1915. 188 p.   PZ3.A8234Re

1045
Attaway, William. Blood on the forge, a novel. Garden City, N.Y., Doubleday, Doran, 1941. 279 p.   PZ3.A882Bl

1046
Baldwin, James. Another country. New York, Dial Press, 1962. 436 p.
    PZ4.B18An2

1047
Baldwin, James. Giovanni's room; a novel. New York, Dial Press, 1956. 248 p.   PZ4.B18Gi

1048
Baldwin, James. Go tell it on the mountain. New York, Knopf, 1953. 303 p.   PZ4.B18Go

1049
Baldwin, James. Going to meet the man. New York, Dial Press, 1965. 249 p.   PZ4.B18Gq
   Contents.—The rockpile.—The outing.—The man child.—Previous condition.—Sonny's blues.—This morning, this evening, so soon.—Come out the wilderness.—Going to meet the man.

1050
Baldwin, James. Tell me how long the train's been gone; a novel. New York, Dial Press, 1968. 484 p.   PS3552.A45T4

1051
Baltimore Afro-American. Best short stories by Afro-American writers, 1925-1950, selected and edited by Nick Aaron Ford and H. L. Faggett. Boston, Meador Pub. Co. [1950] 307 p.   PZ1.B23Be

1052
Bennett, Hal. A wilderness of vines. Garden City, N.Y., Doubleday, 1966. 345 p.   PZ4.B4696Wi

1053
Boles, Robert. Curling, a novel. Boston, Houghton Mifflin, 1968 [c1967] 259 p.   PZ4.B6883Cu

1054
Bontemps, Arna W. Black thunder. New York, Macmillan, 1936. 298 p.   PZ3.B64442Bl

1055
Bontemps, Arna W. Chariot in the sky; a story of the Jubilee Singers. Illustrations by Cyrus Leroy Baldridge. Philadelphia, Winston [1951] 234 p. illus. (Land of the Free series)   PZ7.B6443Ch

1056
Bontemps, Arna W. Drums at dusk; a novel. New York, Macmillan, 1939. 226 p. illus.   PZ3.B64442Dr

1056a
Bontemps, Arna W. God sends Sunday. New York, Harcourt, Brace [c1931] 199 p.   PZ3.B64442Go

1057
Bosworth, William. The long search, a novel. Great Barrington, Mass., Advance Pub. Co. [1957] 303 p.   PZ4.B7475Lo

1058
Brooks, Gwendolyn. Maud Martha, a novel. New York, Harper [1953] 180 p.   PZ4.B872Mau

1059
Brown, Frank L. Trumbull Park, a novel. Chicago, Regnery [1959] 432 p.   PZ4.B8774Tr

1060

Brown, Lloyd L. Iron City, a novel. New York, Masses & Mainstream,
1951. 255 p.   PZ4.B879Ir

1061

Brown, William W. Clotel. New York, Arno Press, 1969. 245 p. illus.
(Afro-American culture series)   DLC

    Reprint of the 1853 ed.
    The first novel written by a Negro.

1062

Chastain, Thomas. Judgment day. Garden City, N.Y., Doubleday, 1962.
213 p.   PZ4.C489Ju

1063

Chesnutt, Charles W. The colonel's dream. New York, Doubleday, Page,
1905. 294 p.   PZ3.C4253Cl

1064

Chesnutt, Charles W. The conjure woman. Ridgewood, N. J., Gregg Press
[1968] 229 p. (Americans in fiction)   PZ3.C4253C5

    Reprint of the 1899 ed.
    Contents.—The goophered grapevine.—Po' Sandy.—Mars Jeem's
nightmare.—The conjurer's revenge.—Sis' Becky's pickaninny.—The gray
wolf's ha'nt.—Hot-Foot Hannibal.

1065

Chesnutt, Charles W. The house behind the cedars. Boston, Houghton,
Mifflin, 1900. 294 p.   PZ3.C4253H

1066

Chesnutt, Charles W. The marrow of tradition. New York, Arno Press,
1969. 329 p. (The American Negro, his history and literature)
                                                              PZ3.C425M5
    Afro-American culture series.
    Reprint of the 1901 ed.

1067

Chesnutt, Charles W. The wife of his youth, and other stories of the color
line. With illustrations by Clyde O. De Land. Boston, Houghton, Mifflin, 1899. 323 p. plates.   PZ3.C4253W

    Contents.—The wife of his youth.—Her Virginia mammy.—The
sheriff's children.—A matter of principle.—Cicely's dream.—The passing

of Grandison.—Uncle Wellington's wives.—The bouquet.—The web of circumstance.

1068
Clarke, John H., *ed.* American Negro short stories. New York, Hill and Wang [1966] xix, 355 p. PZ1.C563Am

1068a
Cotter, Joseph S. Negro tales. New York, Cosmopolitan Press, 1912. 148 p. port. PZ3.C8274N

1069
Crump, Paul. Burn, killer, burn! Chicago, Johnson Pub. Co. [1962] 391 p. illus. PZ4.C9563Bu

1070
Cullen, Countee. My lives and how I lost them, by Christopher Cat in collaboration with Countee Cullen, with drawings by Robert Reid Macguire. New York, Harper [c1942] xiv, 160 p. illus. PZ3.C89761My

1071
Cullen, Countee. One way to heaven. New York, Harper, 1932. 230 p. PZ3.C89761On

1071a
Daly, Victor. Not only war, a story of two great conflicts. Boston, Christopher Pub. House [c1932] 106 p. PZ3.D179No

1072
Davis, Christopher. First family. New York, Coward-McCann [1961] 253 p. PZ4.D2596Fi

1073
Demby, William. Beetlecreek, a novel. New York, Rinehart [1950] 223 p. PZ3.D3923Be

1074
Demby, William. The catacombs. New York, Pantheon Books [1965] 244 p. PZ3.D3923Cat

1075
Dodson, Owen. Boy at the window, a novel. New York, Farrar, Straus and Young [1951] 212 p. PZ4.D647Bo

Paperback ed. (New York, Popular Library, 1965) has title: *When Trees Were Green.*

1076

DuBois, William E. B. Dark princess, a romance. New York, Harcourt, Brace [c1928] 311 p.   PZ3.D8525Da

1077

DuBois, William E. B. Mansart builds a school. New York, Mainstream Publishers, 1959. 367 p. (*His* The black flame, a trilogy, book 2)

PZ3.D8525Man

1078

DuBois, William E. B. The ordeal of Mansart. New York, Mainstream Publishers, 1957. 316 p. (*His* The black flame, a trilogy, book 1)

PZ3.D85250r

1079

DuBois, William E. B. The quest of the silver fleece; a novel. Illustrated by H. S. DeLay. Chicago, A. C. McClurg, 1911. 434 p. plates.

PZ3.D8525Q

1080

DuBois, William E. B. Worlds of color. New York, Mainstream Publishers, 1961. 349 p. (*His* The black flame, a trilogy, book 3)   PZ3.D8525Wo

1081

Dunbar, Paul L. The fanatics. New York, Dodd, Mead, 1901. 312 p.

PZ3.D911F

1082

Dunbar, Paul L. Folks from Dixie. With illustrations by E. W. Kemble. New York, Dodd, Mead, 1898. 263 p. plates (part col.)

PZ3.D911Fo3

Contents.—Anner' Lizer's stumblin' block.—The ordeal at Mt. Hope. —The colonel's awakening.—The trial sermons on Bull-Skin.—Jimsella. —Mt. Pisgah's Christmas 'possum.—A family feud.—Aunt Mandy's investment.—The intervention of Peter.—Nelse Hatton's vengeance.—At Shaft 11.—The deliberation of Mr. Dunkin.

1083

Dunbar, Paul L. The love of Landry. New York, Dodd, Mead [1900] 200 p.   PZ3.D911L

1084

Dunbar, Paul L. The sport of the Gods. New York, Arno Press, 1969. 255 p. (The American Negro, his history and literature)   PZ3.D911Sp6

Afro-American culture series.
Reprint of the 1902 ed.

1085
Dunbar, Paul L. The strength of Gideon and other stories. New York, Arno Press, 1969. 362 p. (The American Negro; his history and literature) PZ3.D911St7

Afro-American culture series.
Reprint of the 1900 ed.

1086
Dunbar, Paul L. The uncalled; a novel. New York, Dodd, Mead, 1898. 255 p. PZ3.D911U3

1087
Ellison, Ralph. Invisible man. New York, Random House [1952] 439 p.
PZ4.E45In

1088
Fauset, Jessie R. The chinaberry tree; a novel of American life. New York, F. A. Stokes Co., 1931. 341 p. PZ3.F276Ch

1089
Fauset, Jessie R. Comedy, American style. New York, F. A. Stokes Co., 1933. 326 p. PZ3.F276Co

1090
Fauset, Jessie R. There is confusion. New York, Boni and Liveright, 1924. 297 p. PZ3.F276Th

1091
Fisher, Rudolph. The conjure-man dies; a mystery tale of dark Harlem. New York, Covici, Friede [c1932] 316 p. PZ3.F5367Co

1092
Fisher, Rudolph. The walls of Jericho. New York, Knopf, 1928. 307 p.
PZ3.F5367Wa
Reprint issued by Arno Press, 1969.

1093
Graham, Lorenz B. South Town. Chicago, Follett Pub. Co. [1958] 189 p.
PZ4.G74So

1094
Graham, Shirley. Jean Baptiste Pointe de Sable, founder of Chicago. New York, J. Messner [1953] 180 p. PZ7.G757Je

1095

Graham, Shirley. The story of Phillis Wheatley; illustrations by Robert Burns. New York, J. Messner [1949] 176 p. illus., port.   PZ7.G757St

"Sources": p. 172.

1096

Griggs, Sutton E. The hindered hand; or, The reign of the repressionist. Nashville, Orion Pub. Co., 1905. 303 p.   PZ3.G888H

1096a

Griggs, Sutton E. Pointing the way. Nashville, Orion Pub. Co., 1908. 233 p.   PZ3.G888P

1097

Harper, Frances E. W. Iola Leroy; or, Shadows uplifted. Philadelphia, Garrigues Bros., 1892. 282 p. port.   PS1799.H7I6

1098

Henderson, George W. Jule. New York, Creative Age Press [1946] 234 p.
PZ3.H3845Ju

1099

Henderson, George W. Ollie Miss, a novel. Blocks by Lowell Leroy Balcolm. New York, F. A. Stokes Co., 1935. 276 p. illus., plates.
PZ3.H3845Ol

1100

Hill, John H. Princess Malah. Washington, Associated Publishers [c1933] 330 p.   PZ3.H5521Pr

1101

Himes, Chester B. Blind man with a pistol. New York, W. Morrow, 1969. 240 p.   PZ3.H57Bl

1102

Himes, Chester B. Cast the first stone, a novel. New York, Coward-McCann [1952] 346 p.   PZ3.H57Cas

1103

Himes, Chester B. If he hollers let him go. Garden City, N.Y., Doubleday, Doran, 1945. 249 p.   PZ3.H57If

1104

Himes, Chester B. Lonely crusade. New York, Knopf, 1947. 398 p.
PZ3.H57Lo

1105

Himes, Chester B. Pinktoes. Paris, Olympia Press [1961] 207 p. (The Traveller's companion series, no. 87)   PZ3.H57Pi

1106

Himes, Chester B. The primitive. [New York] New American Library [1955] 151 p. (A Signet book, 1264)   PZ3.H57Pr

1107

Himes, Chester B. The third generation. Cleveland, World Pub. Co. [1954] 350 p.   PZ3.H57Th

1108

Hughes, Langston. The best of Simple. Illustrated by Bernhard Nast. New York, Hill and Wang [1961] 245 p. illus. (American century series, AC39)   PS3515.U274B4

1109

Hughes, Langston, *ed.* The best short stories by Negro writers; an anthology from 1899 to the present. Boston, Little, Brown [1967] xvii, 508 p.   PZ1.H849Be

1110

Hughes, Langston. Laughing to keep from crying. New York, Holt [1952] 206 p.   PZ3.H87313Lau

Short stories.

1111

Hughes, Langston. Not without laughter. New York, Knopf, 1930. 324 p.
                                                          PZ3.H87313No

1112

Hughes, Langston. Simple speaks his mind. [New York] Simon and Schuster [1950] 231 p.   PS3515.U274S53

1113

Hughes, Langston. Something in common, and other stories. New York, Hill and Wang [1963] 236 p. (American century series)
                                                          PZ3.H87313So

1114

Hughes, Langston. Tambourines to glory, a novel. New York, J. Day Co. [1958] 188 p.   PZ3.H87313Tam

1115

Hughes, Langston. The ways of white folks. New York, Knopf, 1934.
248 p.   PZ3.H87313Way

   Short stories.

1116

Hunter, Kristin. God bless the child. New York, Scribner [1964] 307 p.
                                          PZ4.H9457Go

1117

Hunter, Kristin. The landlord. New York, Scribner [1966] 338 p.
                                          PZ4.H9457Lan

1118

Hurston, Zora N. Seraph on the Suwanee, a novel. New York, Scribner,
1948. 311 p.   PZ3.H9457Se

1119

Hurston, Zora N. Their eyes were watching God; a novel. Philadelphia,
Lippincott [c1937] 286 p.   PZ3.H9457Th

1120

[Johnson, James W.] The autobiography of an ex-colored man. Boston,
Sherman, French, 1912. 207 p.   PZ3.P633Au

1121

Jones, LeRoi. The system of Dante's Hell; [a novel]. New York, Grove
Press [1965] 154 p.   PZ4.J774Sy

1122

Jones, LeRoi. Tales. New York, Grove Press [1967] 132 p.   PZ4.J774Tal

1123

Kelley, William M. Dancers on the shore. Garden City, N.Y., Doubleday,
1964. 201 p.   PZ4.K285Dan

   Short stories.

1124

Kelley, William M. Dem. Garden City, N.Y., Doubleday, 1967. 210 p.
                                          PZ4.K285De

1125

Kelley, William M. A drop of patience. Garden City, N.Y., Doubleday,
1965. 237 p.   PZ4.K285Dr

1126

Killens, John O. And then we heard the thunder. New York, Knopf, 1963 [c1962] 485 p.   PZ4.K48An2

1127

Killens, John O. 'Sippi. New York, Trident Press, 1967. 434 p.   PZ4.K48Si

1128

Killens, John O. Youngblood. New York, Dial Press, 1954. 566 p.
                                                          PZ4.K48Yo

1129

Larsen, Nella. Passing. New York, Knopf, 1929. 215 p.   PZ3.L33Pas

1130

Larsen, Nella. Quicksand. New York, Knopf, 1928. 301 p.   PZ3.L33Qu

1131

Lee, George W. River George. New York, Macaulay Co. [c1937] 275 p.
                                                        PZ3.L5123Ri

1132

Marshall, Paule. Brown girl, brownstones. New York, Random House [1959] 310 p.   PZ4.M369Br

1133

Mayfield, Julian. The grand parade. New York, Vanguard Press [1961] 448 p.   PZ4.M47Gr

1134

Mayfield, Julian. The hit, a novel. New York, Vanguard Press [1957] 212 p.   PZ4.M47Hi

1135

Mayfield, Julian. The long night. New York, Vanguard Press [1958] 156 p. illus.   PZ4.M47Lo

1136

Micheaux, Oscar. The story of Dorothy Stanfield, based on a great insurance swindle, and a woman! A novel. New York, Book Supply Co., 1946. 416 p. col. front.   PZ3.M5809St

1137

Miller, Warren. The cool world, a novel. Boston, Little, Brown [1959] 241 p.   PZ4.M65Co

1138
Motley, Willard. Knock on any door. New York, Appleton-Century Co.
[1947] 503 p.   PZ3.M8573Kn

1139
Motley, Willard. Let no man write my epitaph. New York, Random House
[1958] 467 p.   PZ3.M8573Le

1140
Motley, Willard. Let noon be fair, a novel. New York, Putnam [c1966]
416 p.   PZ3.M8573Lg

1141
Motley, Willard. We fished all night. New York, Appleton-Century-Crofts
[1951] 560 p.   PZ3.M8573We

1142
Ottley, Roi. White marble lady. New York, Farrar, Straus and Giroux
[1965] 278 p.   PZ4.O894Wh

1142a
Parks, Gordon. The learning tree. New York, Harper & Row [1963]
303 p.   PZ4.P249Le

1143
Paynter, John H. Fugitives of the Pearl. Washington, Associated Publishers
[c1930] 209 p. ports.   PZ3.P2938Fu

   "Descendants of Paul and Amelia Edmonson": p. [203]-209.

1144
Petry, Ann L. Country place. Boston, Houghton Mifflin, 1947. 266 p.
                                                         PZ3.P44904Co

1145
Petry, Ann L. The Narrows. Boston, Houghton Mifflin, 1953. 428 p.
                                                         PZ3.P44904No

1146
Petry, Ann L. The street. Boston, Houghton Mifflin, 1946. 435 p.
                                                         PZ3.P44904St
   "A Houghton Mifflin literary fellowship novel."

1147
Pharr, Robert D. The book of numbers. Garden City, N.Y., Doubleday
1969. 374 p.   PS3566.H3B6 1969

1148

Pickens, William. The vengeance of the gods, and three other stories of real American color line life. Introduction by Bishop John Hurst. Philadelphia, A.M.E. Book Concern [c1922] 125 p.   PZ3.P5853Ve

Contents.—The vengeance of the gods.—The superior race.—Passing the buck.—Tit for tat.

1149

Polite, Carlene H. The flagellants. New York [Farrar, Straus & Giroux, 1967] 214 p.   PZ4.P7674Fl

1150

Redding, Jay Saunders. Stranger and alone, a novel. New York, Harcourt, Brace [1950] 308 p.   PZ3.R246533St

1151

Rogers, Joel A. She walks in beauty. Los Angeles, Western Publishers, 1963. 316 p.   PZ4.R727Sh

1152

Rollins, Bryant. Danger song. Garden City, N.Y., Doubleday, 1967. 280 p.   PZ4.R753Dan

1153

Savoy, Willard W. Alien land. New York, E. P. Dutton, 1949. 320 p.   PZ3.S2695Al

1153a

Schuyler, George S. Black no more; being an account of the strange and wonderful workings of science in the land of the free, A.D. 1933-1940. New York, Macaulay Co. [c1931] 250 p.   PZ3.S3972Bl

1154

Smith, William G. Anger at innocence. New York, Farrar, Straus [1950] 300 p.   PZ3.S6638An

1155

Smith, William G. Last of the conquerors. New York, Farrar, Straus, 1948. 262 p.   PZ3.S6638Las

1156

Smith, William G. The stone face, a novel. New York, Farrar, Straus [1963] 213 p.   PZ3.S6638St

1157

Thurman, Wallace. The blacker the berry; a novel of Negro life. New York Macaulay Co., 1929. 262 p.   PZ3.T4258B

1158

Thurman, Wallace. Infants of the spring. New York, Macaulay Co. [c1932] 284 p.   PZ3.T4258In

1158a

Thurman, Wallace, *and* Abraham L. Furman. The interne. New York, Macaulay Co. [c1932] 252 p.   PZ3.T4258Int

1159

Toomer, Jean. Cane. With a foreword by Waldo Frank. New York, University Place Press [1967, c1951] 239 p.   PZ3.T6184Can5

First published in 1923.
Prose interspersed with poetry.

1160

Turpin, Waters E. O Canaan! A novel. New York, Doubleday, Doran, 1939. 311 p.   PZ3.T8670

1161

Turpin, Waters E. The rootless. New York, Vantage Press [1957] 340 p.
                                    PZ3.T867Ro

1162

Turpin, Waters E. These low grounds. New York, Harper, 1937. 344 p.
                                    PZ3.T867Th

1163

Van Dyke, Henry. Blood of strawberries. New York, Farrar, Straus and Giroux [1969] 277 p.   PZ4.V24Bl

1164

Van Dyke, Henry. Ladies of the Rachmaninoff eyes. New York, Farrar, Straus and Giroux [1965] 214 p.   PZ4.V24Lad

1165

Walker, Margaret. Jubilee. Boston, Houghton Mifflin, 1966. 497 p. map.
                                    PZ4.W1814Ju

1166

Walrond, Eric. Tropic death. New York, Boni & Liveright, 1926. 282 p.
                                    PZ3.W166Tr

Contents.—Drought.—Panama gold.—The yellow one.—The wharf rats.—The palm porch.—Subjection.—The beach pin.—The white snake. —The vampire bat.—Tropic death.

1167
Ward, Thomas P. The right to live. New York, Pageant Press [1953] 249 p.   PZ7.W216Ri

1168
Webb, Frank J. The Garies and their friends. New York, Arno Press, 1969. 392 p. (Afro-American culture series)   PZ3.W382332Ga5

The American Negro, his history and literature.
Reprint of the 1857 ed.

1169
West, Dorothy. The living is easy. Boston, Houghton, Mifflin, 1948. 347 p.
                                           PZ3.W5174Li

1170
White, Walter F. The fire in the flint. New York, Knopf, 1924. 300 p.
                                           PZ3.W5857Fi

1171
White, Walter F. Flight. New York, Knopf, 1926. 300 p.   PZ3.W5857Fl

1172
Williams, Chancellor. Have you been to the river? A novel. New York, Exposition Press [1952] 256 p.   PZ3.W67143Hav

1173
Williams, John A. The man who cried I am; a novel. Boston, Little, Brown [1967] 403 p.   PZ4.W72624Man

1174
Williams, John A. Night song. New York, Farrar, Straus and Cudahy [1961] 219 p.   PZ4.W72624Ni

1175
Williams, John A. Sissie. New York, Farrar, Straus and Cudahy [1963] 277 p.   PZ4.W72624Si

1176
Wright, Charles S. The messenger. New York, Farrar, Straus [1963] 217 p.
                                           PZ4.W9477Me

1177

Wright, Charles S. The wig, a mirror image. New York, Farrar, Straus and Giroux [1966] 179 p.   PZ4.W9477Wi

1178

Wright, Richard. Eight men. Cleveland, World Pub. Co. [1961] 250 p.
                                                   PZ3.W9352Ei
    Short stories.

1179

Wright, Richard. Lawd today. New York, Walker [1963] 189 p.
                                                   PZ3.W9352Law

1180

Wright, Richard. The long dream, a novel. Garden City, N.Y., Doubleday, 1958. 384 p.   PZ3.W9352Lo

1181

Wright, Richard. Native son. New York, Harper, 1940. 359 p.
                                                   PZ3.W9352Nat

1182

Wright, Richard. The outsider. New York, Harper [1953] 450 p.
                                                   PZ3.W9352Ou

1183

Wright, Richard. Uncle Tom's children, five long stories. New York, Harper [c1938] xxx, 384 p.   PZ3.W935Un2

    Contents.—The ethics of living Jim Crow; an autobiographical sketch.—Big boy leaves home.— Down by the riverside.—Long black song.—Fire and cloud.—Bright and morning star.

1184

Yerby, Frank. Captain Rebel. New York, Dial Press [1956] 343 p.
                                                   PZ3.Y415Cap

1185

Yerby, Frank. The devil's laughter. New York, Dial Press, 1953. 376 p.
                                                   PZ3.Y415De

1186

Yerby, Frank. Fairoaks, a novel. New York, Dial Press [1957] 405 p.
                                                   PZ3.Y415Fai

1187

Yerby, Frank. Floodtide. New York, Dial Press, 1950. 342 p.
                                                   PZ3.Y415Fl

1188
Yerby, Frank. The foxes of Harrow. New York, Dial Press, 1946. 534 p.
PZ3.Y415Fo

1189
Yerby, Frank. The Garfield honor. New York, Dial Press, 1961. 347 p.
PZ3.Y415Gar

1190
Yerby, Frank. Gillian. New York, Dial Press, 1960. 346 p.   PZ3.Y415Gi

1191
Yerby, Frank. The golden hawk. New York, Dial Press, 1948. 346 p. map.
PZ3.Y415Go

1192
Yerby, Frank. Griffin's Way, a novel. New York, Dial Press, 1962. 345 p.
PZ3.Y415Gr

1193
Yerby, Frank. Jarrett's Jade, a novel. New York, Dial Press, 1959. 342 p.
PZ3.Y415Jar

1194
Yerby, Frank. The old gods laugh, a modern romance. New York, Dial
Press, 1964. 408 p.   PZ3.Y415Ol

1195
Yerby, Frank. Pride's castle. New York, Dial Press, 1949. 382 p.
PZ3.Y415Pr

1196
Yerby, Frank. The serpent and the staff. New York, Dial Press, 1958.
377 p.   PZ3.Y415Se

1197
Yerby, Frank. The treasure of Pleasant Valley. New York, Dial Press,
1955. 348 p.   PZ3.Y415Tr

1198
Yerby, Frank. The vixens, a novel. New York, Dial Press, 1947. 347 p.
PZ3.Y415Vi

1199
Yerby, Frank. A woman called Fancy. New York, Dial Press, 1951. 340 p.
PZ3.Y415Wo

Humor

1200

Gregory, Dick. From the back of the bus. Photographs by Jerry Yulsman. Introduction by Hugh M. Hefner. Edited by Bob Orden. New York, Dutton, 1962. 125 p. illus.   PN6231.S485G7

1201

Gregory, Dick. What's happening? Photographs by Jerry Yulsman. New York, Dutton, 1965. 125 p. illus.   PN6231.N5G68

1202

Hughes, Langston, ed. The book of Negro humor. New York, Dodd, Mead [1966] 265 p.   PN6231.N5H8

1203

Sterling, Philip, ed. Laughing on the outside; the intelligent white reader's guide to Negro tales and humor. Introductory essay by Saunders Redding. Cartoons by Ollie Harrington. New York, Grosset & Dunlap [1965] 254 p. illus.   PN6231.N5S7

   Bibliography: p. [251]-254.

1204

That passing laughter; stories of the Southland, written by those who lived it. Drawings by Harry Maddox. Photography by Gertrude Gibson [and] Mattie Lou Stribling. Portrait by Marie Hull. Birmingham, Ala., Southern University Press, c1966. 140 p. illus.   PN6231.N5T5

Plays

1205

Baldwin, James. The amen corner; a play. New York, Dial Press, 1968. xvii, 91 p.   PS3552.A45A8

1206

Baldwin, James. Blues for Mister Charlie, a play. New York, Dial Press, 1964. xv, 121 p.   PS3552.A45B5

1207
Connelly, Marcus C. The green pastures, a fable, suggested by Roark Bradford's southern sketches, "Ol' man Adam an' his chillun." New York, Farrar & Rinehart [c1929] xvi, 173 p.   PS3505.O4814G7 1929

In dramatic form, with cast of characters as presented at the Mansfield Theatre, New York, 1930.
Attempts "to present certain aspects of a living religion in the terms of its believers . . . thousands of Negroes in the deep South."—p. xv.

1208
Cotter, Joseph S. Caleb, the degenerate, a play in four acts; a study of the types, customs, and needs of the American Negro. Louisville, Ky., Bradley & Gilbert Co., 1903. 57 p. port.   PS3505.O862C3 1903

1209
Couch, William, *comp*. New black playwrights, an anthology. Baton Rouge, Louisiana State University Press [1968] xxiii, 258 p.
PS634.C684

1210
Davis, Ossie. Purlie victorious; a comedy in three acts. New York, S. French [c1961] 90 p.   PS3507.A7444P8

1211
Duberman, Martin B. In white America, a documentary play. Boston, Houghton Mifflin, 1964. 112 p.   PS3554.U25I5

1212
D'Usseau, Arnaud, *and* James Gow. Deep are the roots. New York, Scribner, 1946. xxvi, 205 p. plates.   PS3507.U925D4

1213
Edmonds, Randolph. The land of cotton, and other plays. Washington, Associated Publishers [c1942] 267 p.   PS3509.D56L3

Contents.—The land of cotton.— Gangsters over Harlem.—Yellow death.—Silas Brown.—The High court of Historia.

1214
Edmonds, Randolph. Shades and shadows. Boston, Meador Pub. Co., 1930. 171 p.   PS3509.D56S5 1930

Contents.—The devil's price.—Hewers of wool.—Shades and shadows.—Everyman's land.—The tribal chief.—The phantom treasure.

1215

Edmonds, Randolph. Six plays for a Negro theatre. Foreword by Frederick H. Koch. Boston, W. H. Baker Co. [c1934] 155 p.

PS3509.D56S6 1934

Contents.—Bad man.—Old man Pete.—Nat Turner.—Breeders.
—Bleeding hearts.—The new window.

1216

Grimke, Angelina W. Rachel, a play in three acts. Boston, Cornhill Co.
[c1920] 96 p.   PS3513.R744R3 1920

1217

Hansberry, Lorraine. A raisin in the sun; a drama in three acts. New York,
Random House [1959] 142 p. illus. (A Random House play)

PS3515.A515R3

1218

Heyward, Dorothy H. K., *and* Du Bose Heyward. Mamba's daughters, a
play. Dramatized from the novel Mamba's daughters by Du Bose Heyward. New York, Farrar & Rinehart [c1939] 182 p. plates.

PS3515.E97M3 1939

1219

Hughes, Langston. Five plays. Edited with an introduction by Webster
Smalley. Bloomington, Indiana University Press [1963] 258 p.

PS3515.U274A19 1963

Contents.—Mulatto.—Soul gone home.—Little Ham.—Simply
heavenly.—Tambourines to glory.

1220

Jones, LeRoi. Dutchman and The slave, two plays. New York, Morrow,
1964. 88 p.   PS3519.O4545D8

1221

Locke, Alain L., *and* Montgomery Gregory, *eds.* Plays of Negro life; a
source-book of native American drama. Decorations and illustrations by
Aaron Douglas. New York, Harper, 1927. 430 p. illus., plates.

PS627.N4L6

"Bibliography of Negro drama": p. 424-430.

1222

Peters, Paul, *and* George Sklar. Stevedore, a play in three acts. New York,
Covici, Friede [c1934] 123 p.   PS3531.E826S7 1934

1223
Richardson, Willis, *comp.* Plays and pageants from the life of the Negro. Washington, Associated Publishers [c1930] 373 p. illus., plates.

PS627.N4R5

Contents.–Plays: Sacrifice, by Thelma M. Duncan. Antar of Araby, by Maud Cuney-Hare. Ti Yette, by John Matheus. Graven images, by May Miller. Riding the goat, by May Miller. The black horseman, by Willis Richardson. The king's dilemma, by Willis Richardson. The house of sham, by Willis Richardson.–Pageants: Two races, by Inez M. Burke. Out of the dark, by Dorothy C. Guinn. The light of the women, by Frances Gunner. Ethiopia at the bar of justice, by Edward J. McCoo.

1224
Richardson, Willis, *and* May Miller, *eds.* Negro history in thirteen plays. Washington, Associated Publishers [c1935] 333 p.   PS627.N4R47

1225
Sackler, Howard O. The great white hope. New York, Dial Press, 1968. 264 p.   PS3537.A156G7

In 1908, Jack Johnson became the first Negro heavyweight champion of the world. This is an epic drama based on his life.

1226
Torrence, Frederic R. Granny Maumee, The rider of dreams, Simon the Cyrenian; plays for a Negro theater. New York, Macmillan, 1917. 111 p.   PS3539.O63G7 1917

1227
Wright, Richard. Native son (the biography of a young American), a play in ten scenes by Paul Green and Richard Wright, from the novel by Richard Wright. A Mercury production by Orson Welles, presented by Orson Welles and John Houseman. New York, Harper [c1941] 148 p. front.   PS3545.R815N25

   Includes songs with music.

Poetry

1228
Adoff, Arnold, *comp.* I am the darker brother; an anthology of modern poems by Negro Americans. Drawings by Benny Andrews. Foreword by Charlemae Rollins. New York, Macmillan [1968] 128 p. illus.

PS591.N4A65

1229

Bontemps, Arna W., *ed.* American Negro poetry. New York, Hill and Wang [1963] 197 p.   PS591.N4B58

1230

Bontemps, Arna W., *comp.* Golden slippers, an anthology of Negro poetry for young readers. With drawings by Henrietta Bruce Sharon. New York, Harper [c1941] 220 p. illus., plates.   PS591.N4B6

"Biographies": p. 200-215.

1231

Braithwaite, William S. B. The house of falling leaves, with other poems. Boston, J. W. Luce, 1908. 112 p.   PS3503.R246H7 1908

Partly reprinted from various periodicals.

1232

Braithwaite, William S. B. Lyrics of life and love. Boston, H. B. Turner, 1904. 80 p. port.   PS3503.R246L8 1904

1233

Braithwaite, William S. B. Selected poems. New York, Coward-McCann [1948] 96 p.   PS3503.R246A6 1948

1234

Brewer, John Mason, *ed.* Heralding dawn; an anthology of verse, by [!] selected and edited, with a historical summary on the Texas Negroes' verse-making, by J. Mason Brewer, and with a preface by Henry Smith. [Dallas, June Thomason, Print., c1936] 45 p. ports.   PS591.N4B65

Includes biographical sketches of the authors.
"Bibliography and acknowledgment": 3d prelim. leaf.

1235

Brooks, Gwendolyn. Annie Allen. [Poems]. New York, Harper [1949] 60 p. port.   PS3503.R7244A7

1236

Brooks, Gwendolyn. In the Mecca; poems. New York, Harper & Row [1968] 54 p.   PS3503.R7244I5

1237

Brown, Sterling A. Southern road, poems; drawings by E. Simms Campbell. New York, Harcourt, Brace [c1932] xv, 135 p. plates.

PS3503.R833S6 1932

1238
Charters, Samuel B. The poetry of the blues. With photographs by Ann Charters. New York, Oak Publications [1963] 111 p. illus.
PS591.N4C4

1239
Cullen, Countee. The black Christ & other poems. With decorations by Charles Cullen. New York, Harper, 1929. 110 p. illus., plates.
PS3505.U287B6 1929

1240
Cullen, Countee, *ed.* Caroling dusk, an anthology of verse by Negro poets. Decorations by Aaron Douglas. New York, Harper, 1927. xxii, 237 p.
PS591.N4C8

1241
Cullen, Countee. Color. New York, Harper, 1925. xvii, 108 p.
PS3505.U287C6 1925

1242
Cullen, Countee. Copper sun. With decorations by Charles Cullen. New York, Harper, 1927. 89 p. illus.
PS3505.U287C65 1927

1243
Cullen, Countee. On these I stand; an anthology of the best poems of Countee Cullen. Selected by himself and including six new poems never before published. New York, Harper [1947] 197 p.
PS3505.U287A6 1947

1244
Cuney, Waring, Langston Hughes, *and* Bruce M. Wright, *eds.* Lincoln University poets; centennial anthology [1854-1954]. Foreword by Horace Mann Bond; introduction by J. Saunders Redding. New York, Fine Editions Press [1954] 72 p.
PS591.N4C84

1245
Dodson, Owen. Powerful long ladder. New York, Farrar, Straus, 1946. 103 p.
PS3507.O364P6

1246
Dunbar, Paul L. The complete poems of Paul Laurence Dunbar, with the introduction to "Lyrics of lowly life," by W. D. Howells. New York, Dodd, Mead, 1913. xxxii, 289 p. port.
PS1556.A1 1913

1247
Dunbar, Paul L. Lyrics of lowly life. New York, Arno Press, 1969. xx, 208 p. (The American Negro, his history and literature)
PS1556.L6 1969

Afro-American culture series.
Reprint of the 1899 ed.

1248
Dunbar, Paul L. Oak and ivy. Dayton, Ohio, Press of United Brethren Pub.
House, 1893. 62 p.   DHU

First ed. of Dunbar's first work; includes 13 poems not in *The
Complete Poems* (1913).

1249
Hayden, Robert E. A ballad of remembrance. London, P. Breman, 1962.
72 p. (Heritage, 1)   PS3515.A9363B3

1250
Hayden, Robert E. Heart-shape in the dust; poems. Detroit, Falcon Press
[c1940] 63 p.   PS3515.A9363H4 1940

1251
Hayden, Robert E., *comp.* Kaleidoscope; poems by American Negro poets,
edited and with an introduction by Robert Hayden. New York, Harcourt, Brace & World [1967] xxiv, 231 p. ports. (Curriculum-related
books)   PS591.N4H3

1252
Hayden, Robert E. Selected poems. New York, October House [1966]
79 p.   PS3515.A9363A6 1966

1253
Hughes, Langston. Fields of wonder. New York, Knopf, 1947. 114 p.
                                                     PS3515.U274F45

1254
Hughes, Langston. Fine clothes to the Jew. New York, Knopf, 1927. 89 p.
                                                 PS3515.U274F5 1927

1255
Hughes, Langston. New Negro poets U.S.A. Foreword by Gwendolyn
Brooks. Bloomington, Indiana University Press [1964] 127 p.
                                                       PS591.N4H8

1256
Hughes, Langston. One-way ticket [poems]; illustrations by Jacob
Lawrence. New York, Knopf, 1949 [c1948] xvii, 136 p. illus.
                                                     PS3515.U274O5

1257

Hughes, Langston. The panther & the lash; poems of our times. New York, Knopf, 1967. 101 p.   PS3515.U274P3

1258

Hughes, Langston, *and* Arna W. Bontemps, *eds.* The poetry of the Negro, 1746-1949; an anthology. Garden City, N.Y., Doubleday, 1949. xviii, 429 p.   PN6109.7H8

1259

Hughes, Langston. Selected poems. Drawings by E. McKnight Kauffer. New York, Knopf, 1959. 297 p. illus.   PS3515.U274A6 1959

1260

Hughes, Langston. Shakespeare in Harlem. With drawings by E. McKnight Kauffer. New York, Knopf, 1942. 124 p. illus.   PS3515.U274S5

"A book of light verse."—4th prelim. leaf.

1261

Hughes, Langston. The weary blues. With an introduction by Carl Van Vechten. New York, Knopf, 1926. 109 p.   PS3515.U274W4 1926

1262

Johnson, Georgia D. An autumn love cycle. New York, H. Vinal, 1928. xix, 70 p. front.   PS3519.O253A8 1928

1263

Johnson, Georgia D. The heart of a woman, and other poems. With an introduction by William Stanley Braithwaite. Boston, Cornhill Co., 1918. 62 p.   PS3601.J6H4 1918

1264

Johnson, James W., *ed.* The book of American Negro poetry, chosen and edited, with an essay on the Negro's creative genius. New York, Harcourt, Brace [c1931] 300 p. music.   PS591.N4J6 1931

"Revised edition."

"Books suggested for collateral reading": p. 295-296.

1265

Johnson, James W. Fifty years & other poems. With an introduction by Brander Matthews. Boston, Cornhill Co. [c1917] xiv, 92 p.

PS3519.O2625F5

Reprinted in part from various periodicals.

1266

Johnson, James W. God's trombones; seven Negro sermons in verse. Drawings by Aaron Douglas, lettering by C. B. Falls. New York, Viking Press, 1927. 56 p. plates.   PS3519.O2625G6 1927

1267

Jones, LeRoi. The dead lecturer; poems. New York, Grove Press [1964] 79 p.   PS3519.O4545D4

1268

Kerlin, Robert T. Negro poets and their poems. 2d ed., rev. and enl. Washington, Associated Publishers [c1935] xxi, 342 p. illus., ports.
   PS591.N4K4 1935
"Index of authors, with biographical and bibliographical notes": p. 323-335.

1269

[Lanusse, Armand], *comp.* Creole voices; poems in French by free men of color, first published in 1845, edited by Edward Maceo Coleman. With a foreword by H. Carrington Lancaster. A Centennial ed. Washington, Associated Publishers, 1945. xlvi, 130 p.   PQ3937.L8L32

This anthology, compiled by Armand Lanusse, who was also one of the principal contributors, was originally published in New Orleans under title: *Les cenelles, choix de poésies indigènes.*
Present edition includes poems of V. E. Rillieux and P. A. Desdunes, two later poets (p. [109]-128).

1270

Major, Clarence, *comp.* The new black poetry. New York, International Publishers [1969] 156 p.   PS591.N4M3

1271

Murphy, Beatrice M., *ed.* Ebony rhythm; an anthology of contemporary Negro verse. Freeport, N.Y., Books for Libraries Press [1968, c1948] 162 p. (Granger index reprint series)   PS591.N4M76 1968

1272

Murphy, Beatrice M., *ed.* Negro voices; illustrations by Clifton Thompson Hill. New York, H. Harrison [c1938] 173 p. illus.   PS591.N4M8

At head of title: An anthology of contemporary verse.

1273

Pipes, James. Ziba. With decorations by Edith Mahier. Norman, University of Oklahoma Press, 1943. 188 p. illus.   PS3531.I79Z3

1274

Pool, Rosey E., *ed.* Beyond the blues, new poems by American Negroes. Lympne, Kent, Hand and Flower Press [1962] 188 p.   PS591.N4P6

Bibliography: p.186-188.

1275

Rollins, Charlemae H., *comp.* Christmas gif'; an anthology of Christmas poems, songs, and stories, written by and about Negroes. Line drawings by Tom O'Sullivan. Book design by Stan Williamson. Chicago, Follett Pub. Co. [1963] 119 p. illus.   PS509.C56R6

1276

Tolson, Melvin B. Harlem gallery. With an introduction by Karl Shapiro. Book 1. The curator. New York, Twayne [1965] 173 p.

PS3539.O334H3

1277

Tolson, Melvin B. Libretto for the Republic of Liberia. New York, Twayne Publishers [1953] 1 v. (unpaged)   PS3539.O334L5

1278

Tolson, Melvin B. Rendezvous with America. New York, Dodd, Mead, 1944. 121 p.   PS3539.O334R4

1279

Turner, Lucy M. 'Bout cullud folkses; poems. New York, H. Harrison [1938] 64 p.   PS3601.T8B6 1938

1280

Walker, Margaret. For my people. With a foreword by Stephen Vincent Benét. New Haven, Yale University Press, 1942. 58 p. (The Yale series of younger poets, [41])   PS3545.A517F6

1281

Wegelin, Oscar. Jupiter Hammon, American Negro poet; selections from his writings and a bibliography; with five facsimiles. New York, Ninety-nine copies printed for C. F. Heartman, 1915. 51 p. facsims., front. (Heartman's historical series, no. 13)   PS767.H15Z8

"No. 90 of 91 copies printed on Alexandra Japan paper."

1282

Wheatley, Phillis. Poems. Edited, with an introduction, by Julian D. Mason, Jr. Chapel Hill, University of North Carolina Press, 1966. lviii, 113 p. facsims., port.   PS866.W5 1966

1283

Wheatley, Phillis. Poems and letters; first collected edition, ed. by Chas. Fred. Heartman; with an appreciation by Arthur A. Schomburg. New York, C. F. Heartman [1915] 111 p. port. (Heartman's historical series, no. 8) PS866.W5 1915

No. 20 of 350 copies printed on Ben Day paper.

1284

Wheatley, Phillis. Poems on various subjects, religious and moral. London, Printed for A. Bell, Bookseller, Aldgate; and sold by Messrs. Cox and Berry, King-street, Boston, 1773. 124 p. port. PS866.W5 1773

1284a

White, Newman Ivey, *and* Walter C. Jackson, *eds.* An anthology of verse by American Negroes, edited with a critical introduction, biographical sketches of the authors, and bibliographical notes. With an introduction by James Hardy Dillard. Durham, N.C., Trinity College Press, 1924. 250 p. (Trinity College publications) PS591.N4W5

"Bibliographical and critical notes": p. 214-237.

1285

Wilson, Joseph T. Voice of a new race. Original selections of poems, with a trilogy and oration. Hampton, Va., Normal School Steam Press, 1882. 43 p. PS3334.W58

MEDICINE AND HEALTH

1286

Cobb, William Montague. The first Negro medical society; a history of the Medico-Chirurgical Society of the District of Columbia, 1884-1939. Washington, Associated Publishers, 1939. 159 p.   R15.M573C6

"Publications by society and members": p. 104-119. Bibliography: p. 135.

1287

Cobb, William Montague. Medical care and the plight of the Negro. New York, National Assn. for the Advancement of Colored People, 1947. 38 p. illus.   E185.88.C7

"Literature cited": p. 37-38.

1288

Cobb, William Montague. Progress and portents for the Negro in medicine. New York, National Assn. for the Advancement of Colored People, 1948. 53 p. illus., map, ports.   E185.82.C6

"Literature cited": p. 46-47.

1289

Cornely, Paul B., *and* Stanley K. Bigman. Cultural considerations in changing health attitudes. [Washington] 1961. 3 v. (185 leaves). tables.

RA448.W3C6

"Research grant 5357 (C1, C2). Division of General Medical Sciences. National Institutes of Health. U.S. Public Health Service, Department of Health, Education, and Welfare."
Bibliographical footnotes.

1290

Corwin, Edward H. L., *and* Gertrude E. Sturges. Opportunities for the medical education of Negroes. With an introduction by Dr. Walter L. Niles and a foreword by Walter White. New York, Scribner, 1936. xv, 293 p. tables.   RA982.N5H35

Report of a biracial group of medical experts and laymen on conditions at Harlem Hospital.

1291

DuBois, William E. B., *ed.* The health and physique of the Negro American. Report of a social study made under the direction of Atlanta University; together with the Proceedings of the Eleventh Conference for the Study of the Negro Problems, held at Atlanta University, on May the 29th, 1906. Atlanta, Atlanta University Press, 1906. 112 p. plates, tables. (Atlanta University publications, no. 11)
                                                   E185.5.A88 no. 11
"Bibliography of Negro health and physique": p. [6]-13.

1292

Dummett, Clifton O., *ed.* The growth and development of the Negro in dentistry in the United States. [Chicago?] National Dental Association [1952] 124 p.   E185.82.D8

1293

Grier, William H., *and* Price M. Cobbs. Black rage. Foreword by Fred R. Harris. New York, Basic Books [1968] 213 p.   E185.625.G68

The Negro authors indicate that rioting is indicative of Negro recovery rather than ill health.

1294

Grossack, Martin M., *ed.* Mental health and segregation; a selection of papers and some book chapters by David P. Ausubel [and others]. New York, Springer Pub. Co. [c1963] 247 p. tables.   E185.625.G7

Bibliography: p. 231-237.

1295

Joint Health Education Committee, *Nashville.* Rural Negro health; a report on a five-year experiment in health education in Tennessee, by Michael

J. Bent, M.D., and Ellen F. Greene, M.A., for the Joint Health Education Committee. Nashville, Julius Rosenwald Fund, 1937. 85 p. diagrs.
RA420.J73
"General references": p. 79-83.

1296
Kardiner, Abram, *and* Lionel Ovesey. The mark of oppression; explorations in the personality of the American Negro. With the assistance of William Goldfarb [and others]. Cleveland, World Pub. Co. [1962, c1951] 396 p. illus. (Meridian Books, M141)   E185.625.K3 1962

1297
Karon, Bertram P. The Negro personality; a rigorous investigation of the effects of culture. Foreword by Silvan S. Tomkins. New York, Springer Pub. Co., 1958. 184 p. illus.   E185.625.K35
Bibliography: p. 176-177.

1298
Kenney, John A. The Negro in medicine. [Tuskegee Institute, Ala., Printed by the Tuskegee Institute Press, c1912] 60 p. plates (part fold.), ports.
E185.82.K36

1299
Lott, Albert J., *and* Bernice E. Lott. Negro and white youth; a psychological study in a border-state community. New York, Holt, Rinehart and Winston [1963] 236 p.   BF731.L6
Includes bibliographies.

1300
Lynk, Miles V. Sixty years of medicine; or, The life and times of Dr. Miles V. Lynk, an autobiography. Memphis, Twentieth Century Press, c1951. 125 p. ports.   R154.L96A3

1301
Malzberg, Benjamin. Statistical data for the study of mental disease among Negroes in New York State, 1949-1951. Albany, 1959. 405 p. tables.
RC444.N4M3
"This study is reprinted from *Mental Hygiene,* volume 43, no. 3, July 1959."

1302
Morais, Herbert M. The history of the Negro in medicine. New York, Publishers Co. [1967] xiv, 317 p. illus., facsims., ports. (International library of Negro life and history)   R695.M6

Published under the auspices of the Association for the Study of Negro Life and History.

Bibliography: p. 281-304.

1303

National Medical Fellowships. Opportunities for Negroes in medicine. Chicago, 1959. 29 p.   E185.82.N38

1304

Negro Health Survey, *Pittsburgh.* Tuberculosis and the Negro in Pittsburgh; a report of the Negro health survey, by Elsie Witchen, director, Negro Health Survey. [Pittsburgh] Tuberculosis League of Pittsburgh, 1934. 120 p. diagrs., maps, plates, tables.   RC313.A57N4

1305

Parker, Seymour, *and* Robert J. Kleiner. Mental illness in the urban Negro community. New York, Free Press [c1966] xiv, 408 p. illus.

RC451.5.N4P35

"Financial assistance received from the National Institutes of Health (grant numbers M-3047, M-5661, and MH-07494-01) and from the Pennsylvania Mental Research Foundation."

Bibliography: p. 349-362.

1306

Pettigrew, Thomas F. A profile of the Negro American. Princeton, Van Nostrand [1964] xiv, 250 p. illus.   E185.625.P4

Bibliography: p. 202-235.

1307

Peyton, Thomas R. Quest for dignity; an autobiography of a Negro doctor. [Rev. reprinting] Los Angeles, Publishers Western, 1963 [c1950] 160 p. illus.   R154.P49A3 1963

1308

Reitzes, Dietrich C. Negroes and medicine. Cambridge, Published for the Commonwealth Fund by Harvard University Press, 1958. 400 p. illus.

E185.82.R46

1309

Rohrer, John H., *and* Munro S. Edmonson, *eds.* The eighth generation: cultures and personalities of New Orleans Negroes. Co-authors: Harold Lief, Daniel Thompson [and] William Thompson. New York, Harper [1960] 346 p. diagrs., tables.   E185.625.R6

"This volume reports a research project carried out during the years 1953-1956 at the Urban Life Research Institute of Tulane University ... The responsibility for its direction rested with Dr. John H. Rohrer." Bibliographical footnotes.

1310
Spencer, Gerald A. Cosmetology in the Negro: a guide to its problems. [New York, Arlain Print. Co., 1944] 127 p. illus.　　　RL71.S65
Bibliographical footnotes.

1311
Spencer, Gerald A. Medical symphony, a study of the contributions of the Negro to medical progress in New York. [New York, c1947] 120 p. ports.　　　R292.N7S63
"References": p. 9.

MILITARY SERVICE

1312
Aptheker, Herbert. The Negro in the Civil War. New York, International
Publishers [c1938] 48 p.   E453.A67
"Suggested readings": p. 47-48.

1313
Brown, Earl L., and George R. Leighton. The Negro and the war. [New
York, Public Affairs Committee] 1942. 32 p. diagrs. (Public affairs
pamphlets, no. 71)   E185.61.B877
"For further reading": p. 32.

1314
Brown, William W. The Negro in the American rebellion, his heroism and
his fidelity. Boston, Lee & Shepard, 1867. xvi, 380 p.   E540.N3B8

1315
Cashin, Herschel V., and others. Under fire. With the Tenth U.S. Cavalry.
Being a brief, comprehensive review of the Negro's participation in the
wars of the United States. With introduction by Major-General Joseph
Wheeler. Illustrated with over one hundred fine engravings from original
photographs. New York, F. T. Neely [c1899] xv, 361 p. illus., plates,
ports.   E725.5.C33
Reprint issued by Arno Press, 1969.

1316
Cornish, Dudley T. The sable arm; Negro troops in the Union Army, 1861-1865. New York, W. W. Norton [1966, c1956] 337 p. (The Norton library, N334)   E540.N3C77 1966

Bibliography: p. 316-332.

1317
Emilio, Luis F. History of the Fifty-fourth Regiment of Massachusetts Volunteer Infantry, 1863-1865. Boston, Boston Book Co., 1891 xvi, 410 p. maps (part fold.), ports.   E513.5 54th

Cover title: A Brave Black Regiment.
Reprint issued by Arno Press, 1969.

1318
Francis, Charles E. The Tuskegee airmen; the story of the Negro in the U.S. Air Force. Boston, Bruce Humphries [1956, c1955] 225 p. illus.
                                                        D810.N4F76

1319
Heywood, Chester D. Negro combat troops in the World War; the story of the 371st Infantry. With maps, photographs and illustrations; pen and ink drawings by D. Lester Dickson. Worcester, Mass., Commonwealth Press [c1928] 310 p. illus., 2 fold. maps (in pocket)
                                                        D570.33 371st.H4

1320
Higginson, Thomas W. Army life in a black regiment. With an introduction by Howard Mumford Jones. [East Lansing] Michigan State University Press, 1960 [i.e. 1961] 235 p.   E492.94 33d H5 1961

First published in 1870.

1321
Johns Hopkins University. Operations Research Office. Utilization of Negro manpower in the Army: a 1951 study. A team research study by staff members, consultants, and subcontractors of the Operations Research Office of the Johns Hopkins University. Alfred H. Hausrath, project director. McLean, Va., Research Analysis Corp., 1967. 1 v. (various pagings) illus.   E185.63.J6

A condensed and unclassified ed. of a 7-vol. draft report (1951) based on a study conducted in Korea and the U.S. as Project CLEAR. "References": p. R1-R7.

1322

Leckie, William H. The buffalo soldiers; a narrative of the Negro cavalry in the West. Norman, University of Oklahoma Press [1967] xiv, 290 p illus., maps, ports.   UA31 10th.L4

Bibliography: p. 262-276.

1323

Lee, Irvin H. Negro Medal of Honor men. New York, Dodd, Mead [1967] 139 p. illus., ports.   UB433.L4

Bibliography: p. 131-132.

1324

Lee, Ulysses G. The employment of Negro troops. Washington, Office of the Chief of Military History, United States Army; [for sale by the Supt. of Docs., U.S. Govt. Print. Off.] 1966. xix, 740 p. illus., map (part fold., part col.), ports. (United States Army in World War II Special studies)   D810.N4L4

Bibliographical footnotes.

1325

McConnell, Roland C. Negro troops of antebellum Louisiana; a history of the Battalion of Free Men of Color. Baton Rouge, Louisiana State University Press [c1968] 143 p. facsim., map. (Louisiana State University studies. Social science series, no. 13)   UA220.M3

Bibliography: p. 135-140. Bibliographical references included in "Notes" (p. 116-133).

1326

Mandelbaum, David G. Soldier groups and Negro soldiers. Berkeley, University of California Press, 1952. 142 p.   E185.63.M35

Bibliography: p. 133-138.

1327

Mason, Monroe, *and* Arthur Furr. The American Negro soldier with the Red Hand of France. Boston, Cornhill Co. [c1920] 180 p. plan, plates port.   D639.N4M3

1328

Miller, Kelly. Kelly Miller's history of the world war for human rights being an intensely human and brilliant account of the World War and why and for what purpose America and the allies are fighting and the important part taken by the Negro. Washington, Austin Jenkins Co. [c1919] 608 p. plates, ports.   D523.M46

Published also with slight variations in text, under title: *Our War for Human Rights.*

1329
Nell, William C. The colored patriots of the American Revolution. New York, Arno Press, 1968. 396 p. illus. (The American Negro, his history and literature)   E269.N3N4 1968

Reprint of the 1855 ed.

1330
Quarles, Benjamin. The Negro in the American Revolution. Chapel Hill, Published for the Institute of Early American History and Culture, Williamsburg, Va., by University of North Carolina Press [1961] 231 p.
                                    E269.N3Q3
Bibliography: p. [201]-223.

1331
Quarles, Benjamin. The Negro in the Civil War. Boston, Little, Brown [1953] xvi, 379 p. illus.   E540.N3Q3

Bibliography: p. [349]-360.

1332
Scott, Emmett J. Scott's official history of the American Negro in the World War. Prefaced with highest tributes to the American Negro by Hon. Newton D. Baker, Gen. John J. Pershing, and the late Theodore Roosevelt. [Chicago, Homewood Press, c1919] 511 p. illus., plates, ports.   D639.N4S3

Reprint issued by Arno Press, 1969.

1333
Sherman, George R. The Negro as a soldier. By George R. Sherman, [captain Seventh United States Colored Infantry and brevet-lieut.-colonel United States Volunteers] Providence, The Society, 1913. 34 p. ports. (Personal narratives of events in the War of the Rebellion, being papers read before the Rhode Island Soldiers and Sailors Historical Society. 7th ser., no. 7)   E464.R47
                                    E540.N3S55
                                    E492.9 7th

1334
Singletary, Otis A. Negro militia and Reconstruction. Austin, University of Texas Press [1957] 181 p. illus.   E668.S59

Bibliography: p. 153-166.

1335
Steward, Theophilus G. The colored regulars in the United States Army. New York, Arno Press, 1969. 344 p. illus., ports. (The American Negro; his history and literature)   E725.5.N3S8 1969

Reprint of the 1904 ed., with a new preface by W. L. Katz.

1336
Stillman, Richard J. Integration of the Negro in the U.S. Armed Forces. New York, Praeger [1968] 167 p. illus. (Praeger special studies in U.S. economic and social development)   E185.63.S7 1968

Includes bibliographical references.

1337
Taylor, Susie K. Reminiscences of my life in camp. New York, Arno Press, 1968. 82 p. illus., ports. (The American Negro; his history and litera-ture)   E492.94 33d.T3 1968

Reprint of the 1902 ed.

1338
U.S. *Commission on Civil Rights. South Dakota Advisory Committee.* Negro airmen in a northern community; discrimination in Rapid City, South Dakota; a report. [Washington, U.S. Govt. Print. Off.] 1963. 50 p.   F659.R2U5

Cover title: *Report on Rapid City.*

1339
U.S. *President's Committee on Equal Opportunity in the Armed Forces.* Equality of treatment and opportunity for Negro military personnel stationed within the United States; initial report. [Washington] 1963. 93 p.   E185.63.U63

1340
Wesley, Charles H., *and* Patricia W. Romero. Negro Americans in the Civil War; from slavery to citizenship. New York, Publishers Co. [1967] 307 p. illus., facsims., maps, ports. (International library of Negro life and history)   E540.N3W4

Published under the auspices of the Association for the Study of Negro Life and History.

Bibliography: p. [273]-285.

1341

Wesley, Charles H. Ohio Negroes in the Civil War. [Columbus] Ohio State University Press for the Ohio Historical Society [1962] 46 p. (Publications of the Ohio Civil War Centennial Commission, no. 6)

E525.O337 no. 6

Includes bibliography.

1342

Williams, George W. A history of the Negro troops in the War of the Rebellion, 1861-65; preceded by a review of the military services of Negroes in ancient and modern times. New York, Bergman Publishers [1968] xvi, 353 p. illus., port.   E540.N3W7 1968

Reprint of the 1888 ed.
Bibliographical footnotes.

1343

Wilson, Joseph T. The black phalanx. New York, Arno Press, 1968. 528 p. illus. (The American Negro; his history and literature)

E185.63.W815 1968

Reprint of the 1890 ed.
Bibliography: p. 517.

MUSIC

1344

Allen, William F., *comp.* Slave songs of the United States; the complete
original collection (136 songs) collected and compiled by William
Francis Allen, Charles Pickard Ware, and Lucy McKim Garrison in
1867, with new piano arrangements and guitar chords by Irving Schlein
[New York] Oak Publications [1965] 175 p. illus.   M1670.A42 196

Includes facsim. of title page and preface of 1st ed. (New York,
Simpson, 1867).

1345

Bradford, Perry. Born with the blues; Perry Bradford's own story. The true
story of the pioneering blues singers and musicians in the early days of
jazz. New York, Oak Publications [c1965] 175 p. illus.

ML410.B779B

1346

Carawan, Guy, *and* Candie Carawan. Ain't you got a right to the tree of
life? The people of Johns Island, South Carolina, their faces, their
words, and their songs, recorded by Guy and Candie Carawan. Photo
graphed by Robert Yellin. Music transcribed by Ethel Raim, with a
preface by Alan Lomax. New York, Simon and Schuster [1967, c1966]
190 p. illus., map.   E185.93.S7C

Includes melodies with words.
Bibliography: p. [11].

1347

Chambers, Herbert A., *ed.* The treasury of Negro spirituals. [Foreword by Marian Anderson] New York, Emerson Books [1963, c1959] 125 p. illus. M1670.C45T7

Contains 30 well-known spirituals, arranged for voice and piano, and six modern compositions, two of which are arranged for male quartet.

1348

Charters, Samuel B. The bluesmen; the story and the music of the men who made the blues. New York, Oak Publications [1967+] illus., music, ports. ML3561.J3C425

Contents.–v. 1. "The singers and the styles from Mississippi, Alabama, and Texas up to the Second World War, with a brief consideration of some of the traceable relationships between the blues and African song."

1349

Courlander, Harold. Negro folk music, U.S.A. New York, Columbia University Press, 1963. 324 p. illus., music. ML3556.C7

"The music" (melodies with words): p. [221]-287.
Bibliography: p. [299]-301. Discography: p. [302]-308.

1350

Dennison, Tim. The American Negro and his amazing music. New York, Vantage Press [1963] 76 p. ML3556.D45

1351

Dett, Robert Nathaniel, *ed.* Religious folk-songs of the Negro as sung at Hampton Institute. Hampton, Va., Hampton Institute Press, 1927. xxvii, 236 p. M1670.H3 1927

1352

Fisher, Miles M. Negro slave songs in the United States. New York, Russell & Russell [1968, c1953] xv, 223 p. ML3556.F58

Foreword by Ray Allen Billington.
Includes texts of the songs, without the music.
Bibliography: p. 193-213.
Reprint also issued by Citadel Press, 1963.

1353

Handy, William C., *ed.* Blues; an anthology. With an introduction by Abbe Niles. Illustrations by Miguel Covarrubias. New York, A. & C. Boni, 1926. 180 p. illus.   M1630.18.H26B5 1926
                                              ML30.25e.H35
Music: p. 49-180.

1354

Handy, William C., *ed.* A treasury of the blues; complete words and music of 67 great songs from Memphis blues to the present day. With an historical and critical text by Abbe Niles. With pictures by Miguel Covarrubias. [New York?] C. Boni; distributed by Simon and Schuster [1949] 258 p. illus.   M1630.18.H26B5 1949

First ed. published in 1926 under title: *Blues, an Anthology.*
"A selective bibliography": p. 254-255.

1355

Hare, Maud C. Negro musicians and their music. Washington, Associated Publishers [1936] 439 p. plates, ports.   ML3556.H3N4

Includes music.
Bibliography: p. 419-423.

1356

Hayes, Roland. My songs; Aframerican religious folk songs arranged and interpreted by Roland Hayes. Boston, Little, Brown, 1948. 128 p.
                                              M1670.H4M9
"An Atlantic Monthly Press book."

1357

Jackson, Clyde O. The songs of our years; a study of Negro folk music. New York, Exposition Press [1968] 54 p. (An Exposition-University book)   ML3556.J39

Bibliography: p. [53]-54.

1358

Jackson, George P. White and Negro spirituals, their life span and kingship tracing 200 years of untrammeled song making and singing among our country folk, with 116 songs as sung by both races. New York, J. J Augustin [1944] 349 p. illus., music, ports.   ML3551.J17

"The tune comparative list. One hundred and sixteen melodies of white people paired with same number of Negro-sung variants". p. [145]-227.

1359
Johnson, James W., *ed.* The book of American Negro spirituals, edited with an introduction of James Weldon Johnson; musical arrangements by J. Rosamond Johnson, additional numbers by Lawrence Brown. New York, Viking Press, 1925. 187 p.   M1670.J67

1360
Johnson, James W., *and* John Rosamond Johnson, *eds.* The books of American Negro spirituals, including The book of American Negro spirituals and The second book of Negro spirituals. New York, Viking Press, 1940. 2 v. in 1.   M1670.J67B65

For voice and piano.
A reissue of the volumes first published separately in 1925 and 1926. Each volume has special t.p.
Musical arrangements by J. Rosamond Johnson, additional numbers by Lawrence Brown.

1361
ones, LeRoi. Black music. New York, W. Morrow, 1967. 221 p. illus.
          ML3556.J728

1362
ones, LeRoi. Blues people; Negro music in white America. New York, W. Morrow, 1963. 244 p.   ML3556.J73

1363
eil, Charles. Urban blues. Chicago, University of Chicago Press [1966] 231 p.   ML3556.K43

1364
irkeby, W. T. E. Duncan P. Schiedt, *and* Sinclair Traill. Ain't misbe-havin'; the story of Fats Waller. New York, Dodd, Mead [1966] 248 p. ports.   ML417.W15K6 1966a

"The music of Thomas 'Fats' Waller; a selective discography compiled by the 'Storyville Team'": p. 233-248.

1365
rehbiel, Henry E. Afro-American folksongs; a study in racial and national music. New York, F. Ungar Pub. Co. [1962] 176 p. music.
          ML3556.K9 1962
Reprint of the 1914 ed.

1366

Locke, Alain L. The Negro and his music. Port Washington, N.Y., Kenn
kat Press [1968] 142 p. (Kennikat Press series in Negro culture an
history)   ML3556.L6N4 196

   Reprint of the ed. first published in 1936.

   "Reading references" at end of each chapter. "Record illustrations
at end of most of the chapters.

1367

Lomax, John A., *and* Alan Lomax, *eds.* Negro folk songs as sung by Lea
Belly, "king of the twelve-string guitar players of the world," long-tin
convict in the penitentiaries of Texas and Louisiana. New York, Ma
millan Co., 1936. xiv, 242 p. port.   ML1670.L84N

   "The main body of the song-texts consists of transcriptions fro
records we made with an instantaneous aluminum recording machin
the property of the Archive of American Folk-song of the Library of
Congress. This machine and these records were used through the cou
tesy of the Library of Congress. Dr. George Herzog transcribed th
melodies, as herein printed, from these same discs."—Introductio
p. xiii.

1368

Lucas, John. Basic jazz on long play. The great soloists: ragtime, folkson
blues, jazz, swing, and the great bands: New Orleans, swing, dixielan
Northfield, Minn., Carleton Jazz Club, Carleton College, 1954. 103
(Carleton College, Northfield, Minn. Carleton Jazz Club. Bulletin no.
                                                ML3561.J3L

1369

Nathan, Hans. Dan Emmett and the rise of early Negro minstrelsy. Ne
man, University of Oklahoma Press [1962] xiv, 496 p. illus., facsims.
                                                ML410.E51

   Includes unaccompanied melodies.

   "Bibliography of the works of D. D. Emmett": p. 290-306. "Anth
ogy" (principally melodies with piano accompaniment): p. [311]-49

1370

Niles, John J. Singing soldiers. Illustrated by Margaret Thorniley Willia
son. New introduction by Leslie Shepard. Detroit, Singing Tree Pre
1968. 171 p. illus.   M1629.N675S45 19

   First published in 1927 by C. Scribner's Sons, New York. "No
reissued."

   Contains both accompanied and unaccompanied melodies w
words.

1371
Odum, Howard W., *and* Guy B. Johnson. The Negro and his songs; a study of typical Negro songs in the South. Hatboro, Pa., Folklore Associates, 1964 [c1925] xix, 306 p. ML3556.O3 1964
"Reprinted from the original ed. of 1925."
"Select bibliography of Negro folk songs": p. [297]-300.

1372
Patterson, Lindsay, *comp.* The Negro in music and art. New York, Publishers Co. [1967] xvi, 304 p. illus., facsims., ports. (International library of Negro life and history) ML3556.P38
Published under the auspices of the Association for the Study of Negro Life and History.
Bibliography: p. [291]-296.

1373
Ramsey, Frederic. Been here and gone. New Brunswick, N.J., Rutgers University Press [1960] 177 p. illus. ML3556.R3

1374
Ramsey, Frederic, *and* Charles E. Smith, *eds.* Jazzmen. New York, Harcourt, Brace [1959, c1939] 360 p. illus. (A Harvest book, 30)
ML3561.J3R3 1959

1375
Scarborough, Dorothy. On the trail of Negro folk-songs, by Dorothy Scarborough, assisted by Ola Lee Gulledge. Foreword by Roger D. Abrahams. Hatboro, Pa., Folklore Associates, 1963. 295 p. music.
ML3556.S3 1925a
"Reprinted in facsimile from the original edition of 1925."

1376
Shapiro, Nat, *and* Nat Hentoff, *comps.* Hear me talkin' to ya; the story of jazz as told by the men who made it. New York, Dover Publications [1966, c1955] xvi, 429 p. ML3561.J3S46 1966
"This Dover edition is a reprint of the work originally published by Rinehart and Company, Inc., in 1955."

1377
Talley, Thomas W., *comp.* Negro folk rhymes, wise and otherwise, with a study. Port Washington, N.Y., Kennikat Press [1968, c1922] 347 p. (Kennikat Press series in Negro culture and history) PS595.N3T3 1968
Includes music (principally melodies with words).

1378

Thurman, Howard. Deep river; reflections on the religious insight of ce: tain of the Negro spirituals. Illustrated by Elizabeth Orton Jones. [Rev and enl.] New York, Harper [1955] 93 p. illus.   ML3556.T55 195

1379

Thurman, Howard. The Negro spiritual speaks of life and death. Nev York, Harper [1947] 55 p. (The Ingersoll lecture, Harvard University 1947)   ML3556.T5

1380

Trotter, James M. Music and some highly musical people; containing brie chapers on I. A description of music. II. The music of nature. III. glance at the history of music. IV. The power, beauty, and uses c music. Following which are given sketches of the lives of remarkabl musicians of the colored race. With portraits, and an appendix contaim ing copies of music composed by colored men. Boston, Lee an Shepard, 1878. 353, 152 p. ports.   ML60.T8

Music: Appendix, p. 4-152.

1381

Williams Martin T. Jazz masters of New Orleans. New York, Macmillan C« [1967] xvii, 287 p. ports. (The Macmillan jazz masters series)

ML3561.J3W531

Bibliographies and discographies at ends of chapters.

1382

ell, Inge P. CORE and the strategy of nonviolence. New York, Random House [1968] 214 p. (Random House studies in sociology)

E185.61.B37

Includes bibliographies.

1383

rooks, Charles H. A history and manual of the Grand United Order of Odd Fellows in America. Philadelphia, 1893. 257 p. ports.

HS1171.3.B8

1384

ass, Donn A. Negro freemasonry and segregation; an historical study of prejudice against American Negroes as Freemasons, and the position of Negro Freemasonry in the Masonic fraternity. Chicago, E. A. Cook Publications, 1957. 152 p. illus.   HS883.C3

Bibliography: p. [150]-152.

1385

lark, Alexander G. History of Prince Hall Freemasonry (1775-1945). Des Moines, United Grand Lodge of Iowa, F. & A. M. (Prince Hall Affiliation) [1947] 337 p. port.   HS883.C47

Completed by S. Joe Brown after the death of the author.

"With special reference to the Grand Lodge of Missouri (Prince Hall Affiliation) and the three Iowa Grand Lodges that grew out of it."

1386

Davis, Harry E. A history of freemasonry among Negroes in America. [Cleveland? 1946] 334 p.   HS883.D35

"Published under auspices of the United Supreme Council, Ancient & Accepted Scottish Rite of Freemasonry, Northern Jurisdiction, U.S.A. (Prince Hall affiliation), Incorporated."

Includes bibliographies.

1387

Hughes, Langston. Fight for freedom; the story of the NAACP. New York, Norton [1962] 224 p. illus.   E185.5.N276H8

Bibliography: p. 207-208.

1388

Kellogg, Charles F. NAACP, a history of the National Association for the Advancement of Colored People. v. 1. 1909-1920. Baltimore, Johns Hopkins Press [1967] 332 p. illus., ports.   E185.5.N276K4, v. 1

"Bibliographical notes": p. 309-315.

1389

Matthews, Joseph B. Communism and the NAACP. [Atlanta, Georgia Commission on Education, 1958?] 2 v.   E185.5.M3

1390

Miller, Helen S. The history of Chi Eta Phi Sorority, Inc., 1932-1967. Durham, N.C. [Association for the Study of Negro Life and History, 1968] xvi, 244 p. ports.   LJ105.C45M5

1391

Myers, Phineas B. Ninety-five years after Lincoln; a history of the Urban League of Dayton, Ohio. [2d, rev. ed.] New York, Exposition Press [1959] 103 p. illus.   F499.D2M9 1959

"The 1950 edition was published under the title: *Eighty-five Years after Lincoln.*"

1392

National Urban League. The National Urban League re-examined; a policy to guide the Urban League in its interracial social service program. Statement and recommendations from the board convention of the National Urban League, April 15-17, 1955 . . . Kansas City, Missouri. [New York, 1955] 40 p.   E185.5.N33A44

1393
National Urban League. The Urban League story, 1910-1960; golden 50th anniversary year book. [William R. Simms, editor. New York, c1961] 66 p. illus.   E185.5.N33A53

1394
Record, Wilson. Race and radicalism; the NAACP and the Communist Party in conflict. Ithaca, N.Y., Cornell University Press [1964] xv, 237 p. (Communism in American life)   E185.5.N276R4

Cornell studies in civil liberty.
Bibliographical footnotes.

1395
Strickland, Arvarh E. History of the Chicago Urban League. Urbana, University of Illinois Press, 1966. 286 p.   F548.9.N3S76

Bibliography: p. [265]-272. Bibliographical footnotes.

1396
Voorhis, Harold V. Negro masonry in the United States. New York City, H. Emmerson, 1940. 132 p. facsims., ports.   HS883.V6

Bibliography: p. 126-128.

1396a
Vroman, Mary E. Shaped to its purpose: Delta Sigma Theta—the first fifty years. New York, Random House [1965] 213 p.   LJ145.D58V7

1397
Wesley, Charles H. The history of Alpha Phi Alpha; a development in Negro college life. [3d ed., rev. and enl.] Washington, Foundation Publishers, 1939. xxi, 396 p. illus., ports.   LJ121.A55W4 1939

"National Alpha Phi Alpha hymn" (words and music): p. 313-315.

1398
Wesley, Charles H. History of the Improved Benevolent and Protective Order of Elks of the World, 1898-1954. Washington, Association for the Study of Negro Life and History [1955] 503 p. illus.
                                                                           HS2259.E53W4

1399
Wesley, Charles H. The history of the Prince Hall Grand Lodge of Free and Accepted Masons of the State of Ohio, 1849-1960; an epoch in American fraternalism. Wilberforce, Ohio, Central State College Press [1961] 457 p. illus.   HS887.O3W4

1400
Wynn, Daniel W. The NAACP versus Negro revolutionary protest; a comparative study of the effectiveness of each movement. New York, Exposition Press [1955] 115 p. (Exposition—University book)

E185.61.W9

Bibliography: p. [103]-110.

1401
Zinn, Howard. S N C C , the new abolitionists. Boston, Beacon Pres[1964] 246 p. E185.61.Z4

1402

ikin, Charles, *ed*. The Negro votes. San Francisco, Chandler Pub. Co. [1962] 377 p. illus. (Chandler publications in political science)

DLC-LL

1403

merican Negro Academy, *Washington, D.C.* The Negro and the elective franchise. A series of papers and a sermon. Washington, 1905. 85 p. (Occasional papers, no. 11)   E184.N3A5

Contents.—1. Meaning and need of the movement to reduce southern representation [by] A. H. Grimke.—2. The penning of the Negro (the Negro vote in the States of the revised constitutions) [by] C. C. Cook.—3. The Negro vote in the States whose constitutions have not been specifically revised [by] John Hope.—4. The potentiality of the Negro vote, North and West [by] John L. Love.—5. Migration and distribution of the Negro population as affecting the elective franchise [by] Kelly Miller.—6. The Negro and his citizenship [by] Rev. F. J. Grimke.

1404

shmore, Harry S. The man in the middle. Columbia, University of Missouri Press [1966] 58 p. (The Paul Anthony Brick lectures, 5th ser.)

E846.A8

1405

Bailey, Harry A., *ed*. Negro politics in America. Columbus, Ohio, C. E. Merrill Books [1967] 455 p. illus., maps.   E185.6.B15

Includes bibliographical references.

1406

Banfield, Edward C., *and* James Q. Wilson. City politics. Cambridge, Harvard University Press, 1963. 362 p. illus. (Publications of the Joint Center for Urban Studies of the Massachusetts Institute of Technology and Harvard University)   JS331.B28

Bibliographical footnotes.

1407

Brewer, John Mason. Negro legislators of Texas and their descendants; a history of the Negro in Texas politics from Reconstruction to disfranchisement, with an introduction by Herbert P. Gambrell. Dallas, Tex., Mathis Pub. Co. [c1935] 134 p. map, ports.   E185.93.T4B7

1408

Brogan, Denis W. Politics in America. New York, Harper [c1954] 467 p.
                    JK268.B72 1954a
Bibliography: p. 436-441.
Chapter 3 is on race and politics.

1409

Brooke, Edward W. The challenge of change; crisis in our two-party system. Boston, Little, Brown [1966] xviii, 269 p.   E743.B77

Bibliography: p. 267-269.

1409a

Brown, William G. The new politics, and other papers. Boston, Houghton Mifflin Co., 1914. 234 p. port.   JK271.B67

Contents.—The new politics.—Prophetic voices about America.—The white peril: the immediate danger of the Negro.—The South and the saloon.—President Taft's opportunity.—Greetings to the presidents.

1410

Buni, Andrew. The Negro in Virginia politics, 1902-1965. Charlottesville, University Press of Virginia [1967] 296 p.   E185.93.V8B86

Bibliography: p. [271]-285.

1411

Clayton, Edward T. The Negro politician, his success and failure. With an introduction by Martin Luther King, Jr. Chicago, Johnson Pub. Co., 1964. xiv, 213 p. E185.6.C637

1412

Cornell-Tompkins County Committee for Free and Fair Elections in Fayette County, Tennessee. Step by step; evolution and operation of the Cornell students' civil-rights project in Tennessee, summer, 1964, by Fayette County Project Volunteers. New York, Published for the Fayette County Fund by W. W. Norton[1965] 128 p. illus. F443.F3C6

Edited by Douglas F. Dowd and Mary D. Nichols.

1413

Coulter, Ellis Merton. Negro legislators in Georgia during the Reconstruction period. Athens, Georgia Historical Quarterly, 1968. 209 p. port.
E185.93.G4C6

"This book is limited to 250 copies."

Contains articles which originally appeared in the *Georgia Historical Quarterly*.

Bibliographical references included in "Notes" (p. [181]-196).

Bibliography: p. [197]-201.

1414

Cox, LaWanda C. F., *and* John H. Cox. Politics, principle, and prejudice, 1865-1866; dilemma of Reconstruction America. [New York] Free Press of Glencoe [1963] 294 p. E666.C84

Bibliographical references included in "Notes" (p. 233-281). Bibliography: p. 283-286.

1415

Cromwell, John W. The challenge of the disfranchised; a plea for the enforcement of the 15th amendment. Washington, The Academy, 1924. 10 p. (American Negro Academy. Occasional papers, no. 22)
E185.5.A51 no. 22

1416

De Santis, Vincent P. Republicans face the Southern question: the new departure years, 1877-1897. Baltimore, Johns Hopkins Press, 1959. 275 p. maps. (The Johns Hopkins University studies in historical and political science, ser. 77, no. 1) H31.J6 ser. 77, no. 1
F215.D345

Bibliographical footnotes.

1417

Edmonds, Helen G. The Negro and fusion politics in North Carolina 1894-1901. Chapel Hill, University of North Carolina Press [1951] 260 p. illus., maps.   E185.93.N6E

   Bibliography: p. 239-247.

1418

Fleming, George J. An all-Negro ticket in Baltimore. [New York] Holt Rinehart and Winston [1960] 16 p. (Case studies in practical politics
                                                           JS590.Z5 4th.F

1419

Ford, James W. The Negro and the democratic front. Introduction by A. W. Berry. New York, International Publishers [c1938] 222 p. port.
                                                              E185.6.F6

1420

Gosnell, Harold F. Negro politicians; the rise of Negro politics in Chicago With an introduction by James Q. Wilson. Chicago, University of Chicago Press [1967] xix, 396 p. maps, ports.   F548.9.N3G67 196

   "Originally published in 1935."
   Bibliographical footnotes.

1421

Heard, Alexander. A two-party South? Chapel Hill, University of North Carolina Press [1952] xviii, 334 p. diagrs., maps.   F215.H4

   Bibliographical references included in "Notes" (p. 281-318).

1422

Hirshson, Stanley P. Farewell to the bloody shirt; northern Republicans & the southern Negro, 1877-1893. Introduction by David Donald. Bloom ington, Indiana University Press [1962] 334 p.   E661.H58

   Bibliography: p. 259-273.

1423

Jarrell, Hampton M. Wade Hampton and the Negro; the road not taken Columbia, University of South Carolina Press, 1949. 209 p. port.
                                                          E467.1.H19J

   Bibliography: p. 189-193.

1424

Jarrette, Alfred Q. Politics and the Negro. Boston, Vinjano Educational Publishers, 1964. 54 p. illus., facsims., map, ports.   E185.96.J3

   Bibliography: p. 54.

1425

Keech, William R. The impact of Negro voting; the role of the vote in the quest for equality. Chicago, Rand McNally [1968] 113 p. (American politics research series)   JK1929.A2K4

    Bibliographical footnotes.

1426

Key, Valdimer O. Southern politics in State and Nation. With the assistance of Alexander Heard. New York, Knopf, 1949. xxvi, 675, xiv p. illus., maps, ports.   F215.K45 1949

    Bibliographical footnotes.

1427

Ladd, Everett C. Negro political leadership in the South. Ithaca, N.Y., Cornell University Press [1966] 348 p. fold. map.   E185.61.L22

    Bibliography: p. 333-342.

1428

Lewinson, Paul. Race, class & party; a history of Negro suffrage and white politics in the South. New York, Russell & Russell, 1963 [c1959] 302 p. illus.   JK1929.A2L4 1963

    First issued in 1932.
    Bibliography: p. 283-292.

1429

Logan, Rayford W., *ed.* The attitude of the southern white press toward Negro suffrage, 1932-1940. With a foreword by Charles H. Wesley. Washington, Foundation Publishers, 1940. 115 p.   JK1929.A2L6

1430

Mabry, William A. The Negro in North Carolina politics since Reconstruction. Durham, N.C., Duke University Press, 1940. 87 p. (Historical papers of the Trinity College Historical Society, ser. 23)

                                     F251.D83 ser. 23
    Bibliography: p. [84]-87.

1431

Matthews, Donald R., *and* James W. Prothro. Negroes and the new southern politics. New York, Harcourt, Brace & World [1966] xvi, 551 p. illus.   E185.61.M38

    Bibliographical footnotes.

1432

Moon, Henry L. Balance of power: the Negro vote. Garden City, N.Y., Doubleday, 1948. 256 p.   JK2275.N4M6

  Bibliographical footnotes.

1433

Morton, Richard L. The Negro in Virginia politics, 1865-1902. Charlottes-ville, University of Virginia, 1919. 199 p. fold. maps. (Publications of the University of Virginia. Phelps-Stokes fellowship paper, no. 4)

E185.93.V8M82

  Published also as thesis (Ph.D.), University of Virginia, 1919.
  Bibliography: p. [163]-165.

1434

Nolan, William A. Communism versus the Negro. Chicago, H. Regnery Co., 1951. xvii, 276 p.   E185.61.N87

  Bibliographical references included in "Notes" (p. [207]-267).

1435

Nowlin, William F. The Negro in American national politics. Boston, Strat-ford Co. [c1931] 148 p.   JK2275.N4N6

  Bibliography: p. 145-148.

1436

Ogden, Frederic D. The poll tax in the South. [University] University of Alabama Press, 1958. xiv, 301 p. diagrs., tables.   HJ4931.A13O4

  "Originally submitted as a doctoral dissertation at the Johns Hop-kins University."
  Bibliographical footnotes.

1437

Olbrich, Emil. The development of sentiment on Negro suffrage to 1860. [Madison] University of Wisconsin, 1912. 135 p. (Bulletin of the University of Wisconsin, no. 477. History series, v. 3, no. 1)

H31.W62 v. 3, no. 1
JK1923.O55

  Thesis (M.A.)—University of Wisconsin, 1906.
  Bibliography: p. 129-135.

1438

Perry, Jennings. Democracy begins at home, the Tennessee fight on the poll tax. Cartoons by Tom Little. Philadelphia, J. B. Lippincott Co. [1944] 280 p. illus., diagr.   HJ4931.T4P4

1439
Pike, James S. The prostrate State; South Carolina under Negro government. Edited with an introduction to the Torchbook ed. by Robert F. Durden. New York, Harper & Row [1968] xlii, 279 p. (Harper Torchbooks, TB3085) F274.P632 1968

Reprint of the 1874 ed.
Bibliographical footnotes.

1440
Price, Hugh D. The Negro and Southern politics; a chapter of Florida history. With an introduction by William G. Carleton. [New York] New York University Press, 1957. xviii, 133 p. facsims., maps, tables.
E185.93.F5P7

Based on thesis (M.A.)–University of Florida.
Bibliographical references included in "Notes" (p. 113-124). Bibliography: p. 125-128.

1441
Price, Margaret W. The Negro and the ballot in the South. Atlanta, Southern Regional Council, 1959. 83 p. tables. JK1929.A2P7

Bibliographical footnotes.

1442
Record, Wilson. The Negro and the Communist Party. Chapel Hill, University of North Carolina Press [1951] 340 p. E185.61.R29

Bibliographical references included in "Notes" (p. 317-331).

1443
Riley, Jerome R. The philosophy of Negro suffrage. Hartford, Conn., American Pub. Co., 1895. 110 p. port. E185.61.R57

1444
Schechter, Betty. The peaceable revolution. Boston, Houghton Mifflin, 1963. 243 p. illus. HM278.S35

1445
Smith, Samuel D. The Negro in Congress, 1870-1901. Port Washington, N.Y., Kennikat Press [1966, c1940] 160 p. E185.6.S64 1966

Bibliography: p. 145-151.

1446
Strong, Donald S. Negroes, ballots, and judges; national voting rights legislation in the Federal courts. University, Published for the Bureau of

Public Administration, University of Alabama, by University of Alabama Press [1968] 100 p.   KF4893.S8

Bibliographical footnotes.

1447

Taper, Bernard. Gomillion versus Lightfoot. New York, McGraw-Hill [1963] 131 p. (McGraw-Hill paperbacks, 62855)   JK1348.A2Z5 1963

Charles G. Gomillion, a Tuskegee professor, *v.* Mayor Philip M. Lightfoot, in a singular case, argued before the Supreme Court the denial of Negro voting rights in Tuskegee, Alabama.

1448

Tatum, Elbert L. The changed political thought of the Negro, 1915-1940; with a foreword by Lawrence A. Davis. New York, Exposition Press [1951] 205 p.   JK2275.N4T3

Bibliography: p. 195-205.

1449

U.S. *Commission on Civil Rights.* Voting; hearings. Washington, U.S. Govt. Print. Off., 1959. 325 p. forms.   JK1929.A4U5

Hearings held Dec. 8, 1958, to Jan. 9, 1959, in Montgomery, Alabama.

1450

Vander, Harry J. The political and economic progress of the American Negro, 1940-1963. Dubuque, Iowa, W. C. Brown Book Co. [1968] 111 p. illus.   JK2275.N4V3

Includes bibliographies.

1451

Wallace, Jesse T. A history of the Negroes of Mississippi from 1865 to 1890. Clinton, Miss., 1927. 188 p.   E185.93.M6W2

Thesis (Ph. D.)—Columbia University, 1928.
Vita.
Bibliography: p. 185-187.

1451a

Wardlaw, Ralph W. Negro suffrage in Georgia, 1867-1930. [Athens, Ga., 1932] 91 p. ([Georgia. University] Phelps-Stokes fellowship studies no. 11)   E185.5.G35 no. 11

Bulletin of the University of Georgia, v. 33, no. 2a.
Thesis (M.A.)–University of Georgia.
Bibliography: p. 86-91.

1452
Watters, Pat, *and* Reese Cleghorn. Climbing Jacob's ladder; the arrival of
Negroes in Southern politics. New York, Harcourt, Brace & World
[1967] xvi, 389 p.   JK1929.A2W3

   Includes bibliographical references.

1453
Weeks, Stephen B. The history of Negro suffrage in the South. Boston,
Ginn, 1894. p. [671]-703.   JK1929.A2W5

   Reprinted from *Political Science Quarterly,* v. 9, no. 4.

1454
Weinberg, Kenneth G. Black victory; Carl Stokes and the winning of Cleve-
land. Chicago, Quadrangle Books, 1968. 250 p. facsim., ports.
                                                     F499.C6S85
1455
Wilson, James Q. Negro politics; the search for leadership. Glencoe, Ill.,
Free Press [1960] 342 p.   JK1924.W5

   Bibliographical references included in "Notes" (p. 319-333).

1456

The Black American and the press [by] Armistead S. Pride [and others].
Edited by Jack Lyle. Los Angeles, W. Ritchie Press [1968] xviii, 86 p.
E185.615.B53
Report of a symposium developed by the Department of Journalism,
University of California at Los Angeles.
Bibliographical footnotes.

1457

Brooks, Maxwell R. The Negro press re-examined; political content of
leading Negro newspapers. Boston, Christopher Pub. House [1959]
125 p.   PN4888.N4B7
Includes bibliographies.

1458

Detweiler, Frederick G. The Negro press in the United States. College
Park, Md., McGrath Pub. Co., 1968 [c1922] 274 p.
PN4888.N4D4 1968
Includes bibliographical references.

1459

Graham, Hugh D. Crisis in print; desegregation and the press in Tennessee
[Nashville] Vanderbilt University Press [1967] 338 p. illus.
E185.93.T3G7
Includes bibliographical references.

1459a

Oak, Vishnu V. The Negro entrepreneur. Yellow Springs, Ohio, Printed for the author by the Antioch Press, 1948-49. 2 v. illus.   E185.8.O2

Bibliography: v.1, p. 138-150; v. 2, p. 209-220.

Contents.—v. 1. The Negro newspaper.—v. 2. The Negro's adventure in general business.

1460

Penn, Irvine G. The Afro-American press and its editors. With contributions by Hon. Frederick Douglass, Hon. John R. Lynch [etc.]. Springfield, Mass., Willey, 1891. 565 p. illus., fold. facsim., ports.

PN4888.N4P4

1461

Simpson, George E. The Negro in the Philadelphia press. Philadelphia, 1936. xv, 158 p. diagrs., map, tables.   PN4899.P48S5 1934

Thesis (Ph.D.)—University of Pennsylvania, 1934.

An analysis of Negro material published in the *Philadelphia Record, Public Ledger, Evening Bulletin,* and *Philadelphia Inquirer* during 1908-1932.

Bibliography: p. [153]-156.

1462

Spearman, Walter, *and* Sylvan Meyer. Racial crisis and the press. Atlanta, Southern Regional Council, 1960. 54 p.   PN4893.S65

1463

American Academy of Political and Social Science, *Philadelphia*. The Negro protest. Special editor: Arnold M. Rose. Philadelphia, 1965. 214 p. (*Its* Annals, v. 357)   H1.A4 v. 357
                                                                    E185.61.A45
    Bibliographical footnotes.

1464

American Academy of Political and Social Science, *Phildelphia*. Racial desegregation and integration, edited by Ira De A. Reid. Philadelphia, 1956. 211 p. (*Its* Annals, v. 304)   H1.A4 v. 304
                                                                    E185.61.A46
    Bibliographical footnotes.

1465

Ashmore, Harry S. The other side of Jordan. New York, Norton [1960] 155 p.   E185.61.A73

1466

Atkins, James A. The age of Jim Crow. New York, Vantage Press [1964] 300 p.   E185.97.A84A3

1467

Austin, Frank E. The history of segregation. Winter Park, Fla., Printed by the Rollins Press, c1956. 260 p.   HT1589.A9

1468

Baker, Ray S. Following the color line; American Negro citizenship in the progressive era. Introduction and notes to the Torchbook ed. by Dewey W. Grantham, Jr. New York, Harper & Row [1964] xviii, 311 p. illus., ports. (American perspectives)　　　　　　E185.61.B16　1964

Harper torchbooks. The University library.
"TB 3053."
Chapters 1-8, 10-14, with slight revisions, originally appeared in the *American Magazine*, Apr. 1907-Sept. 1908.

1469

Baldwin, James. The fire next time. New York, Dial Press, 1963. 120 p.
E185.61.B195

1470

Baldwin, James. Notes of a native son. New York, Dial Press, 1963 [c1955] 158 p.　　　　　　　　　　　　　　E185.61.B2　1963

1471

Banton, Michael P. Race relations. New York, Basic Books [c1967] xiv, 434 p. illus., maps.　　　　　　　　　HT1521.B34　1967b
Bibliography: p. [394]-415.

1472

Bennett, Lerone. Confrontation: black and white. Foreword by A. Philip Randolph. Chicago, Johnson Pub. Co., 1965. 321 p.　　　E185.B42
Bibliography: p. [305]-312.

1473

Boyd, Malcolm. You can't kill the dream. Reflections. Photos compiled by Bruce Roberts. The American dream, by Eric Sevareid. Richmond, John Knox Press [1968] 80 p. illus., ports.　　　　E185.61.B776

1474

Boyle, Sarah P. The desegregated heart; a Virginian's stand in time of transition. New York, Morrow, 1962. 364 p.　　　E185.61.B778

1475

Boyle, Sarah P. For human beings only; a primer of human understanding. New York, Seabury Press, 1964. 127 p.　　　E185.61.B779

1476

Braden, Anne. The wall between. New York, Monthly Review Press, 1958. 306 p.　　　　　　　　　　　　　　　F459.L8B7
Autobiographical.

1477

Brink, William J., *and* Louis Harris. The Negro revolution in America; what Negroes want, why and how they are fighting, whom they support, what whites think of them and their demands. New York, Simon and Schuster, 1964 [c1963] 249 p. tables.   E185.61.B795

"Based on the nationwide survey by *Newsweek* magazine."

1478

Bunche, Ralph J. A world view of race. Port Washington, N.Y., Kennikat Press [1968, c1936] 98 p. (Kennikat Press series in Negro culture and history)   HT1521.B78 1968

Includes bibliographies.

1479

Caldwell, Erskine. In search of Bisco. New York, Farrar, Straus and Giroux [1965] 219 p.   E185.61.C2

Story of the author's visits to the deep South in search of his childhood playmate, a Negro boy named Bisco, from whom he was separated by the laws of a segregated society.

1480

Carter, Hodding. The South strikes back. Garden City, N.Y., Doubleday, 1959. 213 p.   E185.61.C28

1481

Center for the Study of Democratic Institutions. Lyndon B. Johnson, Robert C. Weaver, Joseph P. Lyford, and John Cogley on the Negro as an American. [Santa Barbara, Calif., 1963] 18 p. (*Its* Occasional papers)   E185.61.C4

1482

Clark, Dennis. The ghetto game; racial conflicts in the city. New York, Sheed and Ward [1962] 245 p.   E184.A1C53

Includes bibliographies.

1483

Clark, Kenneth B. Dark ghetto; dilemmas of social power. Foreword by Gunnar Myrdal. New York, Harper & Row [1965] xxix, 251 p. illus.
F128.9.N3C65

1484

Clark, Kenneth B. The Negro protest: James Baldwin, Malcolm X, Martin Luther King talk with Kenneth B. Clark. Boston, Beacon Press [1963] 56 p.   E185.61.C62

1485
Cleaver, Eldridge. Eldridge Cleaver; post-prison writings and speeches. Edited and with an appraisal by Robert Scheer. New York, Random House [1969] xxxiii, 211 p.   E185.615.C63

1486
Cleaver, Eldridge. Soul on ice. With an introduction by Maxwell Geismar. New York, McGraw-Hill [1967, c1968] xv, 210 p.   E185.97.C6
"A Ramparts book."

1487
Collins, Winfield H. The truth about lynching and the Negro in the South, in which the author pleads that the South be made safe for the white race. New York, Neale Pub. Co., 1918. 163 p.   E185.65.C7

1488
Conference on Negro-Jewish Relations in the United States, *New York, 1964.* Negro-Jewish relations in the United States; papers and proceedings. New York, Citadel Press, 1966. 71 p.   E185.61.C7545 1964
"Convened by the Conference on Jewish Social Studies, New York City."
First published in *Jewish Social Studies,* v. 27, Jan. 1965.
Bibliography: p. 67-71.

1489
Connecticut. *Commission on Civil Rights.* Attitudes toward racial integration in Connecticut, by Henry G. Stetler, supervisor, Research Division. Hartford, 1961. 50 p. illus.   E185.93.C7A52

1490
Cook, James G. The segregationists. New York, Appleton-Century-Crofts [1962] 376 p.   E184.A1C62

1491
Creger, Ralph. A look down the lonesome road, by Ralph Creger with Erwin L. McDonald. Foreword by Harry Golden. Garden City, N.Y., Doubleday, 1964. xiv, 223 p.   E185.61.C9

1492
Curry, Jesse E., *and* Glen D. King. Race tensions and the police. With a foreword by George Eastman. Springfield, Ill., Thomas [1962] 137 p. (Police science series)   HV8069.C8
Bibliography: p. 135.

1493

Dabbs, James M. The Southern heritage. New York, Knopf, 1958. 273 p.
E185.61.D2

1494

Dees, Jesse W., *and* James S. Hadley. Jim Crow. Ann Arbor, Ann Arbor
Publishers [1951] 529 p. illus.   E185.61.D4

Bibliography: p. 483-495.

1495

Doyle, Bertram W. The etiquette of race relations in the South. Port
Washington, N.Y., Kennikat Press [1968, c1937] xxv, 249 p. (Kennikat
Press series in Negro culture and history)   E185.61.D766

Bibliography: p. 173-190.

1496

DuBois, William E. B. Dusk of dawn; an essay toward an autobiography of
a race concept. New York, Harcourt, Brace [1940] 334 p.

E185.97.D73

1497

Dykeman, Wilma, *and* James Stokely. Neither black nor white. New York,
Rinehart [1957] 371 p.   E185.61.D993

1498

Essien-Udom, Essien U. Black nationalism; a search for an identity in
America. [Chicago] University of Chicago Press [1962] 367 p. illus.,
ports.   E185.61.E75

Bibliography: p. 351-360.

1499

Evers, *Mrs.* Medgar. For us, the living, by Mrs. Medgar Evers with William
Peters. Garden City, N.Y., Doubleday, 1967. 378 p.   E185.97.E94E9

1500

Fager, Charles E. White reflections on black power. Grand Rapids, W. B.
Eerdmans Pub. Co. [1967] 118 p.   E185.615.F3

1501

Fields, Uriah J. The Montgomery story; the unhappy effects of the Montgomery bus boycott. New York, Exposition Press [1959] 87 p.
E185.89.T8F5

1501a

Fontaine, William T. Reflections on segregation, desegregation, power and
morals. Springfield, Ill., Thomas [1967] 162 p. (American lecture

series, publication no. 700. A monograph in the Bannerstone division of American lectures in philosophy)   E185.615.F6

Bibliographical footnotes.

1502

Fortune, T. Thomas. Black and white; land, labor, and politics in the South. New York, Arno Press, 1968. 310 p. (The American Negro, his history and literature)   E185.61.F74 1968

Reprint of work first published in 1884.

1503

Franklin, John H., *comp.* Color and race. Boston, Houghton Mifflin, 1968. xvi, 391 p. (The Daedalus library, v. 13)   HT1521.F65

Includes bibliographies.

1504

Frazier, Edward Franklin. On race relations; selected writings. Edited and with an introduction by G. Franklin Edwards. Chicago, University of Chicago Press [1968] xx, 331 p. illus. (The Heritage of sociology)
                                                                      E185.F835 1968

Includes bibliographical references.
"Bibliography of E. Franklin Frazier": p. 325-331.

1505

Ginzberg, Eli, *and* Alfred S. Eichner. The troublesome presence; American democracy and the Negro. [New York] Free Press of Glencoe [1964] 339 p.   E185.G5

Includes bibliographical references.

1506

Harkey, Ira B. The smell of burning crosses; an autobiography of a Mississippi newspaperman. Jacksonville, Ill., Harris-Wolfe [1967] 208 p.
                                                                      E185.61.H248

1507

Harris, Janet, *and* Julius W. Hobson. Black pride; a people's struggle. New York, McGraw-Hill [1969] 160 p. illus., ports.   E185.H3

Traces the history of black people in America and the struggles of such leaders as Frederick Douglass, Malcolm X, and Martin Luther King to establish a racial identity and equal rights for Negroes as citizens of the United States.

Bibliography: p. 153-157.

1508

Hays, Brooks. A southern moderate speaks. Chapel Hill, University of North Carolina Press [1959] 231 p.   E185.61.H43£

1509

Height, Dorothy I. Step by step with interracial groups. [Rev. ed.] New York, Publications Services, National Board, YWCA [1955] 56 p.
HT1521.H4 195£

1510

Hentoff, Nat. The new equality. New York, Viking Press [1964] 243 p.
E185.61.H4£

1511

Johnson, James W. Negro Americans, what now? New York, Viking Press 1934. 103 p.   E185.61.J6£

1512

Kerlin, Robert T. The voice of the Negro, 1919. New York, Arno Press 1968. 188 p. (The American Negro, his history and literature)
E185.61.K4 196£

Reprint of the 1920 ed.

1513

Killens, John O. Black man's burden. New York, Trident Press, 1965 176 p.   E185.61.K48'

1514

Lester, Julius. Look out, Whitey! Black power's gon' get your mama! New York, Dial Press, 1968. 152 p.   E185.615.L47.

Bibliographical references included in "Notes" (p. 147-149). Bibli ography: p. 151-152.

1515

Lightfoot, Claude M. Ghetto rebellion to black liberation. New York International Publishers [1968] 192 p.   E185.61.L55

1516

Lubell, Samuel. White and black: test of a nation. 2d ed., rev. New York Harper & Row [1966] xiv, 233 p. (Harper colophon books, CN75J)
E185.61.L8 196

Bibliographical references included in "Reading notes" (p. 219-226'

1517
McWilliams, Carey. Brothers under the skin. Rev. ed. Boston, Little,
Brown [1964] xix, 364 p.   E184.A1M19 1964
　　Bibliographical footnotes.

1518
Marx, Gary T. Protest and prejudice; a study of belief in the black com-
munity. New York, Harper & Row [1967] xxviii, 228, 27 p.
　　　　　　　　　　　　　　　　　　　　　　　　　　E185.615.M32
　　"Volume three in a series based on the University of California
Five-year Study of Anti-Semitism in the United States, being conducted
by the Survey of Research Center . . . under a grant from the Anti-
defamation League of B'nai B'rith."

1519
Moody, Anne. Coming of age in Mississippi. New York, Dial Press, 1968.
348 p.   E185.97.M65A3
　　Autobiographical.

1520
Moon, Bucklin. The high cost of prejudice. New York, J. Messner [1947]
xvi, 168 p.   E185.61.M75
　　"Check list for further reading": p. 165-168.

1521
Moton, Robert R. What the Negro thinks. Garden City, N.Y., Doubleday,
Doran, 1929. 267 p.   E185.61.M934

1522
National Association for the Advancement of Colored People. An appeal
to the world; a statement on the denial of human rights to minorities in
the case of citizens of Negro descent in the United States of America
and an appeal to the United Nations for redress. Prepared under the
editorial supervision of W. E. Burghardt Du Bois. [New York, 1947]
94 p.   NcD
　　Includes bibliographical references.

1523
National Urban League. The racial gap, 1955-1965: 1965-1975 in income,
unemployment, education, health [and] housing [by Sylvia Lauter].
New York [1967] 41 p.   E185.615.N3
　　Bibliography: p. 40-41.

1524

Negro and Jew: an encounter in America; a symposium compiled by Mid-stream magazine. Shlomo Katz, editor. New York, Macmillan [1967] xvi, 141 p.   E185.61.N386

1525

New South (*Atlanta*). Changing patterns in the new South; a unique record of the growth of democracy in the South in the last decade, from the pages of the Southern Regional Council's publication New South. [Atlanta, Southern Regional Council, 1955] 116 p.   E185.61.N47

Many of the selections have been condensed. Several of the articles were originally issued in newspapers or adapted from speeches, before being printed in the *New South.*

1526

New York *(State) State Commission for Human Rights. Research Division.* Negroes in five New York cities, a study of problems, achievement, and trends, by Eunice and George Grier. [New York, New York State Commission against Discrimination] 1958. 113 leaves. illus.

E185.93.N56N46
Bibliography: leaves C1-C9.

1526a

Newby, Idus A. Challenge to the Court; social scientists and the defense of segregation, 1954-1966. Baton Rouge, Louisiana State University Press [1967] 239 p.   E185.61.N46

Bibliographical footnotes.

1527

Newby, Idus A. Jim Crow's defense; anti-Negro thought in America, 1900-1930. Baton Rouge, Louisiana State University Press, 1965. xv, 230 p.   E185.61.N475

Bibliography: p. 201-221.

1528

Nolen, Claude H. The Negro's image in the South; the anatomy of white supremacy. Lexington, University of Kentucky Press, 1967. xix, 232 p.

E185.61.N872
"Bibliographical essay": p. [211]-218.

1529

Osofsky, Gilbert. The burden of race; a documentary history of Negro-white relations in America. New York, Harper & Row [1967] xvi, 654 p. E185.O8

Bibliography: p. 637-641.

1530

Park, Robert E. Race and culture. Glencoe, Ill., Free Press [1950] xxii, 403 p. port. (*His* Collected papers, v. 1) HT1521.P3

Bibliographical footnotes.

1531

Peck, James. Freedom ride. New York, Simon and Schuster, 1962. 160 p. E185.61.P43

1532

Peters, William. The Southern temper. With a foreword by Harry Golden. Garden City, N.Y., Doubleday, 1959. 283 p. E185.61.P47

Bibliographical references included in "Acknowledgments" (p. [9] - 10).

1533

Petersen, William, *ed*. American social patterns; studies of race relations, popular heroes, voting, union democracy, and government bureaucracy. Garden City, N.Y., Doubleday, 1956. 263 p. illus. (Doubleday anchor books, A86) HN57.P4

Includes bibliographical references.

1534

Phelps-Stokes Fund. Negro status and race relations in the United States, 1911-1946; the thirty-five year report of the Phelps-Stokes Fund, by Anson Phelps Stokes, with contributions from Channing H. Tobias [and others] and a documentary appendix. New York, 1948. 219 p. E185.61.P53

Cover title: *Progress in Negro Status and Race Relations, 1911-1946.* Includes bibliographies.

1535

Pope, Liston. The kingdom beyond caste. New York, Friendship Press [1957] 170 p. HT1521.P6

1535a

Powledge, Fred. Black power, white resistance; notes on the new civil war Cleveland, World Pub. Co. [1967] 282 p.   E185.615.P6

Bibliographical footnotes.

1536

Proudfoot, Merrill. Diary of a sit-in. Foreword by Frank P. Graham Chapel Hill, University of North Carolina Press [1962] 204 p.

F444.K7P95

1537

Putnam, Carleton. Race and reason, a Yankee view. Washington, Public Affairs Press [1961] 125 p.   E185.61.P84

1538

Quint, Howard H. Profile in black and white; a frank portrait of South Carolina. Washington, Public Affairs Press [1958] 214 p.

E185.93.S7Q5

1539

Randel, William P. The Ku Klux Klan; a century of infamy. Philadelphia Chilton Books [1965] xvii, 300 p. illus.   E668.R18

"Bibliographical note": p. 265-294.

1540

Raper, Arthur F. The tragedy of lynching. Chapel Hill, University of North Carolina Press, 1933. 499 p. diagr., map. ([University of North Carolina Social study series])   HV6464.R3

Presented by the Southern Commission on the Study of Lynching

1541

Reuter, Edward B. The American race problem; a study of the Negro. New York, Crowell [c1927] 448 p. diagrs., map, tables. (Crowell's social science series)   E185.61.R44

"Readings" at end of each chapter.

1542

Rogers, Joel A. From "superman" to man. 5th ed. New York, J. A. Rogers Publications [c1941] 132 p.   E185.61.R72 1941

1543

Rowan, Carl T. Go South to sorrow. New York, Random House [1957] 246 p.   E185.61.R855

1544
Rowan, Carl T. South of freedom. New York, Knopf, 1952. 270 p.
E185.61.R86

1545
Rumbough, Constance H. Crumbling barriers. Foreword by Charles S. Johnson. New York, Fellowship Publications [1948] 45 p.
E185.61.R935

1546
Shannon, Alexander H. The racial integrity of the American Negro. Nashville, Printed for the author by Parthenon Press [1951] 264 p.
E185.62.S52 1951
Bibliography: p. 261.

1546a
Silberman, Charles E. Crisis in black and white. New York, Random House [1964] 370 p.
E185.61.S57
Bibliographical footnotes.

1547
Smith, James Wesley. The strange way of truth. New York, Vantage Press [1968] 145 p.
E185.93.V8S55
Bibliography: p. 141-145.

1548
Stanton, William R. The leopard's spots: scientific attitudes toward race in America, 1815-59. [Chicago] University of Chicago Press [1960] 244 p.
GN17.S75
Bibliographical references included in "Notes" (p. 197-238).

1549
Stover, William H. M. Don't just deplore discrimination, do something! New York, Vantage Press [1964] 188 p. form.
E185.61.S9

1550
Talmadge, Herman E. You and segregation. Birmingham, Ala., Vulcan Press [1955] 79 p.
E185.61.T2

1551
Thompson, Edgar T., *ed.* Race relations and the race problem; a definition and an analysis. Contributors: Robert E. Park [and others] New York, Greenwood Press, 1968 [c1939] xv, 338 p. maps.
E184.A1T5 1968
Bibliography: p. [307]-328.

1552

Thurman, Howard. The luminous darkness; a personal interpretation of the anatomy of segregation and the ground of hope. New York, Harper & Row [1965] 113 p. E185.61.T47

1553

Tucker, Sterling. Beyond the burning: life and death of the ghetto. New York, Association Press [1968] 160 p. E185.615.T8

Bibliographical references included in "Notes" (p. 152-160).

1554

Tumin, Melvin M. Desegregation: resistance and readiness, by Melvin M. Tumin, with the assistance of Warren Eason [and others]. Princeton, N.J., Princeton University Press, 1958. xvii, 270 p. tables. E185.61.T88

Bibliographical footnotes.

1555

Vander Zanden, James W. Race relations in transition; the segregation crisis in the South. New York, Random House [1965] 135 p. (Studies in sociology, SS25) E185.61.V33

Bibliographical references included in "Notes" (p. 118-126). "Suggested readings": p. 127-129.

1556

Vaughan, Curtis M. Faubus' folly; the story of segregation. New York, Vantage Press [1959] 160 p. E185.61.V36

1557

Warren, Robert Penn. Segregation, the inner conflict in the South. New York, Random House [1956] 66 p. E185.61.W2

1558

Weatherby, William J. Love in the shadows. New York, Stein and Day [1966] 182 p. E185.61.W35 1966

First published in 1965 under title: *Breaking the Silence.*

1559

Weatherford, Willis D., *and* Charles S. Johnson. Race relations; adjustment of whites and Negroes in the United States. Boston, D. C. Heath [c1934] 590 p. (Social relations series) E185.W42

Bibliography: p. 556-576.

1560
White, Walter F. How far the promised land? New York, Viking Press, 1955. 244 p.   E185.61.W6

1561
White, Walter F. Rope & faggot; a biography of Judge Lynch. New York, Knopf, 1929. 272 p. front., tables.   HV6457.W45

Bibliography: p. 269-272.

1562
Williams, O. R. Segregation and common sense. Boston, Forum Pub. Co. [1961] 217 p.   E185.61.W737

1563
Willlamson, Joel, *comp.* The origins of segregation. Boston, D. C. Heath [1968] xiv, 113 p. (Problems in American Civilization)   E185.615.W5

Contents.—The strange career of Jim Crow, by C. V. Woodward. —The color line, by G. B. Tindall.—Jim Crow laws and miscegenation, by V. L. Wharton.—Social acceptance and unacceptance, by C. E. Wynes.—The separation of the races, by J. Williamson.—Why Negroes were segregated in the new South, by C. V. Woodward.—In summation, by C. E. Wynes.—The debate on school segregation in South Carolina, 1868.—The Negroes in Negroland, by H. R. Helper.—The Negro, by J. R. Sparkman.—The silent South, by G. W. Cable.—Urban segregation during slavery, by R. C. Wade.—Segregation in the antebellum North, by L. F. Litwack.—Why segregation in postwar Philadelphia, by B. H. Hunt.—Ethnic relations in American communities, by R. M. Williams, Jr.—Suggestions of additional reading (p. 111-113).

1564
Wood, Forrest G. Black scare; the racist response to emancipation and Reconstruction. Berkeley, University of California Press, 1968. 219 p. illus.   E185.61.W84

Bibliography: p. [193]-210.

1565
Woodward, Comer Vann. The strange career of Jim Crow. 2d rev. ed. New York, Oxford University Press, 1966. 205 p.   E185.61.W86 1966

"Notes on reading": p. 193-196.

1566
Woofter, Thomas J. Southern race progress, the wavering color line. Intro
duction by Jonathan Daniels. Washington, Public Affairs Press [1957
180 p.   E185.61.W92

1567
Wright, Nathan. Let's work together. New York, Hawthorn Books [1968
271 p.   E185.615.W7

1568
Wright, Nathan. Ready to riot. New York, Holt, Rinehart and Winsto
[1968] 148 p. illus., maps.   HN80.N685W7

Bibliographical footnotes.

1569
Wright, Richard. White man, listen! Garden City, N.Y., Doubleday, 195*
190 p.   HT1581.W

Reprint issued by Anchor Books, 1964.

1569a
Zinn, Howard. The Southern mystique. New York, Knopf, 1964. 267 p.
                                                              E185.61.Z

"Bibliographical notes": p. 265-267.

Riots

1570
Berson, Lenora E. Case study of a riot; the Philadelphia story. With con
mentaries by Alex Rosen and Kenneth B. Clark. New York, Institute o
Human Relations Press, American Jewish Committee [1966] 71 p
maps. ([American Jewish Committee. Institute of Human Relations
Pamphlet series, no. 7)   F158.9.N3B

1571
California. *Governor's Commission on the Los Angeles Riots.* Transcript
depositions, consultants reports, and selected documents. Los Angele
1965. 18 v. illus. (part col.), maps.   F869.L8C

Includes bibliographies.

1572

California. *Governor's Commission on the Los Angeles Riots.* Violence in the city—an end or a beginning? A report. [Los Angeles] 1965. 101 p. plates (part col.), fold. col. map. F869.L8C17

1573

Cohen, Jerry, *and* William S. Murphy. Burn, baby, burn! The Los Angeles race riot, August 1965. Introduction by Robert Kirsch. New York, Dutton, 1966. 318 p. illus., ports. F869.L8C6

1574

Conot, Robert E. Rivers of blood, years of darkness; the unforgettable classic account of the Watts riot. New York, Morrow, 1968 [c1967] 497 p. F869.L8C66 1968

Bibliography: p. 493-497.

1575

Crump, Spencer. Black riot in Los Angeles; the story of the Watts tragedy. Los Angeles, Trans-Anglo Books [1966] 160 p. illus., facsims., maps (part col.), ports. F869.L8C78

"Appendix: The text of the McCone Commission report": p. 125-154.

Bibliography: p. 155.

1576

Gilbert, Ben W. Ten blocks from the White House; anatomy of the Washington riots of 1968 [by] Ben W. Gilbert and the staff of the Washington Post. New York, Praeger [1968] xix, 245 p. illus., maps. (Praeger paperbacks, P-240) F200.G5

1577

Hayden, Thomas. Rebellion in Newark; official violence and ghetto response. New York, Vintage Books [1967] 102 p. maps. F144.N6H27

1578

Heaps, Willard A. Riots, U.S.A., 1765-1965. New York, Seabury Press [1966] 186 p. E178.3.H427

Bibliography: p. 174-182.

1579

Illinois. *Chicago Commission on Race Relations.* The Negro in Chicago; a study of race relations and a race riot in 1919. New York, Arno Press,

1968. xxiv, 672 p. illus., maps. (The American Negro, his history and
literature)   F548.9.N3I2 1968

Reprint of the 1922 ed.

1580

Janowitz, Morris. Social control of escalated riots. [Chicago?] University
of Chicago, Center for Policy Study [1968] 44 p.   HV6477.J3

"Prepared for the Center's conference on 'Short Term and Emer-
gency Measures to Avert Urban Violence.'"
Bibliographical footnotes.

1581

Lee, Alfred M., *and* Norman D. Humphrey. Race riot, Detroit 1943. With
a new introductory essay by Alfred McClung Lee. New York, Octagon
Books, 1968 [c1943] xxxiii, 143 p. illus., maps.   F574.D4L4 1968

Bibliography: p. 142-143.

1582

Momboisse, Raymond M. Riots, revolts, and insurrections. Springfield, Ill.,
C. C. Thomas [1967] xviii, 523 p.   HV8055.M6

1583

Nelson, Truman J. The torture of mothers. Introduction by Maxwell
Geismar. Newburyport, Mass., Garrison Press [1965] 121 p. ports.

F128.9.N3N37

Experiences related by mothers and children who were subjected to
violent treatment at the hands of the police during the Harlem riots of
fall 1964.

1584

Rudwick, Elliott M. Race riot at East St. Louis, July 2, 1917. Foreword
by Oscar Handlin. Carbondale, Southern Illinois University Press
[1964] xvii, 300 p. illus., maps.   F549.E2R8

Bibliography: p. 285-291.

1585

Shogan, Robert, *and* Tom Craig. The Detroit race riot; a study in violence.
Philadelphia, Chilton Books [1964] 199 p.   F574.D4S5

Bibliography: p. 185-188.

1586

Supplemental studies for the National Advisory Commission on Civil Disorders. New York, Praeger [1968] 248 p. forms. (Praeger special
studies in U.S. economic and social development) E185.61.S94 1968b

"The studies were conducted independently of the Commission and of each other by research groups at the University of Michigan, the Johns Hopkins University, and Columbia University."

Bibliographical footnotes.

Contents.–Racial attitudes in fifteen American cities, by A. Campbell and H. Schuman.–Between white and black; the faces of American institutions in the ghetto, by P. H. Rossi, and others.–Who riots? A study of participation in the 1967 riots, by R. M. Fogelson and R. B. Hill.

1587

U.S. *Congress. House. Select Committee on New Orleans Riots.* New Orleans riots. Minority report. [Washington? 1866?] 24 p.　F379.N5U5

Presented by B. M. Boyer.

From *House Report*, no. 16, 39th Congress, 2d session.

1588

U.S. *National Advisory Commission on Civil Disorders.* Report. [Washington, For sale by the Supt. of Docs., U.S. Govt. Print. Off., 1968] xv, 425 p. illus., ports.　HV6477.A56

Commercially published, with an introduction by Tom Wicker, in hard covers by E. P. Dutton and in paperback by Bantam, New York, 1968.

1589

Urban riots: violence and social change. Edited by Robert H. Connery. New York, 1968. 190 p. (Proceedings of the Academy of Political Science, v. 29, no. 1)　HN58.U7

Many of the "papers in this issue . . . were delivered at a conference sponsored by the academy in cooperation with the Columbia University Center on Urban Minority Affairs, April 19, 1968."

Bibliography: p. 183-190.

1590

Walker, Marion E. Black rebellion. Columbia, S.C., National Graphics [1968] 64 p. illus., ports.　HV6477.W34

1591

Waskow, Arthur I. From race riot to sit-in, 1919 and the 1960s; a study in the connections between conflict and violence. Garden City, N.Y., Doubleday, 1966. xviii, 380 p.　E185.61.W24

Bibliography: p. [355]-366.

REGIONAL STUDIES

1592
Allen, James E. The Negro in New York. Foreword by Arthur Levitt. New York, Exposition Press [1964] 94 p.   E185.93.N56A55
   Bibliography: p. [93]-94.

1593
Aukofer, Frank A. City with a chance. Milwaukee, Bruce Pub. Co. [1968] 146 p.   F589.M6A93
   Milwaukee is the city discussed.

1594
Bartlett, Irving H. From slave to citizen; the story of the Negro in Rhode Island. Foreword by Benjamin Crocker Clough. Providence, Urban League of Greater Providence, 1954. 76 p. illus.   E185.93.R4B3
   "Bibliographical note": p. 74-76.

1595
Beasley, Delilah L. The Negro trail blazers of California; a compilation of records from the California archives in the Bancroft Library at the University of California, in Berkeley; and from the diaries, old papers, and conversations of old pioneers in the State of California. Los Angeles, 1919. 317 p. ports.   F870.N38B3 1919b

Photo offset. San Francisco, R and E Research Associates, 1968.
Bibliography: p. [13-14].

1596
Burgess, Margaret E. Negro leadership in a southern city. Chapel Hill,
University of North Carolina Press [1962] 231 p. illus.   E185.61.B95
Bibliography: p. [219]-226.

1597
California. *State Fair Employment Practice Commission.* Negro Califor-
nians; population, employment, income, education. San Francisco,
Division of Fair Employment Practices, 1963. 34 p.   E185.93.C2A5

"Derived principally from the 1960 Census of population, the statistical tables were compiled by the California Division of Labor Statistics
and Research."

1598
Chicago. University. *Chicago Community Inventory.* Chicago's Negro pop-
ulation; characteristics and trends. A report by the Chicago Community
Inventory, University of Chicago, to the Office of the Housing and
Redevelopment Coordinator and the Chicago Plan Commission. [Chi-
cago] 1956. 109 p. maps.   ICU

"This report was prepared by Otis Dudley Duncan, associate director, and Beverly Duncan, research assistant."

1599
Clark, Peter W. Delta shadows, "a pageant of Negro progress in New
Orleans." Illustrated by Numa Joseph Roussève. [New Orleans]
Graphic Arts Studios, 1942. 200 p. illus., ports.   F379.N5C6

1600
Clarke, John H., *ed.* Harlem, a community in transition. New York,
Citadel Press [c1964] 223 p. illus., ports.   F128.68.H3C55

"Much of the material in this book is from the Summer 1963
(Volume III, no. 3) issue of *Freedomways.*"
Bibliographical footnotes.

1601
Claspy, Everett. The Negro in southwestern Michigan; Negroes in the
North in a rural environment. Dowagiac, Mich., 1967. 112 p.
     E185.93.M5C55
Includes bibliographical references.

1602

Crum, Mason. Gullah; Negro life in the Carolina Sea Islands. Durham, N.C., Duke University Press, 1940. xv, 351 p. plates. (Duke University publications)   E185.93.S7C85

Bibliography: p. [345]-351.

1603

Dabney, Wendell P. Cincinnati's colored citizens; historical, sociological and biographical. Cincinnati, Dabney Pub. Co. [c1926] 440 p. illus., ports.   F499.C5D12

1604

Daniels, John. In freedom's birthplace; a study of the Boston Negroes. Boston, Houghton Mifflin Co., 1914. 496 p.   F73.9.N4D2

1605

De Jong, Gordon F., *and* George A. Hillery. Kentucky's Negro population in 1960. Lexington, University of Kentucky, Agricultural Experiment Station, Dept. of Rural Sociology, 1965. 32 p. illus., map. ([Kentucky. Agricultural Experiment Station, Lexington] Bulletin 704)
E185.93.K3D4

Bibliographical footnotes.

1606

Detroit Urban League. *Research Dept.* A profile of the Detroit Negro, 1955-1964. [Detroit] 1965. 62 p. illus., maps.   F574.D4D59

Bibliography: p. 62.

1607

Drake, St. Clair, *and* Horace R. Cayton. Black metropolis; a study of Negro life in a northern city. Introduction by Richard Wright. Introduction to Torchbook ed. by Everett C. Hughes. [Rev. and enl. ed.] New York, Harper & Row [1962] 2 v. illus. (Harper torchbooks, TB1086-1087. The Academy library)   F548.9.N3D68 1962

Bibliographical references included in "Notes and documentation" (p. 783-792). "A list of selected books dealing with the American Negro": p. 793-796. "Suggestions for collateral reading": p. 797-798.

1608

DuBois, William. E. B. The Philadelphia Negro; a social study. Together with a special report on domestic service, by Isabel Eaton. New York, B. Blom [1967] xx, 520 p. illus., 2 fold. col. plans. (Publications of the

University of Pennsylvania. Series in political economy and public law, no. 14)   F158.9.N3D8 1967

Contents.—The Philadelphia Negro.—Appendixes. A. Schedules used in the house-to-house inquiry. B. Legislation, etc., of Pennsylvania in regard to the Negro. C. Bibliography (p. 419-423). Special report on Negro domestic service in the seventh ward, Philadelphia, by I. Eaton.

1608a

Ehle, John. The free men. New York, Harper & Row [1965] 340 p. illus., ports.   F264.C38E4

A portrait of a moderate southern community (Chapel Hill, North Carolina) experiencing an effort at integration in the years 1963-64.

1609

Gay, William T. Montgomery, Alabama, a city in crisis. New York, Exposition Press [1957] 117 p.   F334.M7G3

1610

Green, Constance M. The secret city; a history of race relations in the Nation's Capital. Princeton, N.J., Princeton University Press, 1967. xv, 389 p. illus., ports.   E185.93.D6G7

"Bibliographical note": p. 339-348. Bibliography: p. 349-361.

1611

Handlin, Oscar. The newcomers: Negroes and Puerto Ricans in a changing metropolis. Cambridge, Harvard University Press, 1959. 171 p. illus. (New York metropolitan region study)   F128.9.A1H3

Bibliographical references included in "Notes" (p. [147]-164).
New York City is the metropolis under study.

1612

Harlem Youth Opportunities Unlimited, *New York*. Youth in the ghetto; a study of the consequences of powerlessness and a blueprint for change. New York, 1964. xxi, 614 p. illus., maps, tables.   HN80.N5H3

Bibliographical footnotes.

1613

Hesslink, George K. Black neighbors; Negroes in a northern rural community. Indianapolis, Bobbs-Merrill [1968] xvii, 190 p. maps. F572.C3H4

Bibliography: p. 185-190.
Cass County, Michigan, is the area under study.

1613a

Johnson, Charles S. Shadow of the plantation. Chicago, University of Chicago Press [1934] xxiv, 214 p. diagr., plates.   E185.93.A3J6

Macon County, Alabama, was the area chosen for this survey.

1614

Johnson, Haynes B. Dusk at the mountain; the Negro, the Nation, and the Capital; a report on problems and progress. Garden City, N.Y., Doubleday, 1963. 273 p.   E185.93.D6J56

Bibliography: p. [260]-266.

1615

Johnson, James W. Black Manhattan. New York, Arno Press, 1968 [c1930] 284, xxxiv p. illus., plans, ports. (The American Negro, his history and literature)   F128.9.N3J67 1968

1616

Johnson, William. William Johnson's Natchez; the ante-bellum diary of a free Negro. Edited by William Ransom Hogan and Edwin Adams Davis. [Baton Rouge] Louisiana State University Press [1951] 812 p. illus., facsims. (Source studies in Southern history, no. 1)   E185.97.J697A3

1617

Joiner, William A. A half century of freedom of the Negro in Ohio. Xenia, Ohio, Press of Smith Adv. Co. [1915?] 134 p. illus., ports.

E185.93.O2J6

Cover title: *The Ohio Book for the Lincoln Jubilee.*
"College song, Dear old Wilberforce [by] W.A. Joiner [and] F. J. Work" (close score): p. 134.

1618

Langhorne, Orra H. M. G. Southern sketches from Virginia, 1881-1901. Edited by Charles E. Wynes. Charlottesville, University Press of Virginia [1964] xxxix, 145 p. illus., ports.   F231.L3

"The writings of Orra Langhorne": p. 139-140. Bibliographical footnotes.

1618a

Lee, Frank F. Negro and white in Connecticut Town. New York, Bookman Associates [1961] 207 p. map.   E185.93.C7L4

"Based upon the writer's unpublished doctoral dissertation . . . Yale University, 1953."
"Annotated bibliography": p. 179-199.

1618b
Lee, George W. Beale Street, where the blues began. Foreword by W. C. Handy. New York, R. O. Ballou [c1934] 296 p. ports.   F444.M5L4

1619
Liebow, Elliot. Tally's corner; a study of Negro streetcorner men. With a foreword by Hylan Lewis. Boston, Little, Brown [1967] xvii, 260 p.
E185.93.D6L5 1967
Revision of thesis, Catholic University of America.
Bibliography: p. [257]-260.
Washington, D.C., is the locale.

1620
Logan, Frenise A. The Negro in North Carolina, 1876-1894. Chapel Hill, University of North Carolina Press [1964] 244 p.   E185.93.N6L6
Bibliography: p. [221]-233.

1621
Lyda, John W. The Negro in the history of Indiana. [Terre Haute? Ind., 1953] 136 p.   E185.93.I4L9
Bibliography: p. 131-136.

1621a
McCord, William M. Mississippi: the long hot summer. New York, Norton [1965] 222 p.   E185.93.M6M32
Bibliographical references included in "Notes" (p. 211-215).
The violence of the summer of 1964 as related and interpreted by a sociologist in terms of his own participation.

1622
Maryland. *Commission on Interracial Problems and Relations.* An American city in transition; the Baltimore community self-survey of inter-group relations. [Sponsored by] Maryland Commission on Inter-racial Problems and Relations [and] Baltimore Commission on Human Relations. [Baltimore] 1955. 264 p. illus., map.   F189.B1M25

1623
Michigan. *Freedmen's Progress Commission.* Michigan manual of freed-men's progress. Compiled by Francis H. Warren. Detroit. 1915. [Detroit] J. M. Green [1968] 371, 34 p. illus., ports.
E185.93.M5A43 1968

1624

Minnesota. *Governor's Human Rights Commission.* The Negro and his home in Minnesota; a report to Governor Luther W. Youngdahl of Minnesota by the Governor's Interracial Commission. [St. Paul] 1947. 77 p. illus.   E185.93.M55A5 1947

"Third of a series of reports . . . on various racial situations."

1625

Moore, Geraldine H. Behind the ebony mask. [Birmingham, Ala.] Southern University Press, 1961. 220 p. illus.   F334.B6M57

On the Negro in Birmingham, Alabama.

1626

National Urban League. *Community Relations Project.* A study of the social and economic conditions of the Negro population of Oklahoma City, Oklahoma, conducted for the Oklahoma City Council of Social Welfare by the National Urban League as part of its Community Relations Project, Dept. of Research, June-July, 1945. [Oklahoma City? 1945?] 91 p.   F704.O41N3

1627

National Urban League. *Dept. of Research and Community Projects.* The Negro community of Baltimore; a summary report of a social study conducted for the Baltimore Urban League through the Dept. of Research, National Urban League, by Ira De A. Reid. Drawings by Wilmer Jennings. Baltimore, 1935. 46 p. diagrs.   F189.B1N24

1628

The Negro in Milwaukee; a historical survey. [Milwaukee, Milwaukee County Historical Society, 1968] 32 p. illus., ports.   F589.M6N48

Contents.—The railway porter who wanted to vote, by F. I. Olson. —Negroes in Milwaukee, by W. T. Green.—An incident of early Milwaukee law enforcement, by W. J. Vollmar.—Negro recognition in early Milwaukee, by C. V. Salomon.—Thirty years a slave, by L. Hughes. —Landmark civil rights decision in Wisconsin, by H. H. Anderson. —Milwaukee Negroes elected to public office.

1629

New York *(City) Interdepartmental Neighborhood Service Center.* The poor of Harlem: social functioning in the underclass; a report to the Welfare Administration by Joan Gordon, with the assistance of Carolyn Atkinson [and others]. New York, 1965, c1966. 167 p.   HN80.N5A49

"Welfare Administration project 105."

1630

O'Reilly, Charles T. The inner core—north; a study of Milwaukee's Negro community. [Milwaukee, University of Wisconsin] 1963. 96 p. illus., maps. F589.M6O685

"A project of the School of Social Work, the University of Wisconsin—Milwaukee for the Ford urban program, the University of Wisconsin Extension Division."

Includes bibliographies.

1631

Osofsky, Gilbert. Harlem; the making of a ghetto; Negro New York, 1890-1930. New York, Harper & Row [1966] 259 p. illus., facsims., ports. F128.9.N3O73

Includes bibliographies.

1632

Ottley, Roi, *and* William J. Weatherby. The Negro in New York; an informal social history. New York, New York Public Library, 1967. xix, 328 p. map. F128.9.N3O74

"Edited from manuscripts in the Schomburg Collection of Negro Literature and History, the New York Public Library . . . originally prepared by the Federal Writers Project under the working title, 'Harlem—the Negroes of New York (an informal social history).'"

Bibliography: p.297-312.

1633

Ottley, Roi. New world a-coming. New York, Arno Press, 1968. 364 p. illus. (The American Negro, his history and literature)

F128.9.N3O75 1968

Reprint of the 1943 ed.

Bibliography: p. [348]-354.

The Negro in New York City.

1633a

Patterson, Caleb P. The Negro in Tennessee, 1790-1865. Austin, Tex., University [1922] 213 p. (University of Texas bulletin. no. 2205: Feb. 1, 1922) E445.T3P2

Bibliography: p. 202-209.

1634

Posey, Thomas E. The Negro citizen of West Virginia. Institute, W. Va., Press of West Virginia State College [1934] 119 p. diagrs., plates, ports.

E185.93.W5P6

Bibliography: p. [110]-112.

1634a

Quillin, Frank U. The color line in Ohio; a history of race prejudice in a typical northern State. Ann Arbor, Mich., G. Wahr, 1913. xvi, 178 p. maps. (University of Michigan historical studies. [3]) E185.93.O2Q62

Published also as thesis (Ph.D.), University of Michigan, 1910.
Bibliography: p. [167]-171.

1635

Record, Wilson. Minority groups and intergroup relations in the San Francisco Bay area. [Berkeley, Calif.] 1963. 48 p. F868.S156R4

At head of title: Institute of Governmental Studies, University of California, Berkeley.
The Institute of Governmental Studies presents this monograph as part of its series of Franklin K. Lane papers.

1636

Rose, Willie L. N. Rehearsal for Reconstruction; the Port Royal experiment. With an introduction by C. Vann Woodward. Indianapolis, Bobbs-Merrill [1964] xviii, 442 p. illus., fold. map, ports. F277.B3R6

"Notes on sources": p. 409-433.
Concerns Sea Islands, South Carolina.

1637

Roussève, Charles B. The Negro in Louisiana; aspects of his history and his literature. New Orleans, Xavier University Press, 1937. xvii, 212 p. illus., diagrs., music, plates. E185.93.L6R6

"This work, prepared in 1935 in partial fulfillment of the requirements for the degree of master of arts, makes its appearance . . . substantially as it was originally written, save for . . . several minor alterations and the addition of a few details."—p. vii.
Bibliography: p. 193-201.

1638a

Russell, John H. The free Negro in Virginia, 1619-1865. Baltimore, Johns Hopkins Press, 1913. 194 p. (Johns Hopkins University studies in historical and political science, series 31, no. 3) H31.J6
E185.93.V8R9

Thesis (Ph.D.)—Johns Hopkins University, 1913.
Bibliography: p. 178-186.

1639
Scheiner, Seth M. Negro mecca; a history of the Negro in New York City, 1865-1920. [New York] New York University Press, 1965. 246 p.
F128.9.N3S3
Bibliography: p. 226-242.

1640
Sexton, Patricia C. Spanish Harlem; an anatomy of poverty. New York, Harper & Row [1965] 208 p. map. F128.9.F8S48
Includes bibliographical references.

1641
Silver, James W. Mississippi: the closed society. New York, Harcourt, Brace & World [1964] xxii, 250 p. facsim., map. F345.S5
Bibliographical footnotes.

1642
Spangler, Earl. The Negro in Minnesota. With an introduction by Carl T. Rowan. Minneapolis, T. S. Denison [1961] 215 p. E185.93.M55S7
Bibliography: p. 186-213.

1643
Spear, Allan H. Black Chicago; the making of a Negro ghetto, 1890-1920. Chicago, University of Chicago Press [1967] xvii, 254 p. illus., col. maps, ports. F548.9.N3S65
Bibliographical footnotes.

1644
Steward, William, *and* Theophilus G. Steward. Gouldtown, a very remarkable settlement of ancient date; studies of some sturdy examples of the simple life, together with sketches of early colonial history of Cumberland County and southern New Jersey and some early genealogical records. Philadelphia, Press of J. B. Lippincott Co., 1913. 237 p. plates, ports. F144.G69S8
Gouldtown was one of the earliest all-Negro settlements.

1645
Tate, Thaddeus W. The Negro in eighteenth-century Williamsburg. Williamsburg, Va., Colonial Williamsburg; distributed by the University Press of Virginia, Charlottesville [c1965] xiv, 256 p. (Williamsburg research studies) F234.W7T3
Bibliography: p. [237]-246.

1646

Thornbrough, Emma L. The Negro in Indiana; a study of a minority. [Indianapolis] Indiana Historical Bureau, 1957. 412 p. (Indiana historical collections, v. 37)   F535.N4T5

Cover title and half-title: *The Negro in Indiana Before 1900.*
Bibliographical footnotes.

1647

Tindall, George B. South Carolina Negroes, 1877-1900. Columbia, University of South Carolina Press, 1952. 336 p. illus., ports.   E185.93.S7T5

Bibliography: p. 311-326.

1648

United Community Services of Metropolitan Boston. Black and white in Boston; a report based on the Community Research Project. [By] Donald D. Dobbin, Norma J. Emond [and] Janine G. O'Grady. [Boston, Research Dept., United Community Services of Metropolitan Boston] 1968. 44 p. map.   F73.9.N4U5

1648a

U.S. *Commission on Civil Rights.* Hearings before the United States Commission on Civil Rights. Hearings held in Detroit, Michigan, December 14, 1960 [and] December 15, 1960. Washington, U.S. Govt. Print. Off., 1961. 511 p. illus., fold. maps.   E185.93.M5A5

1648b

Warner, Robert A. New Haven Negroes, a social history. New Haven, Published for the Institute of Human Relations by Yale University Press, 1940. xiv, 309 p. facsim., maps, plates, port.   F104.N6W27

Bibliographical footnotes.

1649

Washington, Nathaniel J. Historical development of the Negro in Oklahoma. Tulsa, Okla., Dexter Pub. Co. [1948] 71 p. illus., maps.
E185.93.O4W3

Bibliography: p. 69-71.

1650

Waynick, Capus M., John C. Brooks, *and* Elsie W. Pitts, *eds.* North Carolina and the Negro. Raleigh, North Carolina Mayors' Co-operating Committee, 1964. xvii, 309 p. illus. (part col.), maps, ports. (part col.)
E185.93.N6W3

Bibliography: p. 271-287.

1651
Whaley, Marcellus S. The old types pass; Gullah sketches of the Carolina
Sea Islands. Illustrated by Edna Reed Whaley. Boston, Christopher Pub.
House [c1925] 192 p. music, plates.   E185.93.S7W6

1652
Wharton, Vernon L. The Negro in Mississippi, 1865-1890. Chapel Hill,
University of North Carolina Press, 1947. 298 p. (The James Sprunt
studies in history and political science, v. 28)   F251.J28 v. 28
Bibliography: p. [277]-292.

1653
Wightman, Orrin S. Early days of coastal Georgia. Photographs by Orrin
Sage Wightman. Story by Margaret Davis Cate. St. Simons Island, Ga.,
Fort Frederica Association [1955] 235 p. illus., maps.   F286.W6

1654
Wright, James M. The free Negro in Maryland, 1634-1860. New York,
Columbia University, 1921. 362 p. (Studies in history, economics and
public law, v. 97, no. 3; whole no. 222)   H31.C7 v. 97
                                                         E185.W95
Bibliography: p. 348-362.

1655
Wynes, Charles E. Race relations in Virginia, 1870-1902. Charlottesville,
University of Virginia Press, 1961. 164 p.   E185.93.V8W9
Bibliography: p. 151-160.

1656

Adams, C. C., *and* Marshall A. Talley. Negro Baptists and foreign missions. Philadelphia, Foreign Mission Board of the National Baptist Convention, U.S.A. [c1944] 84 p.   BV2521.A85

1657

Bragg, George F. History of the Afro-American group of the Episcopal Church. Baltimore, Church Advocate Press, 1922. 319 p. plates, ports.
                                                          BX5979.B7
  "Negro ordinations from 1866 to present": p. [267]-287.
  Clerical directory: p. [285]-292.

1658

Brawley, E. M., *ed.* The Negro Baptist pulpit; a collection of sermons and papers on Baptist doctrine and missionary and educational work, by colored Baptist ministers. Philadelphia, American Baptist Publication Society [1890] 300 p.   BX6447.B7

1659

Brotz, Howard. The black Jews of Harlem: Negro nationalism and the dilemmas of Negro leadership. [New York] Free Press of Glencoe [1964] 144 p.   F128.68.H3B7
  Bibliographical references included in "Notes" (p. 133-140).

1660
Campbell, Will D. Race and the renewal of the church. Philadelphia, Westminster Press [1962] 90 p. (Christian perspectives on social problems)
BT734.C3
1661
The Church and the urban racial crisis, edited by Mathew Ahmann and Margaret Roach. Techny, Ill., Divine Word Publications [1967] 262 p.
E185.615.C58
"The major addresses and background papers prepared for the August, 1967, convention of the National Catholic Conference for Interracial Justice held at Rockhurst College in Kansas City, Missouri."

1662
Culver, Dwight W. Negro segregation in the Methodist Church. New Haven, Yale University Press, 1953. 218 p. (Yale studies in religious education, 22)
BX8382.A17C8

Based on the author's thesis, Yale University, 1948.
Bibliography: p. [191]-206.

1663
Daniel, Vattel E. Ritual in Chicago's South Side churches for Negroes. Chicago, 1940. 155 leaves. mounted col. map.
BR563.N4D29

Thesis—University of Chicago.
Typescript (carbon copy).
Bibliography: leaves 144-150.

1664
Day, Helen C. Color, ebony. New York, Sheed & Ward, 1951. 182 p.
BX4668.D34
Concerns converts to Catholicism.

1665
DuBois, William E. B., *ed.* The Negro church; report of a social study made under the direction of Atlanta University; together with the Proceedings of the Eighth Conference for the Study of the Negro Problems, held at Atlanta University, May 26th, 1903. Atlanta, Atlanta University Press, 1903. 212 p. (Atlanta University publications, no. 8)
E185.5.A88 no. 8
E185.7.D81
"Select bibliography of Negro churches": p. vi-viii.

1666
Fauset, Arthur H. Black gods of the metropolis; Negro religious cults of the urban North. Philadelphia, University of Pennsylvania Press, 1944.

126 p. plates, ports. (Publications of the Philadelphia Anthropological Society, v. 3)   BR563.N4F3 1944a

Brinton memorial series, [no. 2].

Issued also as thesis (Ph.D.), University of Pennsylvania.

"A study of five Negro religious cults in the Philadelphia of today."
—Preface.

1667

Felton, Ralph A. Go down, Moses; a study of 21 successful Negro rural pastors. [Madison, N.J., Dept. of the Rural Church, Drew Theological Seminary [1952] 95 p. illus.   BR563.N4F38

1668

Felton, Ralph A. These my brethren; a study of 570 Negro churches and 1542 Negro homes in the rural South. Madison, N.J., Dept. of the Rural Church, Drew Theological Seminary [1950] 102 p.   BR563.N4F4

1669

Fisk University, *Nashville. Social Science Institute.* God struck me dead; religious conversion experiences and autobiographies of Negro ex-slaves. Nashville, 1945. 218 leaves. (*Its* Social science source documents, no. 2)
BV4930.F5

1670

Frazier, Edward Franklin. The Negro church in America. New York, Schocken Books [1964, c1963] 92 p. (Studies in sociology)
BR563.N4F7

Bibliographical footnotes.

1671

Fuller, Thomas O. History of the Negro Baptists of Tennessee. [Memphis, Tenn., Haskins Print, c1936] 346 p. plates, ports.   BX6444.T4F8

1672

Gillard, John T. The Catholic Church and the American Negro; being an investigation of the past and present activities of the Catholic Church in behalf of the 12,000,000 Negroes in the United States, with an examination of the difficulties which affect the work of the colored missions. Baltimore, St. Joseph's Society Press, 1929 [i.e. 1930] xv, 324 p. diagr., map, tables (part fold.)   BX1407.N4G5

Bibliography: p. 291-301.

1673

Harrison, William P. The gospel among the slaves. A short account of missionary operations among the African slaves of the Southern States.

Compiled from original sources. Nashville, Pub. House of the M. E. Church, South. 1893. 394 p. illus., ports. BV2783.H3

1674
Haynes, Leonard L. The Negro community within American Protestantism, 1619-1844. Boston, Christopher Pub. House [1953] 264 p.
BR563.N4H38

1675
Hough, Joseph C. Black power and white Protestants; a Christian response to the new Negro pluralism. New York, Oxford University Press, 1968. 228 p. BT734.2.H63

Bibliographical footnotes.

1676
Ingram, Tolbert R., *ed.* Essays on segregation. Boston, St. Thomas Press, 1960. 106 p. BT734.3.I5

1677
Johnston, Ruby F. The development of Negro religion. New York, Philosophical Library [1954] 202 p. illus. BR563.N4J6

1678
Joint Survey Commission of the Baptist Inter-convention Committee. The Negro Baptist ministry; an analysis of its profession, preparation, and practices, by Ira De A. Reid. Report of a survey conducted by the Joint Survey Commission of the Baptist Inter-convention Committee: the American Baptist Convention, the National Baptist Convention [and] the Southern Baptist Convention. [Philadelphia, H. and L. Advertising Co.] 1951 [i.e. 1952] 145 p. BV4080.J6

1679
Jones, Howard O. Shall we overcome? A challenge to Negro and white Christians. Westwood, N.J., F. H. Revell Co. [1966] 146 p. BT734.2.J6

1680
Jordan Lewis G. Negro Baptist history, U.S.A., 1750, 1930. Nashville, Sunday School Pub. Board, N.B.C. [1930] 394 p. plates, ports.
BX6443.J6
"Minutes of the Baptist Foreign Mission Convention of the United States of America held in Montgomery, Ala., November 24, 25, 26, 1880" (p. [153]-170) and "Minutes of the fourth annual session of the Baptist Foreign Mission Convention of the United States of America,

held with the First Baptist Church, Manchester, Virginia, September 19-22, 1883" (p. [217]-236) have special title pages.
Bibliography: p. 392-394.

1680a
King, Martin Luther. Strength to love. New York, Harper & Row [1963]
146 p.   BX6452.K5

1681
Koger, Azzie B. Negro Baptists of Maryland. [Baltimore, Clarke Press]
c1946. 78 p. illus., ports.   BX6444.M3K6 1946

First published in 1936 under title: *History of the Negro Baptists of Maryland.*

1682
Lincoln, Charles Eric. The Black Muslims in America. Foreword by Gordon Allport. Boston, Beacon Press [1961] 276 p.   E185.61.L56

"This book originated as a dissertation . . . in the Graduate School of Boston University."
Includes bibliography.
This black separatist group, also called the Nation of Islam, under the leadership of Elijah Mohammad, has a widespread following in the United States.

1683
Lincoln, Charles Eric. My face is black. Boston, Beacon Press [1964]
137 p.   E185.61.L57

Bibliographical references included in "Notes" (p. [134]-137).
Includes further discussion of the Black Muslims.

1684
Loescher, Frank S. The Protestant church and the Negro. Philadelphia, 1948. 159 p.   BR563.N4L6 1948a

Essential portion of thesis—University of Pennsylvania.
Bibliographical footnotes.

1685
Mays, Benjamin E., *and* Joseph W. Nicholson. The Negro's church. New York, Institute of Social and Religious Research [c1933] 321 p. maps.
                                                              BR563.N4M3
1686
Millea, Thomas V. Ghetto fever. Milwaukee, Bruce Pub. Co. [1968] 166 p.
                                                              F548.9.N3M5
Concerns church and race problems in Chicago.

1687

Payne, Daniel A., *Bp.* History of the African Methodist Episcopal Church. Edited by Rev. C. S. Smith. Nashville, Pub. House of the A.M.E. Sunday-School Union, 1891. xvi, 502 p. ports.　　　　BX8443.P28

1688

Pipes, William H. Say amen, brother! Old-time Negro preaching: a study in American frustration. New York, William-Frederick Press, 1951. 210 p.

　　　　　　　　　　　　　　　　　　　　　　　BR563.N4P53

Bibliography: p. 201-205.

1689

Poole, Elijah. Message to the blackman in America, by Elijah Muhammad. Chicago, Muhammad Mosque of Islam No. 2 [1965] xxvii, 355 p.

　　　　　　　　　　　　　　　　　　　　　　　BP222.P6

On the Black Muslims.

1690

Reimers, David M. White Protestantism and the Negro. New York, Oxford University Press, 1965. 236 p.　　　　　　　E185.6l.R36

Bibliographical references included in "Notes" (p. 190-222). Bibliography: p. 223-227.

1691

Richardson, Harry V. Dark glory, a picture of the church among Negroes in the rural South. New York, Pub. for Home Missions Council of North America and Phelps-Stokes Fund by Friendship Press [1947] xiv, 209 p.　　　　　　　　　　　　　　　BR563.N4R5

"A selected reading list": p. 194-197.

1692

Sellers, James E. The South and Christian ethics. New York, Association Press [1962] 190 p.　　　　　　　　　　E185.61.S48

1693

Singleton, George A. The romance of African Methodism; a study of the African Methodist Episcopal Church. New York, Exposition Press [1952] 251 p. illus.　　　　　　　　　　BX8443.S45

1694

Sleeper, Charles F. Black power and Christian responsibility; some Biblical foundations for social ethics. Nashville, Abingdon Press [1968, c1969] 221 p.　　　　　　　　　　　　　　BS680.E84S5

Bibliography: p. 205-217.

1695

Tyms, James D. The rise of religious education among Negro Baptists; a historical case study. New York, Exposition Press [1966, c1965] xiv, 408 p. (An Exposition-university book)   BX6450.T93

Bibliography: p. [397]-403.

1696

Washington, Joseph R. Black religion; the Negro and Christianity in the United States. Boston, Beacon Press [1964] 308 p.   BR563.N4W3

Bibliographical references included in "Notes" (p. 298-303).

1697

Washington, Joseph R. The politics of God. Boston, Beacon Press [1967] 234 p.   BR563.N4W33

Bibliographical footnotes.

1698

Weatherford, Willis D. American churches and the Negro; an historical study from early slave days to the present. Boston, Christopher Pub. House [1957] 310 p.   BR563.N4W4

1699

Woodson, Carter G. The history of the Negro church. Washington, Associated Publishers [c1921] 330 p. plates, ports.   BR563.N4W6

1700

Woodward, Joseph Herbert. The Negro bishop movement in the Episcopal diocese of South Carolina. McPhersonville, S.C., H. Woodward [c1916] 45 p.   BX5967.W65

1701

Year book of Negro churches, with statistics and records of achievements of Negroes in the United States. 1935/36+ Wilberforce, Ohio, Printed at Wilberforce University.   E185.7.Y43

Editor: Reverdy C. Ransom.
"Published by authority of the bishops of the A.M.E. Church."

1702
Barndt, Joseph R. Why black power? New York, Friendship Press [1968]
122 p.   E185.615.B35

1703
Berry, Brewton. Race and ethnic relations. 3d ed. Boston, Houghton
Mifflin [1965] 435 p. illus.   HT1521.B45 1965

1704
Boggs, James. The American revolution; pages from a Negro worker's note-
book. New York, Monthly Review Press, 1963. 93 p.   E841.B6
"MR9."

1705
Booker, Simeon. Black man's America. Englewood Cliffs, N.J., Prentice-
Hall [1964] 230 p.   E185.6.B76

1706
Clemons, Lulamae, Erwin Hollitz, *and* Gordon A. Gardner. The American
Negro. St. Louis, Webster Division, McGraw-Hill [1965] 138 p. illus.,
ports. (Americans all series)   E185.C6
    Bibliography: p. 122-124.

1707

Cohn, David L. God shakes creation. New York, Harper, 1935. xvi, 299 p. plates.   E185.93.M6C64

At head of title: by David L. Cohn; drawings by Lucian Dent.
"Some of the salient features of . . . society . . . [of the Mississippi] delta."–Foreword.

1708

Cruse, Harold. The crisis of the Negro intellectual. New York, Morrow, 1967. 594 p.   E185.82.C74

Includes bibliographical references.

1709

Davis, Allison, Burleigh B. Gardner, *and* Mary R. Gardner. Deep South; a social anthropological study of caste and class. Directed by W. Lloyd Warner. Chicago, University of Chicago Press [1941] xv, 558 p. diagrs., forms, tables.   HN79.A2D3

1710

Dollard, John. Caste and class in a southern town. 3d ed. Garden City, N.Y., Doubleday, 1957 [c1949] 466 p. (Doubleday anchor books, A95)   F215.D65 1957

Bibliographical footnotes.

1711

Dunbar, Ernest. The black expatriates; a study of American Negroes in exile. New York, Dutton, 1968. 251 p.   E185.94.D8

1712

Eppes, Susan B. The Negro of the old South, a bit of period history. [Rev.] Macon, Ga., J. W. Burke Pub. Co. [c1941] xvi, 203 p. illus.
     E443.E64 1941

1713

Ferman, Louis A., Joyce L. Kornbluh, *and* Alan Haber, *eds.* Poverty in America; book of readings. Introduction by Michael Harrington. Rev. ed. Ann Arbor, University of Michigan Press [1968] xxxiii, 669 p. illus.
     HC110.P6F4 1968

Includes bibliographies.

1714

Frazier, Edward Franklin. Black bourgeoisie. With a new preface by the author. New York, Collier Books [1962] 222 p. illus. (Collier books, AS347)   E185.61.F833 1962

1715
Greer, Scott A. Urban renewal and American cities; the dilemma of democratic intervention. Indianapolis, Bobbs-Merrill [1966, c1965] 201 p.   HT175.U6G7
Bibliographical footnotes.

1716
Griffin, John H. Black like me. Boston, Houghton Mifflin, 1961. 176 p.
E185.61.G8
The author darkened his skin and traveled as a Negro in the deep South.

1717
Hare, Nathan. The black Anglo-Saxons. With an introduction by Oliver C. Cox. [New York] Marzani & Munsell [1965] 124 p.   E185.86.H3
Bibliographical references included in footnotes.

1718
Herskovits, Melville J. The American Negro; a study in racial crossing. Bloomington, Indiana University Press [1964, c1928] 92 p. (A Midland book, MB61)   E185.89A5H5 1964
"Bibliographic appendix": p. 83-87.

1719
Johnson, Charles S. Growing up in the Black Belt; Negro youth in the rural South. With an introduction by St. Clair Drake. Prepared for the American Youth Commission, American Council on Education. New York, Schocken Books [1967, c1941] xxvi, 358 p. map.   E185.86.J6 1967

1719a
Kennedy, Louise V. The Negro peasant turns cityward; effects of recent migrations to northern centers. New York, Columbia University Press, 1930. 270 p. diagr. (Studies in history, economics and public law, no. 329)   H31.C7 no. 329
E185.8.K35
"Research conducted . . . under subsidy by the Social Science Research Council and the Columbia University Council for Research in the Social Sciences."
Published also as thesis (Ph.D.), Columbia University.
"General bibliography": p. 239-255.

1720

Larkins, John R. Alcohol and the Negro: explosive issues. Zebulon, N.C., Record Pub. Co., 1965. 251 p. illus.   E185.86.L36

Includes bibliographical references.

1721

Larsson, Clotye M., *ed.* Marriage across the color line. Chicago, Johnson Pub. Co., 1965. 204 p.   HQ1031.L3

1722

Lewis, Hylan. Blackways of Kent. Chapel Hill, University of North Carolina Press, 1955. xxiv, 337 p. diagrs., tables. (Field studies in the modern culture of the South)   E185.6.L4

Based on thesis, University of Chicago.

1723

McCord, Charles H. The American Negro as a dependent, defective and delinquent. [Nashville, Press of Benson Print. Co., c1914] 342 p.
    E185.65.M13

1724

Miller, Abie. The Negro and the Great Society. New York, Vantage Press [1966, c1965] 209 p.   E185.M64

1725

Moore, Richard B. The name "Negro," its origin and evil use. New York, Afroamerican Publishers, 1960. 82 p. illus.   E185.89.N3M6

1726

Myrdal, Gunnar. An American dilemma: the Negro problem and modern democracy. With the assistance of Richard Sterner and Arnold Rose. 20th anniversary ed. New York, Harper & Row [1962] 1483 p. illus.
    E185.6.M95 1962

Bibliography: p. 1144-1180.

1727

Peterkin, Julia M. Roll, Jordan, roll; the photographic studies by Doris Ulmann. New York, R. O. Ballou [c1933] 251 p. illus., plates.
    E185.6.P46

1728

Powdermaker, Hortense. After freedom; a cultural study in the Deep South. With a new preface by Elliott M. Rudwick. New York, Russell & Russell [1968, c1939] xxi, 408 p. (Studies in American Negro life)
    E185.93.M6P6 1968

Bibliography: p. [375]-380.

1729

Rogers, Joel A. Nature knows no color-line; research into the Negro ances-
try in the white race. New York [1952] 242 p. illus.   HT1581.R6

1730

Rose, Arnold M. The Negro in America. With a foreword by Gunnar
Myrdal. New York, Harper & Row [1964] xxxiv, 324 p. map. (Harper
torchbooks. The University library)   E185.6.R75 1964

"TB3048."
"The condensed version of Gunnar Myrdal's *An American
Dilemma.*"
Bibliographical footnotes.

1731

Stewart, Maxwell S. The Negro in America. [Rev. ed. New York, Public
Affairs Committee, 1962] 28 p. illus. (Public affairs pamphlet no. 95)
                                                E185.6.M952 1962
"[Summarizes Gunnar Myrdal's] two-volume report entitled *An
American Dilemma* (1944), and brings this material up to date on the
basis of recent Supreme Court decisions and the 1960 census."

1732

Thompson, Daniel C. The Negro leadership class. Englewood Cliffs, N.J.,
Prentice Hall [1963] 174 p. (A Spectrum book)   F379.N5T45

Includes bibliography.

1733

U.S. *Bureau of the Census.* Negro population 1790-1915. Washington,
Govt. Print. Off., 1918. 844 p. diagrs., maps, tables.   HA205.A33

"Prepared by Dr. John Cummings in the Division of Revision and
Results, under the general supervision of Dr. Joseph A. Hill."—"Letter
of transmittal," p. 13.
Reprint issued by Arno Press, 1968.

1734

U.S. *Bureau of the Census.* Negroes in the United States. Washington,
Govt. Print. Off., 1904. 333 p. charts, diagrs., front. (*Its* Bulletin 8)
                                                HA201 1900.A12 no. 8
                                                E185.6.U58

1735

U.S. *Bureau of the Census.* Negroes in the United States. Washington,
Govt. Print. Off., 1915. 207 p. diagrs., maps, tables. (*Its* Bulletin 129)
                                                HA201.1900.A12 no. 129
                                                E185.6.U585

1736

U.S. *Bureau of the Census.* Negroes in the United States, 1920-32. Pre
pared under the supervision of Z. R. Pettet, chief statistician for agricu
ture, by Charles E. Hall, specialist in Negro statistics. Washington, U. S
Govt. Print. Off., 1935. xvi, 845 p. diagrs., maps, tables.

HA205.A33 1920-3

"This report supplements the volume, 'Negro Population in th
United States, 1790-1915,' published by the Bureau of the Census i
1918."—p. iii.

1737

Washington, Booker T. The future of the American Negro. Boston, Smal
Maynard, 1899. 244 p. port.   E185.6.W31

1738

Weaver, Robert C. Dilemmas of urban America. Cambridge, Mass., Harvar
University Press, 1965. 138 p. (The Godkin lectures at Harvard Unive
sity, 1965)   HT175.U6W

"Based on the Godkin lectures . . . delivered at Harvard University.
Bibliographical references included in "Notes" (p. [121]-131).

1739

Weaver, Robert C. The urban complex; human values in urban life. Garde
City, N.Y., Doubleday, 1964. 297 p.   HT123.W3

Bibliographical footnotes.

1740

Wiley, Bell I. Southern Negroes, 1861-1865. [2d ed.] New York, Rineha
[1953, c1938] 366 p. illus. (Yale historical publications. Miscellany
31)   E185.2.W65 195

1741

Williams, John G., *of Allendale, S.C.* "De ole plantation." Charleston, S.C
Walker, Evans, & Cogswell Co., Printers, 1895. 67 p.   E185.93.S7W

Contents.—Preface.—An old-time Saturday night meeting.—Brudde
Coteny's sermons.—Glimpses of a vanished past: Two pictures of ol
plantation life.

1742

Woodson, Carter G. A century of Negro migration. New York, Russell &
Russell [1969] 221 p. maps.   E185.9.W89 196

Reprint of the 1918 ed.
Bibliography: p. 193-211.

1743

'oodson, Carter G. The rural Negro. New York, Russell & Russell [1969]
xvi, 265 p. illus.   E185.86.W896 1969

   Reprint of the 1930 ed.

   Bibliographical footnotes.

1744

'oofter, Thomas J., *ed.* Negro problems in cities; a study made under the
direction of T. J. Woofter, Jr. Garden City, N.Y., Doubleday, Doran
[c1928] 284 p. diagrs., form, maps.   E185.86.W91

   "The Institute of Social and Religious Research . . . is responsible for
this publication."

   Contents.–pt. l. Neighborhoods, by T. J. Woofter, Jr.–pt. 2. Housing, by Madge Headley.– pt. 3. Schools, by W. A. Daniel.–pt. 4. Recre-
ation, by H. J. McGuinn.

'hildren

1745

lark, Kenneth B. Prejudice and your child. 2d ed., enl. Boston, Beacon
Press [1963] 247 p. (A Beacon paperback)   BF723.R3C5 1963

   Includes bibliography.

1746

oles, Robert. Children of crisis; a study of courage and fear. Boston,
Little, Brown [1967] xiv, 401 p. illus.   E185.61.C66

   "An Atlantic : Monthly press book."

   Includes bibliographical references.

1747

anshel, David. A study in Negro adoption. Commentary by Alexander J.
Allen. New York, Child Welfare League of America, 1957. 108 p.
tables.   HV875.F2

1748

off, Regina M. Problems and emotional difficulties of Negro children as
studied in selected communities and attributed by parents and children
to the fact that they are Negro. New York, Bureau of Publications,

Teachers College, Columbia University, 1949. 93 p. (Columbia Univer
sity. Teachers College. Contributions to education, no. 960)

E185.89.C3G6 1949s
LB5.C8 no. 96(
Issued also as thesis, Columbia University.
Bibliography: p. 89.

1749

Goodman, Mary E. Race awareness in young children. With an introduc
tion by Kenneth B. Clark. New, rev. ed. New York, Collier Book
[1964] 351 p. map.   BF723.R3G6 1964

"Notes and references": p. 331-342.

1750

Gula, Martin. Quest for equality, the story of how six institutions opened
their doors to serve Negro children and their families. [Washington
U.S. Dept. of Health, Education, and Welfare, Welfare Administration
Children's Bureau; for sale by the Supt. of Docs., U.S. Govt. Print. Off.
1966] 50 p. illus. (U.S. Children's Bureau. Publication no. 441)

HV873.G8
HV741.A32 no. 441
Includes bibliographies.

1751

Henton, Comradge L., *and* Edward E. Johnson. Relationship between self
concepts of Negro elementary-school children and their academic
achievement, intelligence, interests, and manifest anxiety. Baton Rouge
La., Southern University, Dept. of Psychology [1964?] 78 leaves.

LB1131.H38(

Cooperative Research Project no. 1592, performed pursuant to a
contract with the U.S. Office of Education.
Bibliography: leaves [76]-78.

1752

Jackson, Luther P. Poverty's children. [n.p., CROSS-TELL] 1966
42 leaves.   HN80.W3J:

Based on the study findings of the 1960-64 Child Rearing Study
(CRS) of Low Income Families in the District of Columbia.

1753

Price, Arthur Cooper. A Rorschach study of the development of personal
ity structure in white and Negro children in a southeastern community
Genetic psychology monographs, v. 65, Feb. 1962: 3-52. tables.

LB1101.G4 v. 6:

"Based upon a doctoral dissertation at the University of Florida."
Bibliography: p. 51-52.

1754

Sanders, Wiley B., *ed.* Negro child welfare in North Carolina; a Rosenwald study, directed by Wiley Britton Sanders. Montclair, N.J., Patterson Smith, 1968 [c1933] xiv, 326 p. illus. (Patterson Smith reprint series in criminology, law enforcement, and social problems, publication no. 18)

E185.86.S27 1968

"Under the joint auspices of the North Carolina State Board of Charities and Public Welfare and the School of Public Welfare, the University of North Carolina."

Crime and Delinquency

1755

Bonger, Willem A. Race and crime. Translated from the Dutch by Margaret Mathews Hordyk. Montclair, N.J., Patterson Smith, 1969. 130 p. (Patterson Smith reprint series in criminology, law enforcement, and social problems, no. 34)

HV6191.B62 1969

Reprint of the 1943 ed.
Translation of *Ras en misdaad.*
Bibliography: p.[109]-123.

1756

Carter, Dan T. Scottsboro; a tragedy of the American South. Baton Rouge, Louisiana State University Press [1969] 431 p. illus., ports.

KF224.S34C3

Includes bibliographical references.

1757

Chamberlain, Bernard P. The Negro and crime in Virginia. [Charlottesville] University of Virginia, 1936. 132 p. tables. (Publications of the University of Virginia. Phelps-Stokes fellowship papers, no. 15)

E185.93.V8C46

1758

DuBois, William E. B., *ed.* Some notes on Negro crime, particularly in Georgia; report of a social study made under the direction of Atlanta University; together with the Proceedings of the Ninth Conference for

the Study of the Negro Problems, held at Atlanta University, May 24, 1904. Atlanta, Atlanta University Press, 1904. 68 p. diagrs. (Atlanta University publications, no. 9)   E185.5.A88 no. 9
E185.65.D81

Bibliography: p. vi-viii.
Contents—The problem of crime, by F. B. Sanborn.—Crime and slavery.—Crime and the census.—Extent of Negro crime.—Crime in cities, by M. N. Work.—Crime in Georgia.—Atlanta and Savannah, by H H. Proctor and M. N. Work.—Crime in Augusta, by A. G. Coombs and L. D. Davis.— What Negroes think of crime.—Causes of Negro crime —Some conclusions.—The Ninth conference.—Resolutions.—Index.

1759
Kephart, William M. Racial factors and urban law enforcement. Phila delphia, University of Pennsylvania Press [1957] 209 p. tables.
HV8138.K4

Bibliography: p. 207-209.

1759a
Lightfoot, Robert M. Negro crime in a small urban community. [Char lottesville] University of Virginia, 1934. 85, [1] p. plan. (Publication of the University of Virginia. Phelps-Stokes fellowship papers, no. 12
E185.93.V8L

Bibliography: p. [86].

1760
Towler, Juby E. The police role in racial conflicts. Springfield, Ill., C. C Thomas [1964] 119 p. illus.   HV8069.T

1761
U.S. *Commission on Civil Rights.* Law enforcement; a report on equi protection in the South. [Washington, For sale by the Supt. of Docs U.S. Govt. Print. Off.] 1965. 188 p.   DLC-L

Bibliographical footnotes.

1762
Wolfgang, Marvin E. Crime and race; conceptions and misconception New York, Institute of Human Relations Press, American Jewish Cor mittee [1964] 71 p. ([American Jewish Committee] Institute Human Relations. Pamphlet series, no. 6)   HV6197.U5W

"References": p. 64-71.

Family

1763
Bernard, Jessie S. Marriage and family among Negroes. Englewood Cliffs, N.J., Prentice-Hall [1966] 160 p. illus. (A Spectrum book)
E185.86.B4
Bibliographical footnotes.

1764
Billingsley, Andrew. Black families in white America [by] Andrew Billingsley, with the assistance of Amy Tate Billingsley. Englewood Cliffs, N.J., Prentice-Hall [1968] 218 p. illus., map. (A Spectrum book)
E185.86.B5
Bibliographical footnotes.

1765
Frazier, Edward Franklin. The free Negro family. New York, Arno Press, 1968. 75 p. maps. (The American Negro, his history and literature)
E185.86.F73 1968
Reprint of the 1932 ed.
Bibliography: p. 73-75.

1766
Frazier, Edward Franklin. The Negro family in the United States. Rev. and abridged ed. Foreword by Nathan Glazer. Chicago, University of Chicago Press [1966] xxii, 372 p.
E185.86.F74 1966
Revised and abridged edition first published in 1948.
Bibliographical footnotes.

1767
Jeffers, Camille. Living poor; a participant observer study of priorities and choices. With an introduction by Hylan Lewis. Ann Arbor, Mich., Ann Arbor Publishers, 1967. 123 p.
HN80.W3J4
A report to the Child Rearing Study of Low Income Families in the District of Columbia, a project sponsored by the Health and Welfare Council of the National Capital Area.

1768
Rainwater, Lee, *and* William L. Yancey. The Moynihan report and the politics of controversy; a Trans-action social science and public policy report. Including the full text of The Negro family: the case for

national action by Daniel Patrick Moynihan. Cambridge, Mass., M.I.T.
Press [1967] xviii, 493 p. illus.   E185.86.U54R3

Includes bibliographical references.

1769

U.S. *Dept. of Labor. Office of Policy Planning and Research.* The Negro
family, the case for national action. [Washington, For sale by the Supt.
of Docs., U.S. Govt. Print. Off.] 1965. 78 p. illus.   E185.86.U52

Bibliography: p. 51-53.
The Moynihan report.

1770

Wisconsin. *Governor's Commission on Human Rights.* Negro families in
rural Wisconsin; a study of their community life. Madison, 1959. 72 p.
illus.   E185.93.W58A54

1771
Brown, James N. Off my chest, by Jimmy Brown with Myron Cope. Garden City, N.Y., Doubleday, 1964. 230 p. illus., ports.

GV939.B75A3

1772
Cottrell, John. Muhammad Ali, who once was Cassius Clay. New York, Funk & Wagnalls [1968, c1967] 363 p. ports.   GV1132.C55C6 1968

First published in London under title: *Man of Destiny*.

1773
Fleischer, Nathaniel S. Black dynamite, the story of the Negro in the prize ring from 1782 to 1938; with numerous illustrations. [New York, Printed by C. J. O'Brien, c1938-47] 5 v. illus., plates, ports. ("The Ring" athletic library)   GV1131.F65

Vol. 2 has also special title: "Jolting Joe," the amazing story of Joe Louis and his rise to world heavyweight title; "Homicide Hank," the socking saga of Henry Armstrong; v. 3: "The three colored aces," George Dixon, "Little Chocolate," Joe Gans, "The Old Master," Joe Walcott, "The Barbados Demon," and several contemporaries; v. 4: "Fighting furies," story of the golden era of Jack Johnson, Sam Langford and their contemporaries; v. 5: Sockers in sepia; a continuation of the drama of the Negro in pugilistic competition.

1774

Henderson, Edwin B. The Negro in sports. Rev. ed. Washington, Associated Publishers, 1949. xvi, 507 p. illus., ports.   GV161.H4 1949

1775

Louis, Joe. How to box, edited by Edward J. Mallory. Philadelphia, D. McKay Co. [1948] 64 p. illus.   GV1137.L8

1776

Mann, Arthur W. Branch Rickey: American in action. Boston, Houghton Mifflin, 1957. 312 p. illus.   GV865.R45M3

Includes a few pages on Negroes in baseball.

1777

Olsen, Jack. The black athlete: a shameful story; the myth of integration in American sport. New York, Time-Life Books [1968] 223 p.

GV713.O4

1778

Robinson, John R. Baseball has done it. Edited by Charles Dexter. Philadelphia, Lippincott [1964] 216 p.   GV865.R6A2

1779

Robinson, Louie. Arthur Ashe, tennis champion. Garden City, N.Y., Doubleday [1967] 136 p. ports. (Doubleday signal books)

GV994.A7R6

1780

Young, Andrew S. N. Negro firsts in sports. With illustrations by Herbert Temple. Chicago, Johnson Pub. Co. [1963] 301 p. illus.   GV697.A1Y6

1781

Zinkoff, Dave. Around the world with the Harlem Globetrotters, by Dave Zinkoff with Edgar Williams. Foreword by Abe Saperstein; illustrated with photographs. Philadelphia, Macrae Smith Co. [1953] 218 p. illus.

GV885.Z5

INDEX

This is primarily an author and subject index. Numbers refer to entries. References to books about persons or associations are preceded by the word "about," to distinguish them from books by those persons or associations.

Abbott, Martin, 883
Abbott, Robert S., about, 134, 261
Abolitionists, 764, 778, 824, 843, 860, 945
  biography (collective), 100
  biography (individual), 158, 161, 189, 205, 215, 242, 266
  See also Antislavery movements
Abrahams, Roger D., 673, 1375
Abrahamson, Julia, 1
Abrams, Charles, 493-94
Abramson, Doris E., 948
Achille, Louis T., 799
Actors, 140, 184, 247, 667-69, 672, 1615. See also Comedians
Adams, C. C., 1656
Adams, Edward C. L., 674
Adams, John Quincy, about, 251
Adams, Russell L., 98
Adams, Walter, 604
Adler, Mortimer J., ed., 770
Adoff, Arnold, comp., 995, 1228
Adoption, 1747
Aerospace industries, 476
Africa, 783, 869
  bibliography, 14, 34, 63

biography (collective), 98
  colonization, 787, 1000, 1003-4
  history, 758
  music, 1355
  relations with the U.S., 329
  See also Ghana; Liberia; Sierra Leone
African Methodist Episcopal Church, 81, 1687, 1693, 1701
  biography (collective), 81, 149
  biography (individual), 284, 303, 306
Ahmann, Mathew H., ed., 996, 1661
Aikin, Charles, ed., 1402
Airmen, 1318, 1338
Alabama, 684, 1609, 1613a, 1625
  civil rights, 201, 270, 322, 1501
  economic conditions, 409, 553
  education, 540, 553, 556, 601, 652
  folk-lore and folk-tales, 684
  politics, 195, 1425, 1447, 1449
    bibliography, 13
  slavery, 155, 857, 863
  University
    Bureau of Educational Research, 540
    Bureau of Public Administration, 1446
Albany Institute of History and Art, 82

See also Reconstruction; Slavery; names of wars, e.g., Civil War; under names of subjects, places, and regions, e.g., Virginia–history
Hobson, Julius W., 1507
Hodges, Carl G., comp., 752
Hoffman, James, 554
Hogan, William R., 183
  ed., 1616
Holdredge, Helen O., 220
Holland, Annie W., about, 132
Hollander, Barnett, 838
Holley, Joseph W., 596-97
Hollitz, Erwin, 1706
Holmes, Dwight O. W., 598
Holmes, Eugene C., ed., 1019
Holmes, Hamilton, about, 643
Holmes, Samuel J., 411
Holsey, Alban L., 70
Holsey, Lucius H., Bishop, about, 173
Holt, John, 609
Holt, Len, 340
Holt, Rackham, 221-22
Home Missions Council of North America, 1691
Homer, Dorothy R., 33
Hope, John, 469, 1403
Hopkins, Thomas A., 347
Horne, Lena, 223
  about, 140
Horney, Helen, 752
Horowitz, Benjamin, 97
Horton, David S., 1038
Hough, Joseph C., 1675
Housing, 465, 493-539, 1533, 1553, 1593, 1624
  bibliography, 55, 517
  statistics, 528, 534
Houston, Tex., 399
Hoving, Thomas P. F., 95
Howard, James, ed., 853
Howard, Oliver O., about, 241
Howard University
  Gallery of Art, 92
  Graduate School, 454, 799
    Division of the Social Sciences, 1019
  Library, Moorland Foundation, 11, 18
Howe, Mark D., 325a
Howells, William D., 1246
Hoyt, Edwin P., 224
Hubbard, Geraldine H., comp., 35
Hughes, Carl M., pseud. *See* Hughes, John M. C.
Hughes, Everett C., 1607
Hughes, John M. C., 963
Hughes, Langston, 122-23, 225-26, 667, 753, 985, 1108, 1110-15, 1219, 1244, 1253-57, 1259-61, 1387

ed., 696, 1109, 1202, 1244, 1258
  about, 7, 118, 134, 192, 252
  bibliography, 7
Hughes, Louis, 1628
Hughes, William H., ed., 227
Huie, William B., 124, 228
Hull, Marie, illus., 1204
Hullfish, Henry Gordon, ed., 566
Humor, 1200-1204. *See also* Comedians
Humphrey, Hubert H., ed., 599
Humphrey, Norman D., 1581
Hundley, Mary G., 600
Hunt, B. H., 1563
Hunter, Charlayne, about, 643
Hunter, Jane E., about, 114
Hunter, Kristin, 1116-17
Hunter, Thomas L., 705
Hunton, George K., 229
Hurst, John F., Bishop, 1148
Hurston, Zora N., 697, 1118-19
Huson, Carolyn F., 457
Hussey, Edith L., 18a
Hyman, Harold M., comp., 908
  ed., 907

Illinois
  Chicago Commission on Race Relations, 1579
  Emancipation Centennial Commission, 752
  history, 752
  riots, 1584
  University, 907
  See also Chicago
Imari, Brother, 341
Imes, Nella. *See* Larsen, Nella
Income, 525, 636
Indexes, 18b, 37a
Indiana, 1621, 1646
Indiana Co., Pa., 871
Indiana Historical Bureau, 1646
Indians of North America, captivities, 209, 246
Industrial relations, 435, 473
Industrial Relations Counselors, 473
Industry, 415, 433
Inger, Morton, 570
Ingram, Tolbert R., ed., 1676
Institute of Early American History and Culture, Williamsburg, Va., 754, 1330
Institute of Labor and Industrial Relations (University of Michigan–Wayne State University), 490
Institute of Race Relations, 315
Institute of Social and Religious Research, 539, 1685, 1744